NARCISSISM

NARCISSISM

A Critical Reader

edited by
Anastasios Gaitanidis
with Polona Curk

KARNAC

First published in 2007 by
Karnac Books Ltd.
118 Finchley Road, London NW3 5HT

British Library Cataloguing in Publication Data

A C.I.P. for this book is available from the British Library

ISBN-13: 978-1-85575-453-9

Typeset by Vikatan Publishing Solutions, Chennai, India

Printed in Great Britain by Biddles Ltd., King's Lynn, Norfolk

www.karnacbooks.com

CONTENTS

To our parents,
Zografia and Georgios (A.G.),
Nada and Pavel (P.C.)

ACKNOWLEDGEMENTS

Anastasios Gaitanidis: I would like to thank all those that have made this book possible. To begin, my Assistant Editor Polona Curk for all her hard work and constant and inspired criticism. Then all the contributors for producing such extremely interesting and exciting papers and for their patience and creative co-operation. Oliver Rathbone and Christelle Yeyet-Jacquot (from Karnac) for their trust and steadfast support. Josh Cohen for the talks at Aldo's restaurant and elsewhere. Michael Babula for his willingness to contribute to the book, but who was unable to do so due to unforeseen circumstances. All my friends and colleagues at PACE, Goldsmiths College (University of London), especially Tessa Adams whose views and feedback had an important effect on the form and content of my paper. The Director of PACE Len Platt and Professor Dianne Waller for an award which enabled me to engage fully with the process of editing the book. Above all, I would like to thank my wife Maria for all her love, sustenance, advice and solidarity over many years.

Polona Curk: I would first like to thank Anastasios Gaitanidis for inviting me to assist him with the editing of this book–I have learned a lot. I would also like to thank Lynne Segal and Lisa

Baraitser for their comments on the early draft of my paper. Mostly, I would like to thank my family for their continuous support over the years even when I choose unusual directions; and Marian Ursu for his encouragement and assistance throughout the process of editing this book and for his belief that this is but the first one of many.

ABOUT THE CONTRIBUTORS

Editor

Dr Anastasios Gaitanidis is a Permanent Visiting Lecturer in Psychoanalytic Studies at Goldsmiths College (University of London), an Associate Lecturer in Social Sciences at the Open University and a Visiting Lecturer in Cultural Studies at the University of Kent. He is also a Psychodynamic Counsellor/ Psychotherapist in private practice. He is currently co-authoring the book *Male in Analysis* with Tessa Adams and Larry O'Carroll (Palgrave) and co-editing the book *Authoring the Sublime* with Tessa Adams (Karnac). He is also in the process of editing his PhD thesis *"Death, Time & the Unconscious: Representation(s) and/of the Death Drive in French Psychoanalytic Thought"* so as to be published as a book.

Assistant Editor

Polona Curk holds an MA in Psychoanalytic Studies from Goldsmiths College (University of London) and is currently a full-time PhD candidate at Birkbeck College (University of London). Before coming to Britain, she worked as an architect in her country,

1

Slovenia. She also worked as a counsellor-volunteer in a non-governmental organisation against violence. Her research is concerned with the concept of autonomy in the meeting of two subjects and with the feminine and masculine subjectivity and their representations in the social realms, using psychoanalytic approaches and feminist theory.

Contributors

Dr Tessa Adams is a Fellow of the Royal Society of Arts and Visiting Fellow of Goldsmiths College (University of London). She is an Art Theorist and practicing Psychoanalytic Psychotherapist, holding Professional Membership with both the Site of Contemporary Psychoanalysis and the Guild of Psychotherapists. She has published widely on psychoanalysis and contemporary art practice and recently published a co-edited volume, *The Feminine Case: Jung, Aesthetics and Creative Process with Karnac.*

Dr Julia Borossa is a Lecturer in Psychoanalysis, Translator and Editor. She has published several articles on feminist theory and the history of psychoanalysis in journals including the *Oxford Literary Review and Paragraph.* She has edited and introduced Sandor Ferenczi's *Selected Writings* (Penguin, 1999) and is the author of *Hysteria* (Icon Books, 2001).

Dr Josh Cohen is a Reader in English and Comparative Literature at Goldsmiths College (University of London) and a Training Candidate at the Institute of Psychoanalysis. His research interests include philosophy and literature, aesthetic theory, Holocaust writing, 19th and 20th-century American literature and psychoanalysis. He is the author of various books and articles on modern literature, European philosophy and psychoanalysis, most recently *Spectacular Allegories* (2002), *Interrupting Auschwitz* (2003) and *How to Read Freud* (2005).

Christopher Hauke is a Jungian Analyst in private practice, a Lecturer in Psychoanalytic Studies, Goldsmiths College (University of London) and a film-maker. He is the author of *Jung and the Postmodern: The Interpretation of Realities.* (2000) and co-editor of *Jung* *and Film. Post-Jungian Takes on the Moving Image* (2001). He recently published his book *Human Being Human: Culture and the Soul* (2005).

Justin Lorentzen is a member of the British Communications Faculty of the University of Southern California where he teaches a course on Popular Culture and Counter-culture. In addition, he is an Associate Lecturer in Cultural Studies at the University of the Arts, London and a Visiting Lecturer in Psychoanalytic Studies, Goldsmiths College (University of London). He is interested in the fields of social pathology and the sociology of transgression, subjectivity and social relations and postmodernism and consumer cultures. Having published in the field of the sociology of transgression, he is currently researching the counter-cultures of 1960s London.

Emmanouil Manakas has studied Occupational Therapy at the Athens Technological and Educational Institute and holds an MSc in Psychology from the Open University. He is currently a part-time doctoral candidate at the Unit of Psychotherapeutic Studies, Goldsmiths College (University of London). He has been working as a Pediatric Occupational Therapist in private practice for the last ten years. His research interests focus on neuro-psychoanalysis, developmental psychology and occupational science.

Rob Mawdsley holds an MSc in Social Work and a Postgraduate Diploma in Counselling from Goldsmiths College (University of London). He has been working as a Social Worker in Mental Health for the last fifteen years. He is also a Psychodynamic Counsellor in private practice. His research mainly involves the psychoanalytic exploration of the process of ageing and how it affects the psychological well-being of older people.

Larry O'Carroll is a Programme Co-ordinator of Psychodynamic Studies at Goldsmiths College (University of London). He has published articles in journals including *Psychodynamic Counselling* and *Free Associations*. He is currently co-authoring the book *Male in Analysis* with Tessa Adams and Anastasios Gaitanidis (Palgrave). His research interests focus on the history of psychoanalytic theory, the work of Michel Foucault and the pragmatist philosophy of Richard Rorty.

Introduction

When we first conceived of this book, our fundamental aim was to provide contemporary critical examinations of the notion of 'narcissism' by having authors from different disciplines write on this topic as it is approached in their specialist field. In other words, we wanted to critically explore and analyse the different meanings that are conveyed by this term when it is used in current psychoanalytic, sociological, artistic and cultural theories and practices. It was also important for us to offer a multiplicity of perspectives on how and why 'narcissism' is perceived as an important element in the construction and development of the self, a character disorder, a social and cultural phenomenon, a necessary aspect of artistic production, and a sign of our times.

Apart from attempting to accomplish the above aims, however, what we also realised in the process of editing this book was that most of the present papers begun by raising—and evolved around— the question of the difference between 'the who' and 'the what' at the heart of love itself. Do we love someone for the absolute singularity of *who* s/he is or do we love her/him for *what* s/he represents to us? Do we love someone or do we love something about this someone that reminds us of (an aspect of) ourselves? In other words, does our love for someone always involve a narcissistic appropriation of her/him?

It would seem that a possible reply to the above questions could be found by examining how the difference between 'the who' and 'the what' at the heart of love determines how one deals with the loss of a loved one, namely, how the way we love someone determines the way we cope with her/his loss. At least, this is what Freud attempted to do when he realised that the distinction between 'the who' and 'the what' could be used to shed light on the difference between mourning and melancholia. Thus, in mourning we acknowledge the singularity and irreplaceability of the lost loved person—*who* s/he is—and our relationship with her/him—including *what* s/he represents to us—is gradually given up, involving pain and suffering, and is substituted by a restructuring of our internal world which is in consonance with the relinquished relationship. In melancholia, however, we are unable to mourn this loss because we might know *whom* we have lost but not *what* we have lost in us (see Freud, 1917e, p. 254).

Freud further elucidates the above difference by introducing the distinction between narcissistic and anaclitic object choice. In the case of the latter, a choice of love object is made in which it is the persons who are concerned with a child's feeding, care and protection who supply the prototype of the erotic object. Moreover, anaclitic object choice depends on the child's capacity to perceive its carers as separate from itself and unique in their ability to provide care and protection. Conversely, narcissistic object choice refers to the formation of an object relationship on the model of the subject's relationship to her/himself, with the object representing some aspect or other of her/himself (see Freud, 1914). Following this distinction, Freud observes that in melancholia,

> [t]he object choice has been effected on a narcissistic basis, so that the object-cathexis, when obstacles come in its way, can regress to narcissism. The narcissistic identification with the object then becomes a substitute for the erotic cathexis, the result of which is that in spite of the conflict with the loved person the love-relation need not be given up. The substitution of identification for object-love is an important mechanism in the narcissistic affections.... It represents, of course, a regression from one type of object choice to original narcissism. [Freud, 1917e, p. 258]

As the melancholic loves his/her object on the basis of narcissistic identification with it, s/he refuses to accept its absence and attempts to preserve it by *incorporating* it into her/himself (i.e., by devouring it). (see Freud, 1917e, p. 258). As a result, the boundaries between the melancholic's self and his/her object are blurred or tend to vanish. The melancholic therefore wants to return to the state of 'original (primary) narcissism' which is generally understood without reference to libido attachments to objects. There is as yet neither ego nor object. We may speak of an undifferentiated force field which later becomes differentiated into ego and objects.

According to Freud, therefore, our love life develops in such a way that one main current desires and longs for other persons as objects of desire, while the other, more ancient current, remains 'narcissistic' in the sense that it does not recognise boundaries between ego and objects and it creates identity of ego and object. In such identification the subject-object differentiation is suspended or is not activated. It is in this fashion that the ego may enrich itself and 'take into itself' aspects or traits of others. In early childhood, this process plays a prominent part in ego formation and consolidation; but it continues, in far more complex ways, in later developmental stages as well.

For Freud, then, love is a force that not only brings people together, one person loving another, but equally brings oneself together into that one individuality which we become through our identifications. Once the differentiation between ego and object is reasonably well established on one level of our mental life, once there is some sort of self-identity as distinguished from the identity of others, we are able to love ourselves as we are able to love another (and *vice versa*), each different from the other. Object love and self love develop together.

It would seem, therefore, that in self love, love of self, a stage is reached where one becomes an object to oneself, where one can respond to and care for oneself. This involves a split *within* the subject that is analogous to that other split, the ego-object distinction. However, despite the fact that during normal psychosexual development these splits (i.e., ego/object and ego-as-subject/ego-as-object) increasingly overshadow and dominate the psychic scene, the original narcissistic unifying current does not disappear. In fact, it exerts an essential influence on the further development of

psychic life and object relations. Freud has referred to this development as the dissolution of the Oedipus complex, leading to the formation of the superego. For him, it is the enriched complexity of
psychic life brought about by the internalisation of elements of oedipal relations that makes possible the more mature love relations of
adult life. In fact, the internalisation involved in superego development can be described as a narcissistic transformation of object relations. Interactions between child and parents during the oedipal
period are transformed into internal, intrapsychic interactions and
relations. This does not mean, of course, that relations with the
parents and other objects cease, but that object world and object relations gain further depth and new dimensions by virtue of a narcissistic reorganisation of the inner life.

This is in broad outline the story of our (narcissistic and ana-
clitic/object) love life according to Freud and many other analysts
after him. Yet, most of the authors in this book are critical, in one
way or another, of this depiction of our love life. They claim, for
example, that a neat differentiation between narcissistic and anaclitic object love is untenable. It is in the "complete object-love of the
anaclitic type" that Freud observes "the marked over-estimation
which is doubtless derived from the original narcissism of the child,
now transferred to the sexual object." (Freud, 1914, p. 69). The love
object is idealised so as to replace the subject's own lost narcissism.
The subject figures that "if I cannot be perfect let me at least have a
relationship with someone else who can be perfect."

Moreover, Josh Cohen is critical of the postulation of an identificatory, narcissistic love that is more ancient than object love. If
attachment to the others is an effect of attachment to the self, then
the reverse is equally true: the love of self is also a reflection of love
of others. In addition, he questions the assumption that primary narcissism is an objectless, monadological state. By examining carefully
the internal tensions within the original Freudian concept, he suggests
that primary narcissism arises as *a paradoxical structure of enclosure
conditioned by the presence of the other*. Thus, it is clear that the narcissistic position is not only conditioned by the relation to an object, but
that the absence of an object is itself always a disguised relation to
an object.

Polona Curk is critical of the equation of identificatory, narcissistic love with incorporation, the latter being a kind of 'taking in' of

the other until it becomes part of the self, no longer psychically distinct. Adopting the views of recent feminist psychoanalytic theory (Benjamin, 1988, 1998), Curk argues that identificatory love can allow the other to *survive* as a separate entity. Her main focus is on the importance of 'mothering' support in allowing the infant to emerge from a self-enclosed space and encouraging it to reach out for the other. Love for the (m)other is consequently built out of an already existing awareness of the (m)other's existence *as a subject*; that is, it is an 'intersubjective' relationship in which aspects of otherness are accepted and used by the self, without destroying the other in the process. Identificatory love, therefore, is not merely a matter of incorporating the (m)other as ideal, but of having a relationship with the person who embodies the ideal. Curk argues, however, that this love can prosper only if we take seriously the assumption that the human need for empathy and support in the area of imaginative living is essential and legitimate, and if the role of the surviving (m)other in the development of empathic and intimate relationships is fully acknowledged and appreciated.

This optimistic rendering of identificatory, narcissistic love as a way of intimately connecting with the other is one important strand in contemporary psychoanalytic work. However, Anastasios Gaitanidis presents us with a critical alternative which is derived from the work of Lacan, who saw narcissistic identification as an 'imaginary' process of taking on an image and 'appropriating' it as if it represents the self. That is, narcissistic identification is primarily a way of losing oneself in the other; more precisely, the fact that it is at the root of the formation of the ego reveals that the ego is itself 'specious', a false acceptance of an image as real. Hence there is a sense in which narcissistic identification *falsifies* and *alienates*, with the subject 'using' the object to sustain a fantasy of integrity of the self and cover over its fundamental fragmentation (see Lacan, 1977).

But is narcissistic identification *necessarily* an 'inauthentic', 'alienating' process? Emmanouil Manakas does not think so. Adopting the views of recent developmental theory (Britton 2003), he depicts narcissism as a problem in sharing intrapsychic space, where the perspective of another person threatens with invasion both the self and the 'internal other' space. He compares this invasion with a 'foreign mental protein' that may compromise the integrity of the psychic immune system. In this respect, narcissistic identification becomes a fool-proof mechanism which permits otherness to be brought in the intrapsychic space controlling at the same time for unwanted effects (i.e., the colonization of this space by the other).

Christopher Hauke also argues that we should avoid seeing narcissistic identification as the only process which produces integrity and wholeness. Instead, he suggests that we need to focus on the fragments, the parts that constitute the whole. Additionally, we should stop searching for any missing pieces that are required to reconstitute a whole. What is missing is the linking, the *relationship* between the parts. He also points out that, if we see the narcissistic, fragmented pathology as having meaning for the development of the whole personality, its defensive parts, like grandiosity, envy and rage, can also be seen as carrying creative potential. Only if the analyst understands the narcissistic defences in this way, Hauke argues, will s/he be able to see the patient as what s/he is about to become. In the end, it is often because of a dreadful sense of desperation that a person sacrifices the psyche's own defences with a sigh: 'I'm not in my own skin. I want to be in my own skin.'

Apart from offering their critical views on the psychoanalytic notions of narcissism and narcissistic identification, several authors in this book attempt to portray something of the *experience* of narcissism as a seemingly unavoidable response to contemporary social relations. Thus, Gaitanidis claims that the over-strict, authoritarian character structure of early modernity has been superfluous to the 'needs' of late modern social relations and no longer represents the prototype of the bourgeois 'economic man'. Instead, we have the narcissistic, permissive personality who demands immediate gratification and lives in a state of restless, perpetually unsatisfied desire.

Following the same line of argumentation, Rob Mawdsley maintains that the 'culture of narcissism' (Lasch, 1979) forces us to desperately try to preserve our omnipotent, youthful outlook and refuse the limits imposed by ageing and death. Thus, we tend to either represent older people as burdens or idealise them as cuddly grandparents since the unconditional recognition of their individuality would compel us to deal with our own process of aging and death. What seems to be the case, then, is that our current attitude towards old age is an attempt to turn away from the inescapable, and this is the cause of deep-rooted anxiety and ambivalence.

In contrast to Gaitanidis and Mawdsley, Justin Lorentzen argues that the 'culture of narcissism' provides the necessary conditions for the emergence of radical creativity. For instance, he shows how the rock culture of the Sixties produced radical challenges to authoritarian and rigid identities and ideologies. Moreover, he points out that it was this 'culture of narcissism' fused with the disorientating experience of hallucinogenic drugs that led to the recognition that the barriers and cultural divides between individuals were politically spurious and without foundation. It was this *simultaneity* of experience that, despite being corrosive to traditional cultural forms, enabled new forms of interpersonal connection.

Yet, this psychedelic simultaneity can fuel a search for narcissistic reunification which is apparent in creative action as well as in simple regressive longing. Here, however, is the difficult issue: to distinguish between what is creative and what is regressive. Thus, certain psychoanalytic theorists (Chasseguet-Smirgel, 1975, 1984 and Segal, 1975) argue that creativity is a process which has to do with the transformation of materials in the service of the struggle to re-imagine reality, and it should not be replaced by nostalgia, by oceanic experiences and trance-inducing imagery which have more to do with hypnosis than working through. For this is the crux of the argument: creativity, like mental health in general, is concerned with facing reality, with acting upon it, transforming it, regenerating it and the emotions it produces. Narcissism embedded structurally in the attempt of the ego to merge with the other, is the denial of difference in favour of an imagined place in which there is no separation and loss, no unmet desire and, indeed, no work.

However, Tessa Adams questions the validity of the above psychoanalytic approaches to artistic creativity. She underlines the paradox at the heart of this psychoanalytic framing of artistic production: on the one hand, psychological maturity is seen to be related to the capacity for authentic creation and, on the other, at least a level of narcissistic ambition is seen to be effectively furnishing originality and creativity. Moreover, she argues that these approaches seem to seriously ignore the fact that many great artists have suffered psychologically but have produced mature works despite, or because, of their suffering. Indeed, it would seem that it is exactly the artists who usually lead the most unconventional, solitary, 'narcissistic' lives that produce the most advanced works of art.

It seems, therefore, that what is 'good' art is not something that could (or should) be unequivocally defined—just as what is a 'good' life could not (or should not) be uniformly defined. For this reason, Larry O'Carroll warns us against psychoanalytic theories of narcissism which, by indicating what is wrong with narcissistic infants/ patients, unwittingly promote their own versions of a good life. He wonders whether their versions of a good life can become as oppressive as the narcissistic versions they describe and condemn. Therefore, instead of trying to subscribe to a rigid mode of theorising, O'Carroll suggests that we need to be open to different definitions of narcissism and understand how accounts of psychic formation re-centre the subject by using psychological formulations that can be potentially exclusive and oppressive.

Finally, in her examination of Fanon's theoretical contributions to the issue of racism, Julia Borossa also proposes that we should encourage a deep appreciation and understanding of narcissistic woundedness. Thus, we should neither forget our narcissistic wounds nor preserve them as monuments of the past. Instead, we should aim to develop our subjectivity through our growing ability to *live with* our narcissistic wounds and thus accept difference and even love it.

Perhaps, we could conclude here that in order to grow in love-ability we need to accept the boundaries of ourselves and others, while remaining vulnerable, woundable, around the bounds. Exceptional, unbounded love effaces the risk of relation. It denies that there is no love without power; that we are at the mercy of each other's narcissistic appropriation. However, without this narcissistic appropriation, love would not be possible. We hope that this book, by offering a variety of critical, theoretical and clinical perspectives on narcissism, will contribute to the continuous work of love.

Anastasios Gaitanidis
with Polona Curk

CHAPTER ONE

Narcissism and the autonomy of the ego

Anastasios Gaitanidis

The concept of narcissism is regarded as one of Freud's most challenging introductions to psychoanalytic theory. This is because his discovery that the ego is formed through the dynamics of narcissism renders the autonomy of the ego in relation to the id problematic, forcing subsequent psychoanalytic theorists to demand either the (absolute or relative) restoration or the complete abolition of this autonomy. The aim of this chapter, therefore, is to present the problems that have been created by Freud's accounts of the formation of the ego in its relation to narcissism and to critically examine the different theoretical formulations that have been provided by Heinz Hartmann, Jacques Lacan and Paul Ricouer as possible solutions to these problems.

Let us begin with Freud's initial conception of the ego. This conception, which arguably remained most fundamental throughout his career, is already to be found in the *Project for a Scientific Psychology* (1895), when the ego is portrayed as a system which progressively differentiates itself from the rest of the neural network as a result of its perceptual contact with external reality and which consequently becomes the representative of the demands of that reality, charged with controlling the spontaneous impulse of the organism towards a reckless or hallucinatory gratification. From 1914 onwards, however, with the publication of 'On Narcissism: An Introduction", a new group of themes begin to overlay this primary conception of the ego. Freud now suggests that a 'new psychical action' (*eine neue psychische aktion*) should be assumed that unifies the previously disorganised auto-erotic drives and brings about the stage of 'primary narcissism' (Freud, 1914c, p. 77).[1] In fact, he has already alluded to the existence of this stage in his paper 'Psychoanalytic Notes on an Autobiographical Account of a Case of Paranoia' (The Case of Schreber) written in 1911:

> There comes a time in the development of the individual at which he unifies his sexual drives (which have hitherto been engaged in auto-erotic activities) in order to obtain a love-object; and he begins by taking his own body as his love-object and only subsequently proceeds from this to the choice of some person other than himself. [Freud, 1911c, pp. 60–61]

Presumably, the ego in this scheme is formed at the stage of primary narcissism, between the stages of auto-eroticism and object love. But it is not clear in Freud what is this new psychical action that brings about ego formation, though we are told that it can be closely linked to the act of taking one's own body as a love object.

One thing is clear, however, during this initial stage of ego development: the ego itself is the 'great reservoir' (Freud, 1905d, p. 218)[2] in which all the libido is stored and from which some is later given off to objects. Yet, at the same time as the ego can invest some of its libido to objects, another portion of this "original libidinal cathexis ... fundamentally persists" in the ego "and is related to the object-cathexes much as the body of an amoeba is related to the pseudopodia which it puts out". Because of the persistence of this original narcissistic investment, the "pseudopodia" can be "drawn back again" from objects and reinvested in the ego—as a form of secondary narcissism—whenever excessive danger or disappointment is experienced with objects in the external world (Freud, 1914c, p. 75). In this version of the theory, then, cathexis emanates from the ego in primary narcissism to the cathexis of objects and, finally, to the recathexis of the ego in secondary narcissism.

An important point that should be noted here concerning Freud's view of the ego in 1914—despite the fact that it is partially obscured by the use of 'energetic' vocabulary—is his struggle to conceptualise the ego as subject and the ego as object.[3] Thus, although the ego is the object of the sexual drives—indeed, this was one of the momentous discoveries of the narcissism paper in which the ego "found its position among sexual objects and was at once given the foremost place among them" (Freud, 1920: 52)–insofar as it has its own 'ego-instincts' and energy (*Ichtriebenergie*) at its disposal, which are not derived from the sexual drives, the ego is viewed as a subject or agent that can pursue its own 'ego-interest' *(Ichinteresse)* of self-preservation and adaptation to the environment, an interest that is distinct from the aims of the sexual drives.[4]

However, Freud raises the following objection: if the ego can be an object of the sexual drives,

> Why ... is there any necessity for further distinguishing a sexual libido from a nonsexual energy of the ego-instincts? Would not the postulation of a single kind of psychical energy save us all the difficulties ... ? [1914c, p. 76].

The main difficulty that Freud faces here is that although he maintains that psychopathology is the result of conflict, he cannot detect any fundamental conflict between narcissistic libido and ego-instincts as they both aim to preserve the integrity and unity of the ego. However, there is still possibility for conflict: if the primary interest of the ego is its self-preservation, then it cannot achieve this by *loving itself too much*, that is to say, by believing that it exists absolutely in and through itself and finding no reason why its freedom should be limited by the pull of nature and object-bound forms of existence and determination. In other words, if the ego is to account for the seemingly obvious truth that it is dependent both on nature (bodily and external) and others for its survival, then it clearly cannot assume such an omnipotent narcissistic position. Yet, the assumption of this position and its potential opposition to the primary ego-interest of self-preservation are equally untenable from the perspective of narcissistic dynamics. Thus, to the question:" ... whence does that necessity arise that urges our mental life to pass on beyond the limits of narcissism and to attach the libido to objects", Freud replies:

The answer which would follow from our line of thought would once more be that we are impelled when the cathexis of the ego with libido exceeds a certain limit. A strong egoism is a protection against disease, but in the last resort we must begin to love in order that we may not fall ill [1914c, p. 66].

The ego, therefore, needs to give up its narcissistic self-enclosure in favour of forming relations with others—that is, it has to learn how to lean on/love others (what Freud calls 'anaclitic object-choice")—so as not to fall ill. Freud also seems to suggest here that pathological narcissism ensues when the ego cannot invest what it cannot afford to lose, that is to say, its cathexis with libido cannot exceed a certain limit that will impel it to invest its surplus libido in others. This, in turn, implies that either the initial libidinal investment in the ego is insufficient or minimal or the ego's investments in others are not met with their approval and/or their reciprocal investment in the ego. Due to one of these two reasons (or perhaps both), the ego's energy sources are (or become) depleted and the ego has no other option but to retreat to a narcissistic state of self-enclosure and to avoid forming intimate relationships with others. Thus, it is forced to follow the path of least resistance, that is, the path that leads to the avoidance of hard work that is required in dealing successfully with the problems presented in the formation and maintenance of intimate relations with others. Psychoanalysis, in this respect, pushes the ego to the path of maximum resistance as it invites it to work hard so as to *negate* (in the Hegelian sense of transcending by simultaneously destroying and preserving) its narcissistic boundaries that prevent it from investing its libido in others, that is to say, it enables the ego to move from narcissism to object-love. Therefore, if narcissism represents the negation (in the Hegelian sense again) of the original state of autoerotic existence, object-love represents the negation of this negation. Pathological narcissism, therefore, signifies the ego's inability to engage with the systematic and continuous (psychoanalytic) work of dialectical negation.

Moreover, when the ego desperately attempts to attain to an affirmative state where it is no longer in thrall to nature and others, then it positions itself in a realm where its dependency on others provides no obstacles to the realisation of this illusory affirmation. Thus, it develops the tendency to model its object on itself, or to choose an object which possesses precisely those virtues which it feels itself to lack, namely, it picks out objects by identification or by incorporating them into itself—what Freud terms 'narcissistic object-choice'.

A little under a decade after 'On Narcissism: An Introduction", in his key essay on the *Ego and the Id* (1923b), Freud advances even further in this direction, that is, he employs the process of identification to explain not only narcissistic object-choice but also the formation of the ego itself. Thus, he abandons the concept of primary narcissism, arguing that the newly defined id must be seen as the initial reservoir of libido from which cathexes can be sent out to objects, leaving thus the ego with no independent energy sources of its own and also suggests that the ego not only chooses objects which resemble itself, but also models itself to a large extend upon its earliest objects. Specifically, it originates in identifications with objects that were cathected by the id and then lost. Another way of putting this is that the ego is formed by loss of intensely loved objects and by identifying with and taking in the lost objects as part of oneself. As Freud puts it:

> The character of the ego is a precipitate of the abandoned object-cathexes, it contains the history of these object-choices. [1923b, p. 29]

Thus, whereas in the earlier scheme the narcissistic cathexis of the ego always precedes both the cathexis of the object and the secondary narcissistic reinvestments in the ego as a result of the withdrawal of cathexes from objects, in the new scheme "the narcissism of the ego is ... a secondary one, which has been withdrawn from objects", (1923b, p. 55)–i.e., the ego is formed through, indeed it is the product of, secondary narcissism. The ego itself appears to be a vicissitude of libidinal forces, with no independent origins of its own.

In spite of these new theoretical developments, Freud's former belief on the importance of ego's autonomous function remains almost unaltered. He continues to describe the ego as having privileged access to reality and as the much harassed mediator between the claims of reality, super-ego and id. The ego may be severely limited in its autonomy and possibilities for action, yet through its control of motility, its development from "obedience to drives" to the "curbing of drives" and its transformation of "the object-cathexes of the id into ego structures", it appropriates some of the id's energy for its own purposes (1923b, pp. 55–6). Indeed, for Freud "psycho-analysis is a tool which should make possible the ego's progressive conquest of the id". (1923b, p. 56)

However, no sooner has Freud listed these ego strengths than he begins to retract them. With respect to the ego's capacity for reality testing, he simply points to the common situation in which "when-ever possible" the ego engages in rationalisation rather than reality testing—that is, it sacrifices the truth—so as to "remain on good terms with the id". Concerning the ego's control of motility, Freud writes that this power is "a question more of form than of fact". With respect to action, the "ego's position is like that of a constitutional monarch", which is to say, while no wish can be transformed into action without the ego's "sanction", the ego "hesitates long before imposing [its] veto" on the id, just as the monarch is reluctant to exercise veto over the legislation of the parliament. In both the cases, then, the ego "only too often yields to the temptation to become sycophantic, opportunist and lying, like a politician who sees the truth but wants to keep his place in popular favour". (1923b, pp. 55–6) With regards to the ego's ability to appropriate the power of the id for its own purposes, Freud argues that the ego acquires the id's energy and thereby advances its own development seductively, that is to say, libidinously. By assuming the characteristics of the love object, that is, by identifying with it and offering itself to the id as a substitute for that object, the ego entices the id to abandon its sex-ual aims and relinquish its object cathexis. As he puts it:

> When the ego assumes the features of the object, it is forcing itself, so to speak, upon the id as a love-object and is trying to make good the id's loss by saying: Look, you can love me too—I am so like the object [1923b, p. 30].

While this process of transforming object cathexis into a narcissistic one through identification with the object allows the ego to "obtain control over the id and deepen its relations with it", there is neverthe-less a price to be paid for that achievement. The ego must "to a large extent" acquiesce "in the id's experience". (1923b, p. 30)

Yet, despite the above remarks, Freud will repeatedly decline to construe the ego as utterly passive and subservient to the id. For example, in *Inhibitions, Symptoms and Anxiety* (1926d), he dissociates himself from those psychoanalysts who, following his earlier work, made into a *Weltanschauung* the theory of the "weakness of the ego in relation to the id". (Freud, 1926d, pp. 95–6) However, several pages later one can find a statement that 'minimises' the ego's strength in relation to the id: "Although the act of repression demonstrates the strength of the ego, in one particular it reveals the ego's powerlessness and how impervious to influence are the separate instinctual impulses of the id". (1926d, p. 97) Thus, Freud equally refuses to regard the ego (or the id) as the commanding factor in psychic life. He realises that attention to the ego proceeds only at the cost of the id and *vice versa*. This ultimately promotes an unproductive either/or logic. Freud seeks to retain both moments–although he occasionally vacillates between negating the renunciation of unconscious drives as repression contrary to reality and applauding it as beneficial to the ego's adaptation to reality—and, moreover, foresees clearly that a turn to ego or id psychology will entail a renunciation of the specific gains of psychoanalysis. A letter of Freud to Jung in 1909 is a testament to Freud's insight, showing him acutely aware of the dangers of an either/or mentality and of the threat—in Adler and Jung—of ego abstracted from depth psychology:

> We have agreed already that the basic mechanisms of neurosogenesis is the antagonism between the instinctual drives–the ego as the repressing [force], the libido as the repressed. ... It is remarkable though, that we human beings find it so difficult to focus attention equally on both of these opposing drives. ... Thus far I have described only the repressed, which is the novel, the unknown, as Cato did when he sided with causa victa. I hope I have not forgotten that there also exists a victrix. Here Adler's psychology invariably sees only the repressing agency and therefore describes the 'sensitivity', this attitude of the ego toward libido, as the basic cause of neuroses. Now I find you on the same path ... that is because I have not sufficiently studied the ego, you are running the risk of not doing justice to the libido which I have evaluated. [Cited in Schur, 1957, pp. 17–8]

Thus, instead of being loyal to both dimensions, both Adler and Jung choose to prioritise the ego at the expense of libido and the id. Following Adler's and Jung's example, Heinz Hartmann—probably the most important of the ego psychologists–opts to detach the ego, or part of the ego, from the id and its narcissistic libidinal origins; he dubs this the 'conflict-free ego sphere' (Hartmann, 1958, p. 8). The ego, therefore, can perform its rational functions without experiencing any interference from the id. The aim of psychoanalysis, according to Hartmann, is to help the ego "achieve a better functioning synthesis and relation to the environment". (1958, p. 81) However, by excluding the influence of the id—and the conflicts that it creates—from this particular ego sphere, Hartmann advocates the ego's uncritical adaptation to society. The ego, therefore, becomes for him a mere receptacle of social reality because he fails to fully appreciate one of the most important functions of the ego: to facilitate the derivation of pleasure from the satisfaction of id impulses. Once this has been consigned to the repertoire of tricks for adapting to society, without consideration of that moment in pleasure that transcends subservience to social imperatives, the ego's capacity to criticise the social reality which prevents the realisation of pleasure is seriously compromised.

For this reason, Hartmann is accused by Jacques Lacan for recoiling from Freud's utterly subversive discovery—which consists in the demonstration that the unconscious, or the "subject of the unconscious", as he calls it and not the ego, constitutes "the core of our being" (Lacan, 1988, p. 43)—and attempting to rehabilitate the pre-analytic ego. His introduction of autonomous ego functions, so Lacan maintains, amounts to turning back from Freud's decentring of the ego vis-à-vis the unconscious and reinstating the ego of academic psychology: "Ah! Our nice little ego is back again!" (1988, p. 11) Lacan's polemic against Hartmann and his return to Freud are thus meant to reverse this regression. He insists that the disagreement with Hartmann is absolute, without possible mediation. If the latter is correct,

[w]e will have to abandon the notion I tell you to be the essence of the Freudian discovery, the decentering of the subject in relation to the ego and to return to the notion that everything

centres on the standard development of ego. This is an alternative without mediation—if that is true, everything I say is false [1988, p. 148].

In contrast to Hartmann, therefore, Lacan decides to forge a rigid connection between narcissism and the ego. By reducing the ego to narcissism, he refuses to see it as an autonomous agent that has its own independent origins and sources of energy and can thus produce objective knowledge of itself and outside reality. For Lacan, the ego is either the foundation of narcissism or the principle of objective knowledge but not both. For the principle of objective knowledge, he asserts, cannot emerge from narcissism unless it is already there from the start. If the ego is essentially narcissistic, there is no immanent genesis of objective knowledge.

For this reason, Lacan also rejects the assumption of the ego's progressive differentiation and independence from the id generated by the organism's adaptation to the reality principle, arguing that "the reality principle can only be distinguished from the pleasure principle on a gnoseological plane and it is therefore illegitimate to introduce it to the genesis of the ego, since it implies the ego itself in its role as subject of knowledge (*connaisance*)". (Lacan, 1932, p. 324) The cognition of which the ego is the support, however, is inseparable from a process of 'mis-cognition' (*meconnaisance*) which is rooted in the imaginary identification in the mirror stage.

More specifically, in his introduction of the mirror stage, Lacan draws on Freud's theory of biological prematurity, so as to trace the ego's origins to the manic attempt to deny infantile helplessness (*Hilflosigkeit*). He locates that helplessness in the fragmented and unintegrated state of the child's bodily experience—what he calls "the body in bits and pieces" (Lacan, 1953, p. 14)—that results from its "anatomical incompleteness" and manifests itself in "the signs of uneasiness and motor uncoordination of the neo-natal months". (Lacan, 1977, p. 4) During the mirror stage, the child anticipates a future situation in which its helplessness would have been overcome. In contradiction to its actually fragmented and uncoordinated state, in the mirror—or, more precisely, in the mirroring experience—the child becomes aware of its own body as a *Gestalt* (i.e., unified whole). The mirror image is held together, it can come and go with a slight change of the infant's position and the mastery of its image fills it with triumph and joy. (1977, p. 1) The ego is constituted, in turn, through the identification with this unified image. This internalised image, now set up in the psyche, provides the trajectory for further 'maturation', namely, the further unification of the self. Lacan's thesis is that this trajectory 'from insufficiency to anticipation' is 'alienating' and 'fictional' (1977, p. 2) in virtue of the fact that it imposes a rigid structure on—and thereby falsifies the actual state of—the child's corporeal experience, which is in fact fragmented and projects an illusory image of the child as whole. The internalisation of the imago leads "to the assumption of the armour of an alienating identity, which will mark with its rigid structure the subject's entire mental development". (1977, p. 34) It follows, for Lacan, that the "essential function of the ego", which he refers to as its imaginary function because of its specular origins, is not reality testing, but *misrecognition*, that is,

> very nearly the systematic refusal to acknowledge reality which French analysts refer to in talking about the psychoses. [Lacan, 1953, p. 12]

The only reality that needs to be acknowledged, according to Lacan, is that what motivates us to embark on this journey from insufficiency to anticipation—i.e., our desire to deny our fragmentation and recover a sense of wholeness—can never be found. As we are born prematurely, our primary and fundamental state of existence is that of fragmentation, so any future search for imaginary wholeness and completion is destined to fail. One of the functions of the imaginary identification in the mirror stage, therefore, will be to paper over a gap inherent in our relation to this future search. The same scenario is re-enacted in our passage from imaginary to symbolic identifications, that is, our identifications with subject positions made available to us by language and culture. We are constantly trying to capture in these subject positions some-*Thing* that will complete us but which is always already lost.[5] There seems to be a fundamental, constitutive lack which is both the object and the cause of the desire for this search.[6]

Furthermore, this constant deferral of (even relative) completion, the postponement and even rejection of closure, creates a constantly shifting horizon of experience that prioritises the possibility of future unfoldings that can change our understanding and interpretation of our past history and present status. For Lacan, therefore, the effectivity of the past, like that of any present event in our life, cannot be divorced from our orientation towards the future. As he puts it:

> What is realised in my history is not the past definite of what was, since it is no more, or even the present perfect of what has been in what I am, but the future anterior of what I shall have been for what I am in the process of becoming. [Lacan, 1966, p. 86]

Lacan's 'future anterior' attitude towards life, therefore, implies that we should not waste time evaluating our current psychological development by judging and grasping what is actually reasonable and enjoyable in our present reality and measuring this particular actuality against our ideals of rationality and happiness. Since all our ideals are necessarily illusory, we need to come to terms with the disappointment of never realising these ideals. So instead of instructing us 'If at first you don't succeed, try, try, try again", Lacan's advice is to accept the fact that 'You will try, try, try again, but you will always fail'. However, there is no possibility of ever resigning completely to the loss of the ideal that generates this endless search. We will always be deceived by the ego and its ideals. Nevertheless, at the end of analysis, this deception will not generate so much suffering, as we will begin to enjoy it and laugh at (and with) its silly inevitability.

However, an important question arises here: why is it that Lacan always seems to prioritise deception and fragmentation at the expense of transparency and synthesis? The answer has already been indicated above: from the moment he decides to reduce ego to narcissism and its formation in the mirror stage, he has no other choice but to represent the ego as systematically deceiving and misrecognising. There can be no non-narcissistic fundament—nothing outside the ego's relation to the other/counterpart in the mirror—on which the ego could stand so as to produce clear and succinct knowledge of itself and/or others.

An interesting objection to Lacan's insistence on the completely deceiving nature of the ego comes from Paul Ricoeur. The latter provides the distinctions that make it possible to offer a differentiated account of the ego which can deconstruct its self-deceptions, thereby preserving the subversiveness of the Freudian project without, at the same time, repudiating the ego as pure misrecognition. Ricoeur, thus, begins by arguing that traditionally philosophers have assumed that our knowledge is based on fundamental facts which must be taken as self-evident. If this cannot be done, then the whole edifice of knowledge might be uncertain and total scepticism might reign. We would not even know whether we are dreaming or not! For instance, Descartes' proposition *cogito ergo sum* refers to the indubitable fact *that I am* insofar as *I think*, regardless of how delusional that thinking may be. For Ricoeur, however, this fact "tends to be confused with the moment of adequation, in which I am *such* as I perceive myself". (Ricoeur, 1974, p. 241) The adequacy of my consciousness of myself, my self-knowledge, can no longer be taken for granted after psychoanalysis' documentation of the innumerable ruses of desire and its discovery of narcissism, "the great screen between self and oneself". (Ricoeur, 1970, p. 421) On the contrary, after Freud's intervention in the history of Western rationality, Ricoeur argues that the fact "that I am" and the possibility that I am deceived, to one extent or another, whenever I describe "what I am"—namely, that my self-knowledge is "indefinitely dubious"—must be assumed together (see Ricoeur, 1974, p. 242ff; 1970, p. 379ff).

Ricoeur, therefore, maintains that psychoanalysis demands the critique of the immediacy, pretensions and self-deceptions of the naive and therefore illusory, cogito: "Only the *cogito* which has passed through the critical test of psychoanalysis is no longer the one claimed by philosophy in its pre-Freudian naiveté". However, he insists that adequacy of consciousness and expansion of the ego remain the goal: "Psychoanalysis can have no therapeutic ambition other than enlarging the field of consciousness and giving back to the ego some of the strength ceded to its three powerful masters [the id, the super-ego and external reality]". What had been the 'origin' in the philosophical idealist tradition, namely "conscious-being (*Bewusstsein*)", now "becomes task or goal". Thus, rather than abandoning the standpoint of the ego altogether, Ricoeur believes that the deconstruction of naive consciousness can instead initiate a process of creating, through the work of psychoanalysis, a more adequate ego-consciousness:

becoming-conscious (*Bewusstwerden*) remains the task, an interminable one, to be sure, but a task nonetheless. [Ricoeur, 1974, p. 241]

Ricoeur can hold this position because, in contrast to Lacan, who, as we have seen, speaks of the intrinsic and systematic misrecognition of the ego, Ricoeur refers only to the 'indefinitely dubious character' of the ego-cogito. This of course implies that I can always be deceived, but I never know the extent to which I am in fact deceived at any given time.

However, although Ricoeur effectively illustrates how the acquisition of self-knowledge can be seen as an ongoing, open-ended process, he does not sufficiently explain how laying claim to a self-knowledge involves an *attempt* to still this process. Such attempts can sometimes take on particularly strident and intolerant forms in which a 'self' is asserted as absolutely different from and superior to the 'other' (e.g., in racism). Clearly, we need to understand and address the assertion of self-knowledge as something fixed and particular as much as to understand its potential malleability and flux.

Moreover, Ricoeur's insufficient explanation of the fixity of self-knowledge is followed by his misguided belief that *only* the ego-cogito can produce it. In other words, the interminable battle between certainty and doubt (and its provisional outcome) can *only* take place within the boundaries set by the ego-cogito. In this respect, it is only the progressive enlargement of consciousness that can lead to the progressive conquest of doubt—but not to its complete elimination. Thus, despite his initial anti-Cartesian intentions, Ricoeur still subscribes to the view that (relative) self-knowledge and certainty is entirely dependent on the activity of the Cartesian cogito. Yet, what Ricoeur seems to be missing from his account is the fact that at the beginning of our lives we have to experience ourselves through our bodily (self-preservative and/or libidinal) functions and participate in activities with others (i.e., our primary caregivers) before we can 'know' and be 'certain' that we exist. This implies that it is not conscious deliberation but the use of—and the enjoyment derived from—our body and our pleasurable and/or painful interactions with the world and others that are vital for the initial formation and later development of self-knowledge and certainty. Ricoeur's conception of self-knowledge as an exclusive product of the Cartesian cogito does not take into consideration its bodily and intersubjective basis and thus reduces it to a mental activity devoid of any somatic-libidinal and social elements.

Fundamentally distinct philosophical outlooks and practical projects are condensed in Hartmann's, Lacan's and Ricoeur's formulations. Hartmann attempts to establish a 'conflict-free ego sphere' which can produce valid knowledge of itself and outside reality as it remains uncontaminated by libidinal investments. In contrast, Lacan asserts that the ego is infinitely deceiving as its formation through the identification with its (mis-taken) double in the mirror condemns it to exist forever in the realm of the imaginary. Finally, with Lacan and against Hartmann, Ricoeur believes that the adequacy of the ego's self-knowledge cannot be taken for granted after Freud's discovery of narcissism. Yet, against Lacan, he still wants to maintain the relative validity of this self-knowledge based on the ego's inherent inability to determine the extent of its own deception. What all of them have in common, however, is that their accounts of ego are primarily mentalistic and empty of any somatic-libidinal and/or social content. Therefore, they tend to derive immediately out of the (supposedly) immutable facts of the ego's mental constitution (for Hartmann, the ego's uncontested autonomy; for Lacan, its completely deceiving character; for Ricoeur, its indefinitely dubious one) the validity (or not) of its knowledge claims without taking into consideration its somatic-libidinal and/or social origins. In order for the ego to be valid, however, it needs to preserve the moments of its somatic-libidinal and social genesis; they work permanently within it. Moreover, the ego's genesis and validity need to be thought in their simultaneous unity and difference. This implies that the assumption that the validity of the ego's production of knowledge is simply independent of its somatic-libidinal and/or social origins is as false as the reverse assumption that it is simply identical with them.

Therefore, the ego is neither to be reduced to its somatic-libidinal and/or social origins nor totally abstracted from them. Hartmann, Lacan and Ricoeur, however, abstract the ego from its origins because they are unable to comprehend the ego as *dialectical*, that is, as *simultaneously* a psychic and an extra-psychic phenomenon, a quantum of libido and the representative of outside reality (see

Adorno, 1968, pp. 86, 93). Moreover, they cannot understand how the ego's relation to a social dynamic can turn into a libidinal one. The notion of narcissism, therefore, does not only describe a psychical and clinical occurrence but captures the social reality of the modern individual; it expresses the private regression of the ego into the id under the sway of public domination. It also comprehends the dialectical isolation of the modern individual—dialectical in that the isolation that damns the individual to scrape along in a private world derives from a public and social one.

In order to find, therefore, why the individual's energy is directed towards her/himself, rather than towards others, we need to examine not only the problems in the individual's ego formation but also the problems that are generated by a society that puts a premium on the hardening of the individual's ego and promotes her/his naked will to self-preservation. This is exactly what Freud (unintentionally) advises us to do when he decides to change his account of ego formation in its relation to narcissism. By moving away from his early conception of the ego as an autonomous agent that has its own independent origins and sources of energy and into his late one in which the ego loses its autonomy and power and is (but does not necessarily have to be) reduced to narcissism, Freud accurately depicts how recent social changes drive the ego to regression and unconsciousness so as to irrationally subsist. For example, the shift from early to late modernity has been accompanied by a shift in the psychological constitution of the individual whose typical characteristic is not a strong ego but 'ego-weakness' and narcissism. Under the conditions of early modernity the persisting 'I' makes a 'sacrifice of the moment' and preserves itself by the desires it has repressed. Under late modernity, however, self-preservation only appears possible by mimetic adaptation to what is dead. The more obvious it becomes that the economic and social basis of any individual's life is liable to annihilation, the more the individual seeks to identify with, and adapt to, the current economic and social conditions. For the present socio-economic system, however, the individual's self-preservation is not in itself a matter of any importance.

Moreover, the tension between super-ego, ego and id which Freud takes as paradigmatic for the individual is replaced in late modernity by a false reconciliation between ego and id.[7] This false reconciliation—which is a parody of a genuine one that would only be possible with the end of structural social antagonism—succeeds in reducing the effectiveness of the mediating agency of the ego (between the id and the superego). This leads to a weak ego whose regressive, compulsive, blind behaviour, bears all the signs of the id, adheres perfectly to the demands of the superego (the agency of social 'normality') and is therefore already enlisted in the service of the social order. Therefore, instead of internalising and thus both mediating and concealing domination as the strong ego does, the ego-weak and narcissistic personality is ready to respond to *direct* domination at a moment's notice. Self-preservation under late modernity is intimately entangled with unquestionable submission to the existing social order and, ultimately, self-destructiveness.

Self-destructiveness, accordingly, cannot be seen as a mere psychological dysfunction that psychoanalytic therapy could alleviate. It is rather the desperate and miscarried form of self-preservation in a society which lives by destroying. Auschwitz and Hiroshima announce the possibility that this entanglement of self-preservation and self-destructiveness may yet finish off the species entirely. This is a *regression*, a direct celebration of archaic violence and barbarity which in any case existed in a mediated form in early modernity. But as it has already been stated above, this regression cannot simply be attributed to sick or inadequate individuals. It is also a social category. The death-driven, narcissistic qualities of the modern individual are also characteristic of late modernity in general.

In this sense, Lacan's portrayal of the ego as an alienating, rigid and reified structure reflects accurately the conditions of the individual's existence in the present society. The concept of the reification of the ego, however, must not be reified. The psychic and character forms of reification are historically specific and are not insular but dialectically linked to the dynamic of modernity. For this reason, we should not assume that the present form of psychical reification is permanent. And it can be changed only if we come to grips with the recent historical dynamic of the psychical domain.

In order to critically engage with this historical dynamic, however, we need the elements of resistance offered by a strong ego and the possibility that it holds out for autonomy of thought and action. This is what Freud unwittingly instructs us to do by insisting, despite his illustration of how the ego becomes engulfed by the id and narcissistic libido, on the preservation and importance of the ego's strength. This does not mean, however, that we should simply celebrate the strong ego (as Hartmann does). We must never lose sight of the repression, domination and untruth constitutive of it. The strong ego is ineradicably oppressive, but needs this oppression to think how oppression might come to an end in more than thought alone. We must not abandon the hope of reconciliation between the ego and id; their unreconciled antagonism in the strong ego serves their true reconciliation better than their false reconciliation in ego-weakness and narcissism.

It is precisely this hope of true reconciliation, however, that Lacan discards in his account of the formation of the ego in the mirror stage. Once the production of the ego in the mirror begins, there is no way back to the id and the historical world and consciousness, or self-consciousness, is radically severed from its somatic origins and empirical history. The only way the id (as the representative of the soma) and the historical world can establish their presence is by violently and traumatically attacking the totalitarian narcissistic structure of the ego. But if we do not want to lose our hope for future happiness, a sharp break between these realms should not be established; they must be neither rendered identical nor absolutely severed. In the pursuit of this dialectical relationship between these dimensions, we can bear witness to the conditions of our present self-mutilation and resist its perpetuation.

NOTES

1.   Although Freud does not explicitly portray the occurrence of primary narcissism as a 'stage' and certain psychoanalytic theorists perceive it more as a 'state' than a 'stage', there is such an abrupt and radical change in the organisation of the activity of the drives and the structure of psyche during this developmental period that the use of the term 'stage' appears to be justified.

2.   The section in which this term is to be found was added to the *Three Essays* after the formulation of the theory of narcissism in 1914.

3.   Freud's struggle to conceptualise the ego as subject and as object is also highlighted and analysed by Joel Whitebook in his (1995) book *Perversion and Utopia: A Study in Psychoanalysis and Critical Theory. Cambridge*, Mass.: The MIT Press, p. 104.

4.   While the sexual drive later becomes autonomous, it originally 'leans on' self-preservative functions and is, hence, derivative from them; e.g., auto-erotic thumb sucking leans on the nutritive function of drinking milk.

5.   Lacan argues that the subject, divided from itself in language, is continually haunted by a sense of 'absence', a sense that it is not 'fully present'. Lacan refers to this sense of absence as the 'Thing'. Of course, in reality, this is not an 'object' that can be rediscovered, simply a lack that is intrinsic to the subject divided from itself in language. However, this sense of a 'lost object' is said to produce in the subject an endless and nagging desire for something that will 'make good the loss'. Needless to say, for Lacan, this desire is doomed to remain a fantasy since there is no original state of 'wholeness' to which the subject could ever return.

6.   This refers to Lacan's notion of *objet* (*petit*) *a* which denotes the object that can never be attained, which is really the cause of desire rather than that towards which desire tends; this is why Lacan calls it 'the object-cause' of desire. Please See Lacan, J. (1977). *The Four Fundamental Concepts of Psychoanalysis.* [Seminar XI—1964] Trans. A. Sheridan. London: Hogarth Press and Institute of Psycho-analysis.

7.   For an especially direct formulation of the relationship between the increasing concentration of capital and ego-weakness, see Adorno, T.W. & Horkheimer, M. (1944). *Dialectic of Enlightenment.* Trans. J. Cumming. London: Verson, 1979.

CHAPTER TWO

"I-not-I": narcissism beyond the one and the other

Josh Cohen

D uring the early 1940s, in the shadow of and under conditions imposed by, world war, the British Psycho-Analytical Society was conducting an internal war of its own: a protracted series of fierce and often bitter debates over the validity and growing influence of Melanie Klein's contributions.[1] The so-called 'Controversial Discussions' saw Klein's followers (and, towards the end of the Discussions, Klein herself) robustly defend the continuity and coherence of her contributions with Freudian metapsychology against the vehement criticism of her Viennese, Hungarian and some English colleagues in the Society.

The criticisms turned on the elaborate mental and affective life Klein ascribed to the youngest infant. As Susan Isaacs claims in the first of the papers from the group around Klein, all somatic processes are from the outset expressed psychically by the infant in the form of phantasy: "[T]here is no impulse, no instinctual urge, which is not experienced as (unconscious) phantasy". (Isaacs in King & Steiner, 1991, p. 277) According to critics from the Hungarian school such as Barbara Lantos and Michael Balint, this ascription of phantasy to even the youngest infant failed to accord with the findings of infant observation, which could confirm affects of "irritation, pain, anger or fright" in the first few months of life, "but none of hate or anxiety". (Balint in King & Steiner, 1991, p. 347) In other words, the infant's observable affective responses could be more plausibly explained by conscious frustration than by unconscious phantasy.

The more trenchant and thoroughgoing critique of Klein, however, came from Anna Freud and her Viennese allies, who found in the thesis of early phantasy an heretical challenge to the fundamental metapsychological concept of primary narcissism. Anna Freud would attempt to compress this crucial difference in the following formula:

> One of the outstanding differences between Freudian and Kleinian theory is that Mrs Klein sees in the first months of life evidence of a wide range of differentiated object relations, partly libidinal and partly aggressive. Freudian theory on the other hand allows at this period only for the crudest rudiments of object relationship and sees life governed by the desire for instinct gratification, in which perception of the object is only achieved slowly. [Freud, 1943 in King & Steiner, 1991, p. 420]

A later contribution from Kate Friedlander would state this difference more starkly still, characterizing the earliest relationship of infant to mother as "a biological one in the beginning", only "slowly altered" into a psychological one. (Friedlander in King & Steiner, 1991, p. 456)

Such contributions point to the Controversial Discussions as a contest above all over the meaning and implications of primary narcissism. According to the Viennese, Freud's term designates a state of biological enclosure, for which objects exist only as sources of instinctual frustration and satisfaction. Responding to her critics, Isaacs points out that such a construal of primary narcissism involves a highly selective and reductive reading of Freud. For Freud, primary narcissism is not an unbroken condition that "occupies the *whole field* of mental life" for a specified period, but a position that persists in varying degrees throughout the course of life. (Isaacs in King & Steiner, 1991, p. 462)

Yet whilst Isaacs rightly insists that Freud's view of earliest infantile life is more complex and variegated than her Viennese antagonists allow, neither she nor any of her Kleinian colleagues show much interest in developing an alternate reading of primary narcissism. Rather, Kleinian and indeed British psychoanalysis more generally, would tend increasingly to oppose to primary narcissism a primary object relation. In the Kleinian tradition, this would mean that the tumultuous somatic and psychic life of the infant was from the very first experienced through phantasized relations. Thus for Isaacs, the baby's urges, desires and affects are registered through rudimentary, pre-verbal libidinal and, especially, destructive phantasies of the mother: "I want to suck the nipple, to stroke her face, to eat her up, to keep her inside me, to bite the breast, to tear her to bits, to drown and burn her, to throw her out of me". (Isaacs in King & Steiner, 1991, p. 277) Whilst Balint and the other analysts of the Hungarian school objected to what they saw as the excessively elaborate content of such fantasies, insisting that a 'primary love' grounded in the dynamic of frustration and satisfaction preceded hate and anxiety, they were in accord with Klein's premise that the infant's psychic life is shaped from the first by their experience of an object.

As I hope to show in the course of this chapter, it has instead been left to French psychoanalytic authors to think primary narcissism beyond this reductive opposition between biological monad and relating subject, not least by attending carefully to the complex vicissitudes of and internal tensions within the concept as developed across the Freudian corpus. Whilst Isaacs and others recognised narcissism's status as what Jean-Bertrand Pontalis would call "an insurmountable and permanent component of the human being" (Pontalis, 1981, p. 136) the implications of this status were left largely unthought in the British tradition.

In what follows, I will draw on a range of writers, most notably André Green, to delineate a conception of primary narcissism that undoes the opposition between the monadic self-enclosure and dyadic relatedness. In a complex and ambivalent relation to his theoretical and clinical legacy, Green nonetheless acknowledges the central role of Lacan in recognizing the ineradicably paradoxical character of primary narcissism as *a structure of enclosure conditioned by the presence of the other*. I will go on to argue that one of the many virtues of D.W. Winnicott's later contributions is its acknowledgment and development, uniquely within British psychoanalysis, of this richly suggestive paradox.[2] Indeed, it is through the retrospective lens of this paradox that we can make sense of the term's disconcerting instability in Freud's authorship.

Freud's narcissisms

The most cursory survey of Freud's various adumbrations of narcissism will reveal why the concept is so apt to sow confusion. We find contradictory pronouncements on this question not only across different texts in the corpus, but *within* Freud's key theoretical statement of 1914, 'On Narcissism: An Introduction'. The essay's first part offers an account of the prehistory of the individual, defined by what Lacan would call "an original organic chaos" (Lacan, 2006, p. 94) a formless nucleus of "auto-erotic instincts ... there from the very first". (Freud, 1914c, p. 77) Auto-erotism precedes the differentiated unity of the ego and therefore any distinction between self and other. This nebulous reservoir of libido is the source of satisfactions "experienced in connection with vital functions which serve the purpose of self-preservation". (Freud, 1914c, p. 87) The satiation of hunger and thirst in particular become invested with an erotic significance which results in the formation of the ego. The ego, that is, comes into being by being cathected as an object worth looking after.

And yet this developmental story by which, to invoke Friedlander's terms, the 'biological' becomes a 'psychological' being is always implicitly and sometimes explicitly put in question by other passages in Freud. Indeed, prior to 'On Narcissism: An Introduction", a famous footnote to the 1911 paper, 'Two Principles of Mental Functioning", had already acknowledged the hypothesis of a purely narcissistic organisation as strictly untenable: "an organization which was a slave to the pleasure principle and neglected the reality of the external world could not maintain itself alive for the shortest time". (Freud, 1911b, p. 220) Such a 'fiction' is justified only if the care it receives from its mother is incorporated into this description of the infant's inner world. It is the very fact of infantile helplessness which conditions its illusion of autonomous self-enclosure. The objectless state is the paradoxical effect of the maternal object's care.

It is only by attending to the apparent contradictions in Freud's formulations of the earliest infantile states that the force of this paradox can come into focus. Thus, where 'On Narcissism: An Introduction' seems to identify auto-erotic drives as the origin and fundament of psychic life, 'there from the very first", the second of the *Three Essays* derives auto-erotic activity from the experience of maternal care. In such activities, writes Freud, the child is seeking to renew their "first and most vital activity, his sucking at his mother's breast, or at substitutes for it, that must have familiarized him with this pleasure". (Freud, 1905d, p. 181) Once again, erotic self-sufficiency is facilitated by erotic dependence. Indeed, a 1920 footnote to the original 1905 section on auto-erotism makes this point explicit. Acknowledging that the term was coined by Havelock Ellis, Freud is nonetheless concerned to distinguish his own understanding of the term from the sexologist's:

> Havelock Ellis, it is true, uses the word 'auto-erotic' in a somewhat different sense, to describe an excitation which is not provoked from the outside but arises internally. What psychoanalysis regards as the central point is not the genesis of the excitation, but the question of its relation to an object. [Freud, 1905d, p. 181]

No content merely to differentiate himself from Ellis, Freud strikingly *inverts* his definition. If the 'central point' is the question of the excitation's 'relation to an object", then Ellis's concern to determine its source as internal is strictly redundant. This is not because Ellis is wrong–indeed, we might ask how *auto*-erotism can logically sig-nify anything other than internally provoked excitation. The problem is rather that the binary logic of inside and outside is inadequate to the paradoxical logic of the auto-erotic: The infant's pleasure in itself is structured by 'its relation to an object'.

Its title notwithstanding, it is of course not in the 1914 essay that the concept of narcissism is introduced, but in the biographical essay on Leonardo of 1910.[3] A backward glance at this text reveals that Freud had from the outset conceived the narcissistic position as conditioned by the relation to an object. Here, narcissism is posited as the basis for homosexuality. Speculating on Leonardo's early childhood, Freud argues that homosexuality arises when the child is forced by circumstances to repress his attachment to his mother: "The boy represses his love for his mother: he puts himself in her place, identifies himself with her and takes his own person as a model in whose likeness he chooses new objects for his love". (Freud, 1910c, p. 100) Prevented by repression from returning the love he receives, the boy instead redirects his desire for his mother inward in an act of identification which aligns his self-perception with his mother's and renders him an object of his own love. The homosexual is in this respect his mother in disguise, loving boys "the way his other loved *him* when he was a child". (Freud, 1910c, p. 100)[4]

Thus, neither this nor any other of Freud's attempts to exemplify narcissism, to delineate its concrete forms, confirm the picture of monadic self-enclosure suggested by the metapsychological remarks of 'On Narcissism''s first part. Indeed, not even the auto-erotic drives which precede narcissism proper can be said to have their source purely in themselves. The absence of an object is always a disguised relation to an object.

Perhaps the most sustained development of this insight is to be found in the last part of 'On Narcissism's itself. The antagonists of the Controversial Discussions, we recall, sought to advance their own interpretations of primary narcissism by appeal to the direct observation of babies. As if anticipating the dead end to which such contention would lead, Freud writes that "[t]he primary narcissism of children which we have assumed ... is less easy to grasp by direct observation than to confirm by inference elsewhere". (Freud, 1914c, p. 90) Here we have a clear intimation that narcissism is less for Freud a determinate and observable state than a structure, in Pontalis' phrase "an insurmountable and permanent component of the human being". This structure, Freud goes on to suggest, follows from the infant's necessary consignment to parental care:

> If we look at the attitude of affectionate parents toward their children, we have to recognise that it is a revival and reproduction of their own narcissism, which they have long since abandoned. ... The child ... shall once more really be the centre and core of creation—His Majesty the Baby, as we once fancied ourselves. The child shall fulfil those wishful dreams of the parents which they never carried out. ... [Freud, 1914c, pp. 90–1]

Narcissism comes into being only by way of the detour of the parents' projections, so that the child can locate its centre in itself only through such projections. As Jean Laplanche puts it, "It is in terms of parental omnipotence, experienced as such by the child and of its introjection, that the megalomania and the narcissistic state of the child may be understood". (Laplanche, 1976, p. 79) The sovereignty of 'His Majesty' can be constituted and affirmed only by His

Majesty's subjects. As Leonardo showed us, self-love is always the introjected love of the other. It is this insight that drives Serge Leclaire's inquiries into primary narcissism in his *A Child Is Being Killed*. For Leclaire, the work of analysis involves the perpetual killing of the fantasised child of primary narcissism, the *"wonderful (or terrifying)"* creature of "the parents dreams and desires":

> The wonderful child is first of all the nostalgic gaze of the mother who made him into an object of extreme magnificence akin to the Child Jesus majesty, a light and jewel radiating forth absolute power ... the wonderful child is the unconscious, primordial representation in which, more densely than anywhere else, our wishes, nostalgia and hopes come together. [Leclaire, 1998, pp. 2–3]

The killing of the 'wonderful child' of primary narcissism involves the perpetually renewed recognition of the infant's sovereign majesty as an implantation from the parental unconscious rather than a creation of its own.[5] It is for this reason that, "[t]here is for everyone, always, a child to kill". (Leclaire, 1998, p. 3) The implantation of the wonderful child cannot be reversed even by 'killing', inasmuch as it insinuates a structural component into consciousness which can never be destroyed—once a narcissist ...

The question of how to understand primary narcissism speaks to some of the fundamental theoretical and technical disputes in post-Freudian psychoanalysis. As Pontalis has shown with exemplary lucidity, the ego-psychological tradition developed by Viennese émigrés to the United States rests on a very different construal of the concept. Perhaps the premier theorist of this tradition, Heinz Hartmann, read out of Freud 'a non-conflictual sphere of the ego", including such functions as perception and motor co-ordination, autonomous of the drives and the conflicts they engender. (Hartmann, 1964, p. 162) Hartmann's positing of conflict-free sphere of ego functioning has explicit implications for the theory of narcissism. According to Hartmann, we fall into categorical confusion if think of narcissism as cathexis of the ego as psychic system, rather than as, more simply, the *self*:

> The opposite of object cathexis is not ego cathexis, but cathexis of one's own person, that is, self-cathexis. ... It will therefore be

clarifying if we define narcissism as the libidinal cathexis not of the ego but of the self. (Hartmann, 1964, p. 127)

It is worth following Pontalis in asking whether such a differentiation of ego from self–that is, of a specific agency defined by its functions from the whole person—is justifiable psychoanalytically. Pontalis' response, consonant with the view I have sought to develop above, is that it is not justifiable, firstly because the distinction between ego and self serves "*to isolate*, to localize narcissism, in order to purify the functions of the ego. But narcissism is not a phase, nor a specific mode of cathexis; it is a position, an insurmountable and permanent component of the human being". (Pontalis, 1981, p. 136) Nor, Pontalis continues, can self-love be thought apart from the libidinal cathexis of the ego as a system. And perhaps most importantly, "[t]he constitution of the ego is related to a recognition of the other and is used as its model". (Pontalis, 1981, p. 137) It is this last point which seems to put in question the entire theoretical edifice of ego psychology, which posits a partial autonomy of the ego free of instinctual conflict and so of *the structuring force of the other*.

Desire for the one: André Green

My reading of *On Narcissism* has sought to show that for Freud, the notion of an ego free from conditioning by the other's presence can be posited only as a heuristic 'fiction'. In this section, I want to explore the implications of this reading as developed by André Green's work on narcissism, most notably his 1966 essay, 'Primary Narcissism: Structure or State?' Because no contribution of Green's exhibits more explicitly the depth of his debt to Lacan, however, I shall preface this exploration with some indications of the latter's take on this question.

It is of course the famous concept of the 'mirror stage' that grounds Lacan's construal of primary narcissism. According to his celebrated essay, the infant's constitutes his ego by means of self-recognition through "identification with the imago of one's semblable". (Lacan, 1977, p. 79) This process, as Laplanche points out, has little to do with the encounter with "the *instrument* of the mirror"; such an encounter is merely an index of "the recognition of the form of another human and the concomitant precipitation within the individual of a first outline of that form". (Laplanche, 1976, p. 81) The ego, that is, can be differentiated and cathected only through recognition of another, whether in the mirror or elsewhere. In *Aggressiveness in Psychoanalysis*, Lacan refers to this moment of perceptual capture, which appears to suspend the 'dialectical movement' of ego and object, as "similar in strangeness to the faces of actors when a film is suddenly stopped in mid-frame". (Lacan, 2006, p. 90) The comparison, as we shall see, bears illuminatingly on Green's conception of 'negative narcissism', a relation of *decathexis* between the ego and its internal objects.

The 'formal stagnation' of ego and object is what confers on them "the attributes of permanence, identity and substance" (Lacan, 2006, p. 90), that is, their narcissistic coherence. From this perspective, Hartmann's autonomous ego functioning becomes an illusory effect of the dialectic of recognition. The ego's increasing subservience to the reality principle has its source not in a sphere of neutral energy, but in "*narcissistic passion*... the obscure foundation of the will's rational mediations". (Lacan, 2006, p. 95) Self-recognition and the apparently stable, differentiated 'knowledge' it brings, involves a kind of violent effacement of the otherness that conditions it. It is of this effacement that Green seems to speak when he describes the ego's independence as acquired "by transferring desire for the Other on to desire for the One". (Green, 2001, p. xx)

Desire for the One lies at the heart of Green's conception of negative narcissism, a pathology governed by the drive to rid consciousness of the agitating force of the other. It is by means of this pathology that Green guides us to the fundamental logic of primary narcissism. The perhaps surprising Freudian source for this logic is the 1917 'Metapsychological Supplement to the Theory of Dreams'. Here, two narcissisms, that of dreams and of sleep, are distinguished. The narcissism of dreams can be defined as secondary insofar as it incorporates into itself the disturbances of objects, albeit as fantasised imagos deprived of their reality by a glorified ego. The narcissism of sleep, however, strives to draw back into the ego *all* cathexes of the external world: "The wish to sleep endeavours to draw in all the cathexes sent out by the ego and to establish an absolute narcissism". (Freud, 1917d, p. 225)

For Green, this 'absolute narcissism' is the fundamental logic that links the Freud's first dual drive theory (ego and sexual drives) to the second (life and death drives). What would be described in *Beyond the Pleasure Principle* as the organism's will to extinguish all internal tension first appears as the desire for total decathexis of the ego. In many 'secondary' narcissistic forms, this desire is libidinised by the sexual drive and so made to serve the vital order. But even these derived forms are apt to display an underlying negativity which seeks nothing less (or more) than the nullification of all meaning, desire and relation. Green's most famous example in this regard is the 'dead mother' complex, a pathology derived from the infant's unconscious identification with a mother too much in the grip of loss to invest affectively in her child. (see Green, 2001).[6] The subject of such a complex will compulsively repeat in his own relationships the withdrawal of desire experienced in the earliest relationship with his introjected 'dead mother'. Such forms of 'negative narcissism' provide clinical grounding for and confirmation of, Green's metapsychological thesis of an absolute primary narcissism inscribed in the very structure of the ego.

Yet the concept of negative narcissism speaks to far more than certain forms of pathology. As Green argues in his earlier 1966 essay, the tendency to decathexis *"internal to the instinct"* (Green, 2001, p. 65) is realised in the 'aim-inhibited' drives by means of which Freud accounts for such affective phenomena as tenderness, as well as of sublimation. Green points out that the aim-inhibited drive cannot be an effect of repression since "it is precisely the manner in which the drive avoids repression that is the particular feature of this drive vicissitude". (Green, 2001, p. 65) In other words, inhibition of aim is not something that happens secondarily *to* the drive, but which the drive effects in itself. In inhibiting itself, the drive "maintains the object by sacrificing the complete satisfaction of the wish for erotic union with it, yet conserves a form of attachment which fixes the investment of it". (Green, 2001, p. 65) From this perspective, 'genital love' can be understood as a tendency within the drive to contain the radically unbinding effects of the pregenital drives, which know and answer to only the imperative of pleasure. The relation of the genital to pregenital drives reproduces in this sense the relation, delineated in *Totem and Taboo*, of murdered father to the primal horde. Just as the phylogenetic trace of this murder is preserved in the murderers' development of religion, law and moral conscience—"signs which do not so much restore his presence as ensure his perpetuation in absence for ever" (Green, 2001, p. 68), so the drives harbour within themselves the means of their own inhibition.

The significance of this insight for Green is that decathexis is not simply a piece of psychic work performed upon the drives, but a permanent possibility of narcissistic withdrawal *internal to* the drives. This leads him to some very striking inferences with regard to auto-erotism. Pointing to Freud's differentiation of his own definition of the term from Havelock Ellis', I argued above that for the former the auto-erotic was a paradoxical mode of relation to an object. Green's reading of this section in the *Three Essays* richly illuminates this paradox. He identifies in the implicit comment Freud imagines the infant making on his own orality—"It's a pity I can't kiss myself" (Freud, 1905d, p. 182)—the fundamental logic of auto-erotism. Noting that auto-erotism comes into being at the moment of and in compensation for, separation from the mother, Green writes:

> Separation reconstitutes this couple in the subject's own body, since the image of lips kissing themselves suggests the idea of a replication followed by a re-gluing which, in this new unity, traces the line of partition which has enabled the 'subject' to fall back on his own resources. [Green, 2001, p. 73]

In the fantasy of kissing his own lips, the infant enacts the 'relation to an object' which Freud would come to see as structuring auto-erotic activity. The mother's care has been insinuated into her child's bodily self-relation: *"The mother shields the infant's auto-erotism"*. (Green, 2001, p. 74; original emphasis) This intermediary stage between mother-infant fusion and later repression is characterised by an 'intersection' between outside as inside, "so that what is inside may be treated in the same way as that which comes from the outside, provided that the inside is perceived as if it were the inside and *without there being any fusion between the two"*. (Green, 2001, pp. 79–80, original emphasis) With this complex and deceptive structure of relations, akin to Lacan's figure of the Möbius strip which "no longer allows us to speak of a wrong side and a right side, an interior and an exterior" (Green, 2001, p. 88), Green has moved narcissism far beyond the alternatives between the monadic and dyadic conceptions of infantile life promulgated by the antagonists of the Controversial Discussions.

Neither fully differentiated nor magically fused with his interior, the infant's exterior becomes a kind of "*I-not-I*", a formation facilitated by *negative hallucination*, the perceptual nullification of a present object. In order for the infant to experience the object in this way as simultaneously itself and other, it must screen out or 'scotomize' the mother's physical presence:

> He [the infant] treats himself as she treats him once she is no longer an extrinsic part of himself. *The mother is caught in the empty frame of negative hallucination and becomes a framing structure for the subject himself.* [Green, 2001, p. 85, original emphasis]

A necessary component of normal development, this narcissistic introjection of the mother is also the key to some of the most virulent pathologies of psychic life. The negative hallucination of the mother, like the inhibition of the drive by the phylogenetic father, is directed towards the disavowal of desire for the Other in favour of the self-sufficiency of the One, of "*self-begetting abolishing sexual difference*". (Green, 2001, p. 89, original emphasis) With the abolition of sexual difference comes the effacement of all that lies outside the circuit of my control. From this perspective, psychic health would be defined above all by the subject's capacity to tolerate and maintain the insuperable and permanent uncertainty engendered by desire for the other. Narcissistic regression, in contrast, would imply a tendency towards negative hallucination of that other in the service of extinguishing dependence and desire. It is in this respect that we are bound to think of primary narcissism as structure rather than state, a component of psychic life apt to manifest itself whenever the burden of desire on the subject becomes intolerable.

Narcissism and destruction: D. W. Winnicott

I have suggested that it is the Möbius logic of Green's account of primary narcissism, its paradoxical intrication of inner and outer, which has tended to elude British psychoanalytic thinking. In the concluding section of this chapter, I want to point to D.W. Winnicott, not coincidentally a constant point of reference for Green's work, as a notable exception in this regard.

It is no doubt Winnicott's training in and affiliation to a British psychoanalytic tradition that leaves him unwilling to employ the vocabulary of narcissism to describe infantile experience. The term, he suggests, "leaves out the idea of dependence, which is so essential at the earliest stages". (Winnicott, 1971, p. 15) Narcissism, in other words, connotes to Winnicott a mode of psychic closure and self-sufficiency that cannot account for dependence.

Yet despite this apparent dissociation of narcissism from the dependent state, *Playing and Reality* is filled with intimations of their intricate relationship. Acknowledging the influence of Lacan's 'Mirror Stage' article at the outset, Winnicott's 1967 essay, 'Mirror-Role of Mother and Family in Child Development' theorizes the structuring role of the mother in the development of the child's capacity to perceive and conceive itself. When looking at the mother's face, he suggests, "what the baby sees is himself or herself. In other words the mother is looking at the baby and *what she looks like is related to what she sees there*". (Winnicott, 1971, p. 112; original emphasis) Compressed in this enigmatic formulation is the Möbius structure of narcissism as Lacan and Green conceptualize it; the mother's face becomes for the baby a means of experiencing him or herself *as an object.* Self-recognition is attained only through recognition of and by the other.[7]

It is in *The Use of an Object and Relating Through Identifications* (1968), one of Winnicott's most celebrated essays, that this paradox is most fully and richly elaborated. The essay describes the infant's passage out of the illusion of total narcissistic enclosure and into an acknowledgment of the reality of the external. In what seems a deliberate terminological provocation, Winnicott describes this discovery of externality as an act of *destruction.* What the child destroys, in order to give birth to the object as "a thing in itself" is the object as a mere phantasmatic "bundle of projections". (Winnicott, 1971, p. 88) This distinction between the object as projection and as thing in itself is both an extension of and a challenge to, the conceptual vocabulary of object-relations theory. The object as object of *relation* is always an effect of 'the subject as an isolate', for whom the world exists only as an emanation of his or her omnipotence. To feed on the breast as object of relation is in this sense radically narcissistic, a 'feeding on the self' which recognises nothing beyond this self-satisfaction. To feed on the breast as object of *use*, in contrast, is to feed 'from an other-than-me source', to recognise a being outside 'the subject's omnipotent control'.

There is a striking sense in this essay of a need to break free of the subjectivism of object-relations theory, an intimation that in restricting itself to the experience of objects as projective entities, psychoanalysis risks missing the complex and enriching encounter with what Winnicottt calls *"externality itself"*. (Winnicott, p. 91; my emphasis) We should be wary, however, of identifying this sense of externality with a naïve immediacy, as if the Kantian border separating us from the thing itself could be abolished at a stroke. Before elaborating the concept of object-use, Winnicott reminds us of the paradox at the heart of transitional objects and phenomena: "the baby creates the object, but the object was there waiting to be created ... we will never challenge the baby to elicit an answer to the question: did you create that or did you find it?" (Winnicott, p. 89) The creative life has always become such by passing through this indistinct zone (or 'potential space') beyond inner and outer, possession and non-possession. If the infant passes from relating to use, from the experience of the object as projective entity within my control to that of external entity beyond my control, this passage is always imprinted by this indistinction of subjective and objective. To experience the thing in itself is not, for Winnicott, to overcome but to *acknowledge* my finitude, the existence of a zone irreducibly other to me, neither fully subjective nor fully objective insofar as both terms enforce an economy of opposition disrupted by the paradoxical logic of object-use.

This logic is embodied above all in the concept of destruction, insofar as the subject confers reality on the object—that is, *creates* it— by destroying it. Winnicott is here uncannily convergent with Leclaire's conception, briefly outlined above, of the analytic aim as the permanent and ongoing 'killing' of the subject's primary narcissistic representatives. Just as for Leclaire there is 'always' and 'relentlessly' an internal representation to be killed in order to make space for what is other, so for Winnicott the object is forever being killed in fantasy in order to underline its reality.[8] For what the infant discovers in destroying the object as projection is its survival of this destruction in the new form of object in its own right: "This quality of 'always being destroyed' makes the *reality* of the surviving object felt as such". (Winnicott, 1971, p. 93)

The object is, in Winnicott's tantalizingly condensed formula, "destroyed because real ... real because destroyed". (Winnicott, 1971, p. 90) The reality of the object, that is, consists precisely in its no longer existing as my possession. Destruction is in this sense the name for the irrevocable renunciation of the subject as source and guarantor of all meaning, as consummation of 'desire for the One'.

Winnicott thus finds in the capacity to use an object less the discovery of the external as *opposed* to the internal, than the recognition of the previously unrecognised inscription of the external *within* the internal—of the presence of the mother in the subject's self-image, of the thing in itself within the thing as projection. Put another way, he brings to light the structuring presence of the other in narcissism. In this structuring presence of the other within the same can be identified nothing less than the fundamental logic of relation psychoanalytically conceived.

NOTES

1. These so-called 'Controversial Discussions' have been collated and edited by King, P. and Steiner, R. (1991). *The Freud-Klein Controversies* 1941–5. London: Brunner-Routledge. For an informed discussion of the broad historical contexts for the Discussions, including the impact of war, See King and Steiner's interspersed 'Editorial Comments '.

2. This is not to ignore the clear ambivalence Winnicott expresses with regard to the terminology of 'primary narcissism'; I suggest this ambivalence derives in large part from the very restricted understanding accorded to this term within his own tradition.

3. Indeed, significant discussions of narcissism had appeared in other works, most notably the case history of Schreber (1911c) and the second essay of *Totem and Taboo* (1912–3), before the concept was 'introduced' in the 1914 essay.

4. The objection might be justifiably raised here that this is an account of secondary rather than primary narcissism, a cathexis of self deriving from a complex sequence of identifications. Yet what is 'secondary' here is only the specific content of the identifications and their psycho-sexual outcome. The conditioning presence of the mother behind these particular vicissitudes is ineradicable and in this sense 'primary'.

5. I am drawing here on Jean Laplanche's concept of 'implantation' as the transmission by the parent to the infant of indecipherable messages or

'enigmatic signifiers'. See Laplanche, J. (1999) 'Implantation, Intromission' in *Essays on Otherness*. Trans. and Ed. J. Fletcher, London: Routledge.

6. André Green, 'The Dead Mother' in *Life Narcissism, Death Narcissism*. For an excellent collection of essays on Green focused on this motif, See Kohon, G. (ed.) (1999), *The Dead Mother: The Work of André Green*. London: Brunner-Routledge.

7. In noting these intriguing metapsychological convergences between Lacan and Winnicott, I do not seek to elide the very real and evident differences in their conceptions of the function and consequences of mirroring. Where the mother's face of Winnicott's essay is a benign precipitate of ego development and differentiation, in Lacan it is the malevolent fundament of the ego's imaginary unity. Nonetheless, the drawing of such radically different psychical consequences from the same phenomenon points to the essential paradoxicality and ambiguity of mirroring as the basis for narcissism.

8. For still another, more recent elaboration of this phantasmatic 'killing', See Ogden, T. H. (2002) 'A New Reading of the Origins of Object-Relations Theory' in *International Journal of Psychoanalysis*, Vol. 83: "In order to grieve the loss of the object, one must first kill it, that is, one must do the psychological work of allowing the object to be irrevocably dead, both in one's mind and in the external world" (p. 778).

CHAPTER THREE

Tracing the origins, centring on selves: reading Kohut and Kernberg from a developmental perspective

Emmanouil Manakas

What is relevant to a developmental perspective is not a description of states and sequences but an identification of the principles and processes which control transitions (Sroufe 1995). The pure essence of development, if such a thing could be conceptualised, is change and transition (Oyama, 2000). What this paper aims to explore is how the implicit and explicit developmental propositions in Kohut's and Kernberg's thinking—to put it simply, their views on change—have shaped their theories on narcissism and disorders of the self. It also aims to unearth possible effects from 'mutations' in their developmental thinking. The theory of change that will be adopted in this paper will be considered in its loosest form as a hermeneutic scheme and not as an evaluative referential criterion. In other words, it will function as a perspective not a model so as to enable us to move flexibly between compatible perspectives.

Before we commence our discussion, we need to make a distinction between what we may somewhat arbitrarily call theories of development and developmental theory, that is, to distinguish between the 'what' and the 'how' aspects of development as most developmentalists prefer to name them. Developmental theory presents a textually rich discourse on mechanisms of change and explanations of how changes occur (Miller, 2002; Oyama, 2000). The 'what' of development depends on the way theorists decide to study the human mind, what categories are constructed out of their understanding, their points of emphasis and the way their models grasp things at work. There is no doubt that a comprehensive consideration of mechanisms of change can go no further than the generativity of a particular developmental frame of reference allows (Sternberg, 1984). In essence, we can only pretend that the 'how' can be totally free from the 'what'. As Miller (2002) puts it, there are theories that excel on the 'what' aspect of development, such as the Piagetian and the Freudian and others that excel on the 'how' at the expense of the 'what'. Some of the latter have achieved such a high degree of abstraction that can sufficiently serve our pretence that there can exist 'what-free' developmental perspectives.

Gotlieb (1996) introduced the concept of 'probabilistic epigenesis' as a framework accounting for the effects of environmental stimulation on the developing organism. According to Gotlieb, environmental information and stimulation have effects not only on the paths that the development will follow on Waddington's epigenetic landscape[1] but also on the landscape itself, influencing even our genetic material. Experience, for Gotlieb (1996), has three significant developmental effects: Firstly, it maintains an achieved state of development, since otherwise it would decay to a simpler organisational state; secondly, it facilitates the emergence of a new state by speeding up transitions; and, finally, it induces a new state, a change that would not otherwise happen. In other words, dynamic maintenance, transition and state induction are all forms of developmental change regulated by experience. Thelen & Smith (2000), on the other hand, study developmental change within the context of self-organising systems and underscore that the generality of principles of change may span and extend from complex to simple living organisms (or even 'complex, nonliving systems'). Multiple causation and continuity in time suggest the frame of self-organisation. The precision and regularity observed in macroscopically viewed developmental processes is generated on the grounds of local diversity, flexibility and asynchrony.[2] The organisational process is non-linear and, most importantly, transition presumes variability. According to this perspective, emergence of new forms of organisation requires a flexible system able to explore different developmental states. The aftermath of this idea leads to a conclusion that sounds familiar to psychoanalytic ears: change in the state of a substructure may undermine cohesion but frees up components which have the potential to reassemble.

Primary narcissism is a major developmental starting point in the Freudian model reflecting the emergence of an 'I', an 'Ego', a primarily agentive structure (Bourdin, 2000). What makes this organisational change possible is the operation of drives and the id's contact with perceptual 'information' (Freud, 1923). The 'self experience' is one among other ego activities and suggests the product of dynamic conflicts in and between biological forces, the drives and the psychic structures that unfold from their vicissitudes (Sandler et al. 1997). Freud's attention, from the beginning of his psychoanalytic work, was especially oriented towards the discovery of the origins of the experienced and observed 'otherness' in human actions, feelings and thoughts. Engaged, as he was, with the exploration of the instinctual origins of the psychic life and the concurrent development of a structural model of the mind, he did not allow any space in his theory for an articulate conceptualisation of the self as an object of experience (Pulver, 1970). By adopting a third person perspective, Freud built a mechanistic model (Greenberg & Mitchell, 1983), where the power of wish moves an almost undifferentiated apparatus into structuralisation, 'assimilating' the external world. From the perspective of modern developmental theory, where Freud principally failed was, first, in his commitment to a deterministic approach on the unreeling of internal motivational powers and the underestimation of external ones and, second, in his simplistic collapse of all possible psychic function 'motivators' into a ponderous generic dual scheme (Westen, 1997).

The evolving ego cathected with energy is a metapsychological explanatory construct for what one may imaginatively capture as the experience of primary love for the self. Green (1974) notes that in the place of the Freudian transformations of the concept of primary narcissism we may offer two differential perspectives: One in which the predominant feature is the orientation of libidinal forces and the other that takes special note of the unification of autoerotic drives that serves the sense of personal cohesion. However, the primary form of love for the ego, Green (1974) thinks, is marked by the need to zero out all excitation, either discharging the pressing energies or welcoming the void. This idea clearly reflects Freud's thinking about the origins of character and personality in the economy of pleasure. The 'observed' personality of a 'subject', metapsychologically speaking, originates (a) at the pathways that energy finds available to traverse, (b) at the 'no-place' that death creates to a-void the pressure of energy and (c) at the many transformations of the psychic apparatus that drive vicissitudes set out. It would be misguided to suggest that this model is ineffectual in trying to account for the self as experience. Yet, Freud seems to have been uninterested in combining the first and third person perspectives so as to find an experiential centre for the self, other than the externally observed, dynamically drifting under the auspices of psychic economy centre of the ego's conscious experience of itself.

Kohut followed another path. He dipped himself in an empathic grasping of his patients' internal centre, losing thus sight and track of parts of the mind that exist in long distance from this centre but still determining its postures and movements. At the same time that Kohut was developing his theories, the intellectual climate created by the British object relations theorists, especially Winnicott & Fairbairn, on the one hand, and Sullivan in the USA, on the other, led to the emergence of the 'Interpersonals' (Mitchell, 1998). In a similar fashion, Kohut set off to prioritise the 'interpersonal' dimension of development at the expense of the 'intrapsychic' one (Perlow, 1995). Several authors also note that Winnicott's emphasis on the use of the term 'self' had an enormous impact on Kohut's ideas of development (Cooper, 1999; Greenberg & Mitchell, 1983). Winnicott, however, was not very interested (as Kohut was) in anything that resembles an operational definition of the self as evidenced in the collection of his articles on development written between 1958 and 1968 and presented in *Maturational Processes and the Facilitating Environment*; rather, he was interested in the self's clinical manifestations. In any case, Kohut oriented himself towards a clinical understanding of narcissism overemphasizing the self as an initiator of experience and underestimating the importance of an elaborate theoretical model that would equally constrict and enable him to explore possible alternative dimensions to the clinical data.

It seems that it is clear to Kohut that a conflictual understanding of the libidinal and aggressive expressions of narcissism will clinically fail, since the original cause of pathology lies in the defective self (Kohut & Wolf, 1978). This self has a functional role as it suggests both an active agent and a representational matrix and it is not simply the product of ego activity. Further, in the Kohutian understanding of primary narcissism there is no differentiation between the 'I-you' (Kohut, 1966; 1971). The newborn has no self and only in the matrix of parental selfobject functions will the nuclear self gradually develop and crystallize. Kohut suggests that the primary narcissism's equilibrium is disturbed by *maturational processes and painful psychic tensions* originating in the unavoidable maternal failure to offer perfectly contingent ministrations (Kohut, 1978). The pain-pleasure balance here is part of a developmental mechanism, an operative index that will open up the road for the evolving self to search for reparation. The rudimentary self manages the narcissistic disequilibrium by 'building up new systems of perfection' (Greenberg & Mitchell, 1983). One of these systems resembles the Freudian 'purified pleasure-ego'. It will absorb every pleasant experience while everything that is unpleasant and unsettles the equilibrium-searching narcissistic structure will be projected outside. The other system, in contrast to the first, attributes absolute power and perfection to a rudimentary but evolving 'you' reflecting the adult. The 'grandiose and exhibitionistic self images' will evolve in relation to the mirroring selfobject function, while the 'idealising self images' will evolve in relation to the idealised selfobjects' efficiency in facilitating fusion (Greenberg & Mitchell, 1983; Kohut, 1996).

The nuclear self is a primitive but complex structure. Selfobjects are not proper objects but functions performed by real people that help the self to maintain its cohesion. Kohut names the process through which the nuclear self organises itself 'transmuting internalisation'. This process involves the parental empathic response to mirroring and idealising needs and non-traumatic response failures that lead to a gradual transfer of the selfobjects' function within the realm of the self. The nuclear self emerges around the second year of life and is pictured as a bipolar structure that holds together connected—but still separated—in its two poles nuclear archaic ambitions and ideals. In the complex interrelationships between parental mirroring and idealisation functions, Kohut indicates some special form of *environmental selectionism*. The parents' actively encourage or discourage potentialities and rudimentary skills and talents. A 'tension arc' is powered by the bipolar structure that finally defines the selection of skills and talents through which the self will express its creativity.

Mollon (2001) describes the Kohutian self-structuralisation as a process of attributing mental contents to the self while obliterating others to a non-self realm–supposedly through the operation of a primitive pain-pleasure balance mechanism in the context of trans-muting internalisation—and the end product as a centre of initiative and perception integrated with our ambitions and ideals and our sense of unity and continuity. However, Perlow (1995) notes that what Kohut mentions as a self-structure actually makes more sense as a capacity to maintain self-esteem in relation to the self's ideals and ambitions. Selfobjects have, as the case may be, either a struc-tural or a functional role, always serving self-esteem modulation.

Fonagy & Target (2003) summarize the criticisms made by sever-al authors on the naïve environmentalism reflected in Kohut's account of self-organisation. And these are rather justified criticisms, since the Kohutian organised centre of experience and initiative, either agentive or representational, seems unexpectedly malleable to environmental variations. If we had to model this Kohutian organi-sational entity in terms of Gotlieb's probabilistic epigenesis metaphor of the landscape and the stream running through its peaks and val-leys, it would look like a very plastic landscape, like a desert consist-ed of innumerable minute grains of sand that pile up into dunes which the environmental winds may easily throw about or pile them up again into new patterns. Kohut paid little attention to what he fleetingly refers to as maturational processes or the inner creativity that has to be expressed by the skills and talents created in the bipo-lar self's tension arc; rather, it is 'parental empathic attunement' that is the critical factor that shapes the developmental land scape.

The Freudian model, on the other hand, is full of inheritances: Deterministically unfolding drives, Oedipus complex origins in the primal horde (Freud, 1913), resurrected ego-structures that move from the id's primordial mass to inhabit the superego (Freud, 1923). Do we really need all these solid, aplastic structures in a model that accounts for how organisational changes occur in a developing structure? Most change theorists in dynamic systems, cognitive neu-roconstructivism, connectionism and other developmental research areas now think that epigenetic landscapes do not need aplastic forms that strictly constrain developmental paths. They usually prefer to speak about non-specific, representational, architectural and chronotropic biases in developing neural networks (Elman et al. 1999). Reading Freud from this point of view, we can accept that there are innate biases towards phylogenetically inherited paths, but they are susceptible to large ontogenetic variability and, through a series of ontogenetic lines, subject to transformation. We may search, then, for an alternative, a middle ground between the Kohutian implausible over-plasticity of the epigenetic landscape and the Freudian invariability.

Interestingly, this middle ground can be found through the investigation of processes that have not been *traditionally* part of psychoanalytic research. In a review article on the implications for psychoanalysis of research in the socio-cognitive and affective processes involved in autism, Volkmar (2000) notes that "the utility of psychoanalytic therapeutic management of autism is highly limited but the reverse is not true" (p. 1). Nowadays, it is widely accepted that one of the primary deficits in the autistic mind involves a lack of *social-affective processes* that underlie the development of the ability to understand and attribute mental states to other minds (Tomasello, 1998; Baron-Cohen, 2000). Autistic children may have a normal or close to normal learning potential, they do use adults to attain their goals, but they are uninterested in understanding and sharing an adult's attention focus (Blakemore & Frith, 2006). They may express pleasure and enjoyment for objects and idiosyncratic activities (Spitzer, 2003), but they are not interested in representing the other as a separate mental being, i.e., they are not interested in *relatedness*.

Taking into account the above findings, we may construct some sketchy arguments in support of the Fairbairnian view that emphasises relatedness in contrast to the Freudian view that emphasises pleasure in the development of internal structures. But Kohut had actually moved away from the Freudian viewpoint, thinking about pleasure-seeking and aggression not anymore as the building blocks of personality but as the products of severe psychopathology (Greenberg & Mitchell, 1983). Moreover, he was certainly not indifferent to the Fairbairnian viewpoint of relatedness-seeking as a primal motivator of the human psyche. It is highly likely, however, that what he left behind from the Fairbairnian perspective, i.e., the 'internal other', was not its least important aspect.

Arguably, Kohutian selfobjects do suggest a form of relatedness and there is ample evidence showing that parental empathy is crucial for the development of self-regulatory capacities (Schore, 2003). For instance, Schore (2003) notes that the hyperaroused child many times fails to elicit a parental mirroring response to the exhibition of his grandiose self gestures and moves into an inward focused 'passive hypoaroused shame state'. Thus, these parental mirroring failures induce shame experiences and reparative mirroring efforts help the child recover from shame. Kohut (1971) has emphasised the neutralization of grandiosity, exhibitionism and idealisation as a prerequisite for the establishment of a true sense of self. This 'truly me' sense, then, is established by reparations that follow empathic misattunements (Kohut, 1996). Broucek (1982) also emphasises in this process the benefit of self and object differentiation. Shame is a step towards individuation.

While Kohut back in 1971 would have no objections to the suggestion of a developmental transition from selfobjects to real objects, he finally came to believe that the actual transition happens in a line from archaic to mature selfobjects. Perlow (1995) argues that Kohut actually tried to escape from difficulties in accounting for how objects develop into internal structures. Beyond narcissistic libido there is in Kohut an object libidinal line of development where true objects are cathected and which enables the structuralisation of the superego. Kohut (1966; 1971) notes that in narcissistic organisations this superego may be finely structured but not idealised.iii As a result, the person usually fails to experience this special sense of glow and pleasure by living up to her/his superego's moral standards or s/he may ignore them without feeling miserable. In this way, Kohut maintains, a source of pleasure remains outside the self structure and perpetuates the person's dependency on immature selfobject functions.

Moreover, in the developmental advancement from shame to guilt, Kohut does describe a quantum transition from a developmental line originating in love for the self and a line originating in love for the object to a new integrated state. Yet, strangely enough, we know little about this object line of development. Apart from its culmination in superego formation, it remains mostly silent. What we mainly know is that early on in his theory formation, Kohut left unexplained the paradox of a self which was both fused with the object, but was still able to cathect the object (Greenberg & Mitchell, 1983). He tried to remedy the paradox by finally mentioning that we are able to cathect objects only when the self has already achieved some cohesion (Kohut, 1984), while he also mentioned that drive and self psychology may describe two different fates of the human psyche, the Guilty and the Tragic man respectively (Kohut, 1996). However, Kohut did not attempt to close the gap between shame and guilt.

The Kohutian selfobject, then, is more of an interpersonal function and less of a true separate object. Objects, when mentioned in Kohut, are relevant to the structuralisation of the superego but not immediately relevant to the construction of a sense of self. It is also interesting that while Kohut clearly grasped the role of empathy in attunement and in the consolidation of a sense of self, he had not paid much attention to possible bridges of empathy from the emergent self towards the parents. Toddlers of 18 months are already able to 'read' other peoples' distress and exhibit other-oriented compassionate and comforting behaviours (Radke-Yarrow et al. 1984). Parental empathic attunements and failures which open up the road to self-other differentiation facilitate the emergence of the object as a separate mental entity, which is what Kernberg and now Mentalisation theorists (namely, Fonagy, Bateman, Gergely, Target and others) re-introduce as the crucial developmental step towards the creation of a stable authentic self (Levy et al. 2006). In fact, evidence from new developmental research shows that this object line of development may be more archaic than Kohut believes it to be (Stern, 1984). Moreover, the representation of another person as a mental being may not be an all-or-nothing achievement (Fonagy & Target, 2003) since the infant from 8 months onwards is oriented towards understanding the intentions in others' actions (Stern, 1984; Tomasello, 1998). Stern (1984) insists that what Mahler viewed as a process towards autonomy is rather a process towards increased, meaningful and deep relatedness. Kohut (1996) was not very sympathetic to the autonomy perspective; instead, he insisted on our lifelong dependence on selfobjects that become more mature and may even include meaningful activities. But his escape from an autonomy perspective did not lead to an emphasis on the enrichment of relatedness with an internal other, but rather to an altogether escape from objects as an equal part of the self, developing simultaneously with the developing self.

Decety & Sommerville (2003) note that, from the perspective of social neurosciences, the self-other representations are intimately tied together early on in development and that empathy and inter-subjectivity are possible due to this close tie and our capacity to identify with others. At the representational level, the inhibition of a pre-potent self perspective makes it possible, they suggest, to "put ourselves in another person's shoes" (p. 4). The 'internal other's' space may not be very talkative, but does not remain mute when the self pulls back. The 'interpersonal' selfobject, then, is evidently not enough; we need an 'intrapsychic' other to contain the functions of the real other. If the object is not over there right from the start as part of the organisation of the self, there can be no meaningful self-object function. The object is part of the self so as to enable maternal ministrations and failures to shape a sense of self. Empathy and intersubjectivity develop out of the rudimentary 'you' that is able to separate from the 'I', but both share the same internal space. The epi-genetic metaphor of the landscape as a desert has no actual mean-ing, because if no objects can be found within it, there can be no objects outside it either that would be able to reach it in any way. The lack of 'internal' objects—if this can be simplistically equated with innate biases towards social information—in high-functioning autis-tic children, makes them uninterested to parental mirroring. Many high-functioning autistics may show exhibitionistic behaviours, being aroused by their self-interests for which they may continu-ously talk about, but they show little interest in the other's sharing of focus, as either their exhibitionistic hyperarousal or their 'hypoaroused low-keyed states' (Schore, 2003) are usually ineffectu-ally modulated.

However, even in autistic children the 'social' component of the self is not totally absent. Rieffe et al. (2000) have shown that high functioning autistics may pass some tests reflecting an understand-ing of mental states, but they still fail to integrate these skills in real life situations. Rutgers et al (2004) in a meta-analytic review of attachment studies in children with autism conclude that autistic children may even exhibit signs reflecting secure attachment behav-iour patterns counter-checked with physiological markers. Nevertheless, a secure attachment where the selfobject can provide the necessary safety for the child to soothe is not enough for the development of prosocial behaviour. What is missing, among other things, in these children is the ability to reflect the interpersonal to the intrapsychic, an inner receptive field made possible by the existence of an internal object. The next piece missing in the developmental chain is the ability to 'get in' the self or the object as objects of the psychic functions. Interestingly, Radke-Yarrow et al observed signs of child's empathic attunement to the mother at 18 months, the same age that Lewis (1991) notes that the child is able to focus attention on the self, that is, to create meta-representations of the self. As long as the intrapsychic self and other develop, both the self and the real other can become an 'object' of 'mental state attribution' (Fonagy & Target, 2003).

Here it is useful to quote Green (2004) who refers to the 'meaningful investment' of psychic operations as 'objectalising' function. He also refers to a negative form of narcissism which is characterised by the disinvestment of psychic functions, aiming at the a-voidance of any excitations and death-aiding, when maternal function fails and the 'peace-of-satisfaction' is impossible. The Kohutian self turns away from the 'joy of a full self experience' and partially collapses in the 'constricted libidinal pleasure of an erotogenic zone' trying to avoid the void of maternal ministrations (Kohut, 1996). Amazingly, the 'fullness' of the Kohutian self needs something external to sustain itself, while the 'nothingness' of the Greenian ego requires an internal attack against an externally sustained function. Obviously, these two perspectives are not contradictory but complementary. The dynamic maintenance of organisation in the system needs the flow of the external into the system as mentioned; with no flow, the organisation disintegrates and searches for another stable point. What is also interesting in dynamic organisations is that as the system emerges through a non-linear path in qualitatively new forms (Smith & Thelen, 2003), it cannot disintegrate to earlier but simply to less integrated forms. When the system then searches but does not find the fertilizing power of 'emotional scaffolding' (Tronick et al. 1998), it looks for another stable point pulling back from its current integrative organisational state. In such a system, the 'objectalising' function may reflect an organisational movement from simpler forms of investment in the self-other sub-organisation towards more complex ones. Investment here may include affective, motivational and representational processes that move from lower to higher organisations while the self-other system expands respectively as its components become integrated. At a higher organisational level, the self and the object become 'objects' of the most complex forms of investment.

Obviously, returning to autistics, we cannot assume that they lack a functional internal object and, thus, it is the line of the self that mainly develops. The self cannot reach ahead of the object in interpersonal functioning. From the perspective of developing dynamic systems, the various parts of a system do not need a coordinating executive agent and 'no single element has causal priority', while coherence in the system lies in the relationships between components (Smith & Thelen, 2003). *The coherent self, then, might be considered as a coherent internal self-other psychic space.* The other is already part of the system right from the start; it is in this internal self-other relation that the personality hijack[4] happens, through what Kohut (1996) considers a vertical split and does not allow the Freudian 'ego synthetic activity' (Modell, 1985) to occur. Parts of the system may remain out of the 'objectalising' process, entrapped to a 'negative' narcissistic organisation, when the external selfobject function is not qualitatively or quantitatively appropriate. A negative process in the system reflects the disintegration of component parts during the organisational movement and this, as mentioned, does not necessarily imply regression to an earlier state but emergence of a non-functional organisational state. If we come to understand death in dynamic systems as the processes that narrow variability and the external as the power that 'excites' variability, then Freud was right in his illustration of the consequences of death and libido defusion. When death is fused with the desire to move towards the external world, the system emerges and dynamically stabilises in functional, qualitatively new states, whilst when death is defused due to failures of the external environment, the system disintegrates into a state where any further development is compromised. *With no death there can be no love for the other; if there is no love from the other, there exists only death.*

We may now possibly unravel the reasons behind Kohut's failure to connect shame and guilt in the same system. He expatriated the object to a separate line of development and hence collapsed all the possible relations between the intrapsychic self and other into a configuration that appears more as a replica of the selfobject function than as a complex structure. But Kohut's overemphasis on the empathic understanding of the phenomenological entity he calls 'Self', was not handicapping only the fuller understanding of the 'Guilty man', but also the understanding of his 'Tragic man' as he also lacks the benefit of intrapsychic plurality appearing in object relational approaches. It is interesting that Kohut paid little attention to messages conveyed by the psychotic discourse other than examining the meaning of fragmentation.[5] The full richness of internal motivational forces collapses along with the collapse of the internal actors' relations in a configuration that, strangely, seems to occupy the largest part of the psychic space, exactly as it appears in the experiential realm and especially in people with narcissistic preoccupations.

Yet, Mollon (2001) admits that Kohut left us an invaluable legacy: the recognition that the "antidote to unthinkable agonies, fragmentation, shame, aggression and alienation and the midwife to autonomy is empathy from another person" (p. 36). In other words, if Kohut failed to provide us elaborate answers on 'what' develops, he did not equally fail in his attempt to conceptualize the 'how' of development. Empathic attunement, its failures and its reparations, may suggest a good candidate for a mechanism of change that brings the system to qualitatively new organisational states. Empathy though, as described by Kohut, is mainly a unidirectional process, since the internal other is underrepresented and mainly involves parental efforts to sustain communication and consequently change. The 'emotional scaffolding' as described by Tronick et al (1998), however, is a bi-directional process involving repetitive efforts by the child to initiate, sustain and repair communication with the other who is represented within the child's internal psychic space from the beginning. It would be unfair, however, if we treated Kohutian empathy only from the perspective of emotional attunement, as it is certainly a wideband term referring to the treatment of the child as having a self right from the start. Kohut (1996) mentions that the mother of an 'anal' child does not respond to the faeces or the anal region but to her child as a 'whole child' including its 'nice gift'. This notion of empathy seems to refer to the parental ability to remain in contact with the experiential contents of the child's mind, even when the child is unable to give meaning to experience, moulding thus empathy with aspects of containment. Kohut, then, was quite successful in approaching the mechanisms of change that work at the interpersonal level, at least to some extend, but he failed to put on the map the mechanisms of change that work at the intrapsychic level and render 'transmuting internalisation' possible.

On the contrary, Kernberg did turn his attention to those possible intrapersonal catalysts of change that may eventually lead to the emergence of the object as a separate mental entity. Kernberg, building on Magda Arnold's view on affects as a form of appraisal that motivates us to move towards or away from situations, ascribes to affects the role of central motivational forces. Affects signal the pleasurable or non-pleasurable nature of a subjective experience and help us communicate internal states. Moreover, during these pleasurable or painful peak affect states the experience of the self is linked with the representation of an external object which is then stored in memory, while it gradually transforms itself into a dynamic unconscious deposit (Kernberg, 2001). Through experience, affects move from a global and diffuse (Westen, 1997) system of signals or dispositions into an established system of affect states that regulates the integration of object relations and their development into psychic structures and drives (Kernberg, 1984, 2001). Consequently, the self in Kernberg (1984) is always a *relational* construct, a self in relation to significant others and in this sense, critically dependent on experience. In the very early phases of development, splitting protects the good from the bad Self-Affect-Object (S-A-O) units and projective identification predominates. As the self and object representations differentiate, synthetic activity is possible and splitting is replaced by repression that looks more like a permeable membrane. In the next developmental phase, a coherent sense of self emerges, since now an integration of libidinal and aggressive aspects of self is possible (Kernberg, 1984, 1989, 2001).

Kernberg follows, broadly speaking, Rosenfeld's reasoning where narcissistic organisations suggest a constellation of defensive positions against dependence, envy and despair and not a developmental stage. Borderline, narcissistic and neurotic organisations, by and large, suggest a continuum. In narcissistic organisations an adequate level of representational stability has been achieved, but splitting is still extensively used. There are two, more or less, stable self representational poles that alternatively occupy positions in consciousness: the grandiose self, constructed by a mixture of ideal self and object images and real self representations and the devalued

self, constructed by all that remains after most of the internal goodness and power have been projected outside (Kernberg, 1984, 1995).
The relationships to real people are respectively largely polarised
into idealisation and devaluation. Idealisation leaves one depleted
from qualities that are projected outside while devaluation usually
sweeps along many of one's own good qualities as well. This internal depletion contributes to the sense of emptiness that people with
narcissistic organisations experience.

Superego immaturity is another major source of emptiness, since
in narcissistic organisations most idealised representations are fused
in the grandiose self, leaving the primitive superego with prohibi-
tive and destructive representations and the self prey to sadistic
attacks. The poorly organised ego maintains the unrealistic self representations through massive projections. It projects the superego's
attacks and aspects of the self onto the object. The world is thus
transformed into a hostile environment, other people usually resist
or fail to substantiate projected aspects of the person's self and relationships easily break up and empathy is undermined by the pressing need for projections and the poorly integrated or partial internal
objects.

Obviously, this defensive organisation cannot be thought in
terms of developmental arrest. Kernberg constructs a rich panorama
of intrapsychic relations where pathology may bear resemblances to
a developmental stage but certainly does not reflect an arrest or the
existence of a linear relationship between a phase in development
and the experience of an adult (Bradley & Westen, 2005). In his construction of this internal world of relations, Kernberg escapes the
Kohutian naïve environmentalism. While several writers note that
Kernberg occupied the happy medium between Fairbairn who
emphasised the reflection of external objects onto the internal world
and Klein who argued for the role of phantasy in the distortion of
object representations (Perlow, 1995), we may reasonably infer from
his writings that he focused more on mechanisms related to distortion than to reflection. Undoubtedly, he explicitly takes into account
the role of parental love or the disorganising implications of parental
failures and maternal unavailability, but in general he is not very
keen to explore mechanisms which take place at the interpersonal
level. He is not very fond of Ogden's conception of projective identification as including a containment dimension, since he altogether

underemphasises the communicative aspects of projective identification (Kernberg, 1989). Moreover, in Love Relations, a book that for
many of us, students of psychoanalysis, is a masterpiece on human
love relations, it is interesting that there are only three pages which
refer to the matter of shame, while guilt appears in twenty nine
pages. From the perspective of this paper, self-psychologists commit
a fallacy in their conception of shame, as they usually overempha-
sise the interpersonal origins of shame while they show little interest
in the intrapsychic processes that shape our individual developmental experience of shame. Kernberg, in a manner of speaking,
commits an inverted fallacy; he intently studies the intrapsychic
vicissitudes of social emotions, while he loosely explores their interpersonal origins.

There is no easy answer on why Kernberg showed less interest in
the interpersonal, compared to the intrapersonal, catalysts of
change. Most of the criticisms regarding Kernberg's work centre on
his use of drive concepts along the object relational framework
(Greenberg & Mitchell, 1983; Fonagy & Target, 2003). Kernberg
(2001), however, believes that an object relational framework
'devoid of a theory of drives' runs the risk of overemphasizing the
re-enactment of 'aspects of actual past interactions'. On the other
hand, he understands drive models stripped from object relations as
susceptible to develop into 'mythical structures', such as the
Lacanian language-like structure of the unconscious, whilst also
considering that any motivational theory centred on affects alone is
unable to account for the role of fantasy.[6] Fantasy suggests a general but, to a certain extent, satisfactory labelling for the intrapersonal
processes that regulate the self-internal object's 'organisational'
vicissitudes. The building blocks of Kernbergian fantasy are the relations occurring at intense affect states, that is, all the 'feared and
desired relations' between the self and the object. Obviously, motivational processes cannot be reduced to their affective origins in his
thinking and this proposition may suggest a mighty safeguard for
his theory. From our developmental perspective, we also expect the
primal and fundamental affective processes to organise into qualitatively different kinds of processes as the system emerges in more
complex organisational states. It seems unlikely though, as Westen
(1997) notes, that a dual motivational scheme (i.e., Eros and
Thanatos, love and hate, pleasure and pain) is enough to account for

the multitude of human motives that have been shaped by evolutionary processes to promote adaptation. Motives appear to have a conditional specificity that cannot be explained by eroticisation and aggression as (the only and/or) superordinate motivational forces.

Indeed, Kernberg collapses all the rich and varied qualities of affective states onto the pain-pleasure balance mechanism, but this is only one dimension of affect, even if it is the most important one. This crude emphasis on the 'appraisal' aspects of affect that ignores the possibility of multiple affective systems subserving different human needs, runs the risk of reducing all the epigenetic potentialities of emotional development to a hybrid theoretical structure with low predictive and explanatory power. For instance, research conducted by Panksepp (1998) on mammalian brains shows that, while 'appraisal' accounts of affective states are still relevant, there are several 'genetically ingrained emotional systems' that serve different needs and vary from a general appetitive, craving and seeking system to more specific systems for anger, rage and hatred, fear and worry, panic, sadness and separation distress, joy and play, lust and jealousy and, finally, maternal care, love and nurturance.[7] Several emotional or motivational processes emerge epigenetically from these basic systems. Thus, we can agree with Kernberg here who argues that affects are always in relation to something, an object proper, a situation, a self representation, but we also have to disagree with his assertion that these basic affective states are simply bridging entities that link intrapsychic contents with no in-built roles for self and the other, or that their multiple and rich epigenetic products can be collapsed into a dual motivational scheme. As Panksepp and other pioneers of affective neurosciences accumulate evidence for the existence of basic affective systems in the mammalian brain, we may feel more confident to assert that there are innate biases for 'feared and desired' relationships in humans that through developmental experience epigenetically consolidate into multiple specific 'sensitised' ways of relating to people, situations, etc., According to this perspective, therefore, fantasy is not simply something phylogenetically inherited or an unalterable point of departure in personality development, but it becomes an innate potential for appraisals that help us relate to the world, idiosyncratically distorting our experience and which is, in turn, dependent upon experience. Kernberg's conception of fantasy is not that far from this perspective, but where his theory diverges is in his 'reduction' of affect states into linking entities that need the extra power of the purely representational to develop into higher order motivational processes.

It is beyond the scope of this paper to explore the nature of fantasy. Nevertheless, we should mention here that most evolutionary accounts of emotion actually refer to a special instance of fantasy. Take for example Panksepp's PANIC system that is associated with separation distress. Separation causes prolonged stimulation of the system which, in turn, produces 'distress vocalisations' that increase the likelihood of the mother finding her baby. If the mother does not appear, the baby adopts depression-like behaviours that, according to Panksepp's evolutionary thinking, reduce the risk of being hunt out by predators. Obviously, fantasy here has 'boiled down' to a basic affective system's function, consisting of the fantasy that the mother will search for the baby and the fantasy that a persecutory other is out there ready to attack the baby. According to this line of thinking, therefore, emotional appraisals, beyond the pleasure–unpleasure dimension, condense primitive fantasies. In these kinds of fantasies the self and the other have already been integrated in the respective affective circuit. Kernberg's 'affects' linking self and object representations lack these in-built self and other roles.[8] With the risk of becoming speculative, we may argue that the Kernbergian self and object representations are not simply linked by these affective systems' activation, but they are 'created' in a sense by affective movements as they suggest psychic spaces that open up from the activation of these circuits. Panksepp (1998) notes that the primal SELF (*Simple Ego-type Life Form*) is actually a motor system devoted to almost 'instinctually' acting on the world under the guidance of emotional appraisals and, moreover, that this system creates a primitive and vague sense of agency. A protorepresentational self then may emerge from the feedback occurring from the activation of this primitive agent, while a protorepresentational other may emerge as the linking pole dictated by the fantasy condensed in the activated circuit.

The fact that mammalian affective systems open up the psychic space for self and object representations and, consequently, for the development of higher order social emotions such as shame and guilt in humans but not in other mammals, suggests that something more must be in place for social development to proceed. This 'something more' might bring us back to the 'innate biases towards social information'[9] that turn humans from swarm into cultural beings. An intrapsychic space representing the other may initially be filled up and grossly distorted by the primal fantasies condensed in the basic affective systems, but it is also the space where the social feedback promotes integration during development and puts more and more constraints on primal fantasy distortions. According to this perspective, social information railroads the development of primal fantasy into more complex, higher order affective and motivational states, while fantasy continues to distort our understanding of social information. Thus, Stern rightly suggests that the human babies' social developmental task is not related to autonomy but to the mastery of relatedness 'skills' which refers first and foremost to relatedness to an internal other. Kernberg, on the other hand, rightly places narcissism on this level, the level where the intrapsychic 'dialogue' between what we register as self and object-proper has already emerged and both representational entities have achieved some necessary stability. However, for Kernberg, narcissistic organisations appear more or less as 'solutions' against unbearable affects originating in dependence, such as envy and despair, as well as against a surplus of innate aggression. Other in-built affective mechanisms and the role of social feedback do not seem equally important.[10]

From our developmental point of view, there are, roughly speaking, three fates for the intrapsychic self-other space: first, it can be grossly distorted by our idiosyncratic 'primal' expectancies; second, it can lose the benefit of variability in the interactions between the basic affective systems due to inflexibility in social feedback; and, third, it can 'entertain' an 'other' that is 'good enough' to whip up, mould, metabolize and channel our primal expectancies and, consequently, magnify variability and developmental potentialities. Kernberg seems to rate only the first as primary. The other two are not as important and/or seem to have no place in his theoretical edifice.[11]

In contrast to Kernberg, Britton (2003) introduces some ideas that seem to be closer to our developmental perspective. For instance, he introduces apart from an hostile/destructive narcissistic object relatedness, the possibility of a libidinal/defensive narcissistic constellation, shifting thus the focus away from the autonomy/ dependence dimension and towards the dimension of relatedness in the intrapsychic space. According to him, narcissistic object relations are motivated by "the wish to preserve the capacity for love by making the love-object seem like the self", or they may aim at "annihilating the object as the representative of otherness" (p. 157). Moreover, he depicts narcissism as a problem in sharing intrapsychic space, where the perspective of another person threatens with invasion both the self and the 'internal other' space. He compares this invasion with a 'foreign mental protein' that may compromise the integrity of the psychic immune system. Obviously, then, our innate hostility to otherness is a safety valve. Identification processes, Britton maintains, offer a fool-proof mechanism which can bring otherness in the intrapsychic space by controlling at the same time its unwanted effects.

Similarly, Fonagy et al. (2004) propose from the perspective of the 'social biofeedback theory of affect-mirroring' a complementary interpersonal mechanism that may ensure seamless internalisation which they call 'markedness in maternal mirroring display'. When the mother mirrors the child's affective display, she usually marks by exaggeration her emotional displays so as to be 'perceptually differentiable' from her realistic emotional expressions and facilitate the child to internalise the emotion as his own. The authors note that marked but incongruent mirroring, that is, a marked display of an affect other than the infant displays, leads to a distorted second-order representation that through multiple experiences consolidates into what Winnicott calls a 'false self', that is, a self whose function is to hide, protect or even express the real self that equally struggles to rise from obscurity or readily goes forth into the mass of second-order representations.[12] The baby 'identifies' with an internalized malignant 'otherness' to settle those brisk affective movements that 'search but do not find the fertilizing power of emotional scaffolding' (Tronick et al. 1998).

Emptiness—not necessarily the lived experience of something missing inside—may suggest the critical aspect of narcissism. From this perspective, both Kohut and Kernberg captured in sketches the three dimensional moving shape of emptiness. Thus, Kohut's portrayal of emptiness resembles that of a moving shadow on a two-dimensional plane. Kernberg's portrayal is really three dimensional since the rich understanding of the relations between different parts gives his account adequate depth and foreshortening. Britton's adumbration animates the picture. At the heart of emptiness there is abhorrence for otherness, internal or external; the complex interactions between the primal affective movements are treated more and more as alien in the self-other intrapsychic space, or the mitigating 'contained' matter is unwelcome in a space already invaded by the primal matter. However, we are always talking about a polymorphous space. As Britton puts it elegantly: "... when I come to the narcissistic disorders I find they include within them a range of phenomena, some destructive, some libidinal and some defensive" (2003, p. 156). Islets of the space are 'allergic' to external otherness, some spots are colonized by the external that drains the briskness of the primal, while in other places the flora either withers away or bursts into flowers over and over again.

NOTES

1.   Conrad Hal Waddington, biologist and embryologist, used the epigenetic landscape metaphor to describe the complex interactions between genotype and environmental influences in organismic development. The growth of an organism is compared to a stream that in a landscape full of hills and valleys searches for a stable point to acquiesce. Environmental influences change the existing paths of the landscape and may consequently change the course of the moving matter or it may even put into motion matter that has acquiesced in some stable points, opening up new paths. Waddington's landscape–or say the genetic blueprint–macroscopically viewed seems almost static, while for Gotlieb there can be macroscopically observable transformations even in the landscape itself under the influence of environmental information.

2.   Thelen & Smith refer to macroscopically observed behaviours/skills–like sitting, walking, or language skills—whose emergence seems invariable in chronological terms in humans. However, this invariability does not develop on the grounds of normative and prescriptive processes. The assembling sub-organisations may follow very different paths in their way towards the same end point.

3.   Especially in this proposition it is evident that the Kohutian 'object', in contrast to object relational perspectives, does not follow the intrapsychic vicissitudes of the self.

4.   According to Kohut, maternal selective encouragement of attitudes and behaviours hijacks the child's personality and results in a vertical split within the self structure that shows up as opposing mental states and attitudes within the same person (Mollon, 2001).

5. It might be worth noting here that Kohut had little contact with internal psychiatric patients and, as Gabbard (2000) mentions, he usually viewed external patients, in contrast to Kernberg who had contact with more regressed patients.

6. Kernberg follows the tradition of self-psychology and writes fantasy with 'f'. However, when he writes phantasy with 'ph', he usually refers to the Kleinian type.

7. Panksepp names these systems respectively as SEEKING, RAGE, FEAR, PANIC, PLAY, LUST & CARE.

8. Actually, as Solms & Turnbull (2002) argue, Panksepp's basic affective systems–especially the SEEKING system—resemble the Freudian drives.

9. The nature of these biases depends on the theoretical framework one adopts. Fonagy et al. (2003) argue for the existence of a social contingency module that turns the baby's attention initially towards perfect contingencies with maternal behaviour and, later on, towards less perfect contingencies. Other theorists study the nature of several different modules analysing social information (i.e., face recognition, eye-direction detection etc) with no reference to a central analyser.

10. It might be useful to clarify some points regarding Kernberg's affect theory that, as we understand it, influences his conceptualization of the self. The most primitive sense of self in Kernberg (1989) is related to affective experience; an intense affect state *per se* suggests the primary form of experienced consciousness. Projective identification does not appear at this stage but only at the next stage where some kind of reflective awareness on the 'feeling' of a subjective state as different from other states has emerged. In contrast, Panksepp's SELF is a motor 'unit', an agent that acts on affective appraisals. Apparently, a protorepresentational self must register 'how it feels' so as to act on the appraisal. Adopting this perspective, we may infer that a purely interpersonal projective identification mechanism might be operative right from the start. We should agree here with Kernberg though that projective identification is "... an intrapsychic operation with a predominance of fantasy over actual behaviour". However, in our perspective, fantasy is already wired in the primal affective systems, while in Kernberg (1989) fantasy requires the capacity for at least a primitive form of thought, namely, symbolisation. Interestingly, Kernberg believes that symbolisation develops on the grounds of intense affect states as an element of a chain that comes to represent the whole chain. If fantasy though is something wired and condensed in basic affective systems, then right from the start the infant is able to 'give out' its inner state and open up an inner space where comparisons take place between what is expected to come from outside and what finally seems to come in.

11. Kernberg's indifferent attitude towards these two aspects of development can also be observed in his perception of death as a psychological force that undermines the ego's synthetic activity, whereas from our point of view death is

a property of the system, that is to say, death is one of the system's functions that narrows variability and developmental potentialities.

12.   Fonagy et al. (2003) define second-order representations as metarepresentational units in which infants match their physiological experience with maternal vocal and facial mirroring displays.

CHAPTER FOUR

From narcissism to mutual recognition: the "mothering" support within the intersubjective dialectic

Polona Curk

The statement that introducing the concept of narcissism to psychoanalysis created many theoretical problems both to Freud as well as to his more contemporary followers is no less than famous.[1] The idea of narcissism as libidinal energy attached to the ego blurred Freud's distinction between ego and libidinal drives. Despite, or perhaps precisely because of, these problems, narcissism also proves a very fruitful concept to explore. And despite forcing Freud to re-address the *original* conflict of the drives, narcissism ultimately still proves to be deeply about—a conflict.

This paper concentrates mainly on secondary narcissism, which is what the term 'narcissism' will be referring to. But the starting point in the present examination of narcissism will be in the context of the interaction between the newborn and the primary caregiver, thus retaining the link to primary narcissism as its origin. Narcissism will be seen, as it will be explained later, in Kohutian terms as an incomplete or disturbed emergence from the archaic narcissistic state. The paper will focus on the function of the maternal support (mothering) in allowing for the emergence of the infant from a self-enclosed space and encouraging it to reach out for the other, adopting thus the position of object-relations theorists, mainly Winnicott and Kohut. From here, two things will be attempted. First, narcissistic disturbances will be explained through the examination of conflicts in this primary interface, mostly in terms of the child's aggressive and compliant subsequent responses. In order to further comprehend these responses, Jessica Benjamin's model of the dialectic of recognition between the mother and the developing infant will be employed. This dialectic is supported by the Winnicottian and object relational concepts of the 'maturational process' and the importance of the parental response for the establishment of subjectivity. Although Benjamin mentions narcissism, she does not speak extensively about it; nonetheless, her model will be juxtaposed with Kohut's theory on narcissism in an attempt to elaborate on her clues on narcissistic injuries in the dialectic of recognition. Second, the paradoxical function of the mothering subject's employment of her/his resources in understanding and supporting the narcissistic child, in order precisely to break through the child's narcissism, will be outlined. Subsequently, the distinction between the mother-child dialectic and the dialectic between two adults will be pointed out in order to understand the extent of the injury and illusion involved in secondary narcissism and the need to acknowledge the mothering (supporting) function in order to break out of narcissistic illusion.

In order to make the following part clearer, two points should be noted here about the use of the term narcissism in this paper. The first one is that this paper partly follows Mario Jacoby's argument that narcissism in contemporary psychoanalysis can be linked to and even understood as, self-esteem and that, arguably, Freud also came close to this meaning in his writing (Jacoby, 1990). For Freud, self-regard was an expression of the size of the ego (Freud, 1914c, p. 98) generated by the amount of narcissistic libidinal cathexes. Jacoby summarizes the positions of several psychoanalytic theoreticians in order to make a distinction between healthy and pathological narcissism, the former originating in satisfied feelings towards the way one sees oneself and the latter in an unconscious defence against unpleasurable, self-depreciating feelings (overcompensation) (Jacoby, 1990, p. 83). This view implies two components of self-esteem, an outside behavioural component and an inside feeling component; the former should normally follow/match the inside feeling one has about oneself. In Jacoby's description, pathological narcissism shows an obvious mismatch of these two components–narcissistic disorder being depicted as only a pseudo-self-esteem–whilst in self-esteem proper the two components match.

The second point relates to the fact that, because of its strong negative connotations, it seems confusing to use narcissism as a neutral term and it is hardly imaginable to say of someone, with a neutral or benevolent tone, that s/he is narcissistic. However, Jacoby proposes just that (Jacoby, 1990, p. 83). Narcissism stands both for a defensive behaviour and for healthy *narcissistic equilibrium*. The latter term was coined by American psychologist Heinz Kohut whose elaborate theory of narcissism examines precisely the dynamics between these two outcomes. However, I would like to point out again that both the narcissism that Jacoby speaks of and Kohut's dynamics between equilibrium and narcissistic disturbances refer mostly to the narcissism of an adult, that is, secondary narcissism, even when they speak of its development from primary narcissism. The distinction of secondary narcissism and its vicissitudes from the infant's primary narcissism (even when the former is considered a leftover or unmodified derivative of the latter) proves to be essential for the understanding of the narcissistic dynamic of a person, its function and the intersubjective relations that are in place to support it.

Introducing the importance of 'mother-ing'

Freud's notion of narcissism (Freud, 1914c) generated quite a few contradictions with his previous postulations, not least because, coinciding with the infamous split with Jung, it came too close to Jung's proposal of a single non-specific psychic energy. More importantly, it set off Freud's radical subsequent theoretical elaborations that established a new level of instinctual conflict. Besides the hypothesized source of neurosis in the conflict between the ego-libidinal and object-libidinal cathexis, which Freud retained even in his revised theory, now the (forever) narcissistic individual was also facing a 'new' conflict within him/herself—between the life and death drives (Freud, 1920g, 1923b). Interestingly, this situated the conflict not exclusively between the ego and the object but within the individual. Because Freud believed that the drives can never be observed in their pure form but always in a fusion with each other and narcissistic libido and the death drive were seen as influencing each other (Freud, 1920g, p. 54), his theory implies that the life and death conflict within the individual influences the relationship with the object/other but also allows for the reverse to be true: that the relationship with the other could influence the dynamics of the life and death drives. Bearing this in mind, what at first appears as a fundamental difference concerning the origins of psychopathology proposed by Heinz Kohut does have its precursors in Freud's theory.

More specifically, Kohut argued that the primary causes of psychopathology can be located in the disturbed empathic responses from the parental environment with the consequence of establishing a not-secure self in the child. Nonetheless, Kohut's theory is radically different from Freud's views on narcissism in two ways. First, it assumes an individual's experience of her/himself as a unit (even in the case of the self-in-formation) and places it above the conflict of the drives. "Ego enslavement to the drive aims" (Kohut in Jacoby, 1990, p. 64) is seen as taking place only secondarily, as an expression rather than a cause of psychopatology, a substitution or displacement for the missing pleasant inside feelings. Jacoby provides us with an everyday example: "An excessive love of sweets ... in my experience ... often reflects a longing to 'make life sweeter', especially in those cases where ... there is no-one whose caring can give the individual a sense of self-esteem". (Jacoby, 1990, p. 65) The second difference lies in the explicit and almost exclusive emphasis Kohut places on the parental responses for the establishment of the baby's self narcissistic equilibrium. Kohut examines the interaction with the empathic caregiver as a source through which the modification of the infant's initial potentialities forms the origins of the infant's self (Jacoby, 1990, p. 72). With this, Kohut exposes not only the narcissistic needs of the individual, but also establishes the empathic support of these needs by the parental other as a *necessary* condition for the individual to emerge from the compulsiveness of these needs and achieve a narcissistic equilibrium, that is to say, a stable self.

Indeed, empathic resonance seems to be Kohut's greatest 'innovation' in psychoanalytic theory and technique, both in explaining the origins of narcissistic disturbance in childhood as well as in the recommended analyst's response in therapy so as to overcome the narcissistic wound of the patient (Jacoby, 1990, p. 195). In this respect, his theory can be regarded as part of the object-relations tradition that concentrates on the primary interaction between mother and child and accords to a large extent with Winnicott's concept of the function of the 'good-enough' mother. What object-relations theories added to the notion of narcissism is the recognition of how fragile and vulnerable the infant's nascent self is in its terrifying experience of dependency and thus established a perspective that sees empathy and acknowledgement of the mothering person(s)' role as crucial for the development of a healthy sense of self-esteem. In fact, according to Jacoby, this perspective is today generally accepted in depth psychology (1990, p. 177).

Kohut strongly states that the essential part of mothering consists of empathic attention and caring towards the infant *as if there was already a self*; the infant can thus experience itself as a self (Kohut, 1971, 1977; Jacoby, 1990). It is, in a manner of speaking, a borrowed self—which is why Kohut called the mother figure of the baby its 'self-object' (Jacoby, 1990, p. 66)—the mother offers her 'resources' on disposal to the baby. For Kohut, this function of mirroring, providing it is empathic and includes 'a gleam in the mother's eye' (Jacoby, 1990, p. 66), is needed for the establishment of a healthy self-esteem. In fact, we encounter seeds of similar ideas already much earlier with Karen Horney, one of the first independent critics of Freud, who argued strongly in favour of social and cultural explanations for the differences in personalities, spoke about the importance of the human relationships and about the centre-point of the feeling of security for a neurotic personality (Horney, 1992/c1945). Horney discussed the pathological dimension of self-esteem as 'the search for glory' (Horney, 1951, p.38). Arguably, for Kohut this glory indicates the not-received gleam of the approving mother. Horney further argued that whilst a healthy person's " ... live forces of the *real self* urge one toward self-realization" (Horney, 1951, p. 38 my italics), the narcissist has a need to actualize *the idealized* self, another parallel with Kohut's theory.

Winnicott had a comparable idea to that of the 'real' self: he termed it True self and connected it through the dynamics of self-worth injuries to its counterpart–False self. This counterpart has many roles: it is a part of the self which develops partly as a defence to protect the True self and partly as "mannered social attitude" (Winnicott, 1965, p. 143). As such, it is of course to be found in every individual. However, in some people the False self takes over the personality.[2] Not only does life with a predominant False self not feel real for the person in question, but Winnicott argues that the person feels " ... completely at loss when not ... being appreciated or applauded (acknowledged as existing)" (1965, p. 150).

As we shall see shortly, being 'acknowledged as existing' is a human need that also seem to lie at the core of Jessica Benjamin's theory on the need for mutual recognition and the idea of the search for the 'surviving other' to recognize us (Benjamin, 1988). The potential source of narcissistic self-importance, this human need can in the helpless infant perhaps be seen as merely related to safety. Because we are born helpless and dependent, we need the other to show us that we are nonetheless valuable, as if thinking: 'I am helpless but if I am valuable for the parenting environment, *they* will protect me'.[3] Benjamin maintains that the need to be recognized extends from a need to share feelings with the other, to try the limits of the other with destructiveness and self-will. The infant wants to force its acknowledgement. It is as if there were, as Michael Balint proposed, a passive primary object-love with its aim "I shall be loved and satisfied, without being under any obligation to give anything in return'. (Jacoby, 1990, p. 42) But because the infant also needs the other to survive its destructive impulses and recognize it, there is an obvious conflict to be overcome, between forcing its own will (i.e., forcing acknowledgement) and *give the acknowledgement* in return.

Winnicott, drawing strongly on Kleinian terms, suggests that the conflict in the infant requires no less than 'two mothers' in one person to be successfully resolved which he named object-mother and environment-mother. The first one has to sustain attacks backed by instinctual tension of the infant who wants to " ... take possession of the contents of the object". (Winnicott, 1965, p. 76) The environment-mother, on the other hand, has to allow for the reparation to take place, as in Klein, so as for the infant to enter the depressive position. In Benjamin's terms, while forcing its own acknowledgement the infant also wants its forcefulness to be contained by the other, because it is the only way to enter the depressive position.[4] The roots of how the patterns of aggression and compliance are built lie here.

Benjamin emphasizes the achievement of *mutual* recognition in the primary dyad as an important factor in the development of the infant's self. Following Bowlby, she sees the sociability of the infant as a primary and not secondary phenomenon (Benjamin, 1988, p. 17). This compels her to add to the Hegelian need to be recognized an independent need *to recognize* (1988, p. 23). Benjamin stressed the need to recognize as originating in the pleasure of sharing subjectivity. The idea of sharing can be supported by Winnicott's insightful observation that it is the contribution that the infant is able to make to the 'environment-mother' that brings up his/her confidence and makes the anxiety of the love-hate ambivalence tolerable for him/her even after the 'two mothers' join to be recognized as one person. This perspective seems in conflict with the Balint's proposal, quoted above, that the infant does not want to give anything in return. It seems implied in Winnicott's idea, however, that it is the mothering person's empathic acceptance of the infant's attempts that gives the infant the feeling of contribution.

It is precisely in the failure of the empathic parental responses where Kohut located the origins of narcissistic disturbances, a failure with the consequence of an unsuccessful modification of the infant's original narcissistic traits resulting in the unstable establishment of the self. The ideas that seem strikingly close to Winnicott's intuitive insights, were expanded and developed by Kohut into an extensive model of how narcissistic disturbances occur during modifications of the 'idealized' and 'grandiose' selves, which he considered them to be "two facets of the same developmental phase" (Kohut, 1971, p. 107). It is important to note that Kohut saw these selves as determined both by the parental response and by the child's own narcissism, although he mainly focused on the former (1971, p. 65 et passim).[5] Interestingly, his concepts construct a kind of economics of omnipotence which is not so dissimilar to Freud's distributions of the libido.

From Kohut's writings three stages can be extracted through which the baby renounces and reassigns omnipotence. In the first, the omnipotence is ascribed to the primary fusion with the self-object. Because the nascent self includes self-objects, the infant feels omnipotent-grandiose. In Jacoby's words: " ... the perfection of the former also means the perfection of the latter". (Jacoby, 1990, p. 67) In the second phase, due to the awareness of separateness[6] the

omnipotence is ascribed to the self-objects–the parents: " ... the psyche saves a part of the lost experience of global narcissistic
perfection by assigning it to an archaic rudimentary (transitional)
self-object, the idealized parent imago". (Kohut, 1971, p. 37) This is
the phase of great vulnerability when " ... all the power and bliss
now reside in the idealized object, the child feels empty and powerless when he is separated from it and he attempts, therefore, to
maintain a continuous union with it". (1971, p. 37) On the other
hand, for Kohut this developmental phase also indicates the attempt
of the child to assign all the narcissistic perfection and power upon
the self. In the third phase, favourably, some power/value gets
re-internalized by the infant. This happens, for Kohut, because the
parents strip themselves of omnipotence and gradually show their
imperfections to the child, which then allows the child to withdraw
some of its idealizing libido back into its own psychic structures
(1971, p. 41). Similarly, it is with the empathic mirroring from the
significant others that the grandiose self is also modified into a self
that has realistic ambitions and a sense of worth (Jacoby, 1990, p. 84).
Through these empathic responses, both the grandiose and the idealized self are modified and balanced. If the parental response is not
phase-appropriate, the child withdraws all the narcissistic cathexes
back into itself rather than achieving narcissistic equilibrium. As
Balint puts it: "If I am not loved sufficiently by the world, not given
enough gratification, I must love and gratify myself" (Jacoby, 1990,
p. 42). Hence, this perspective sees secondary narcissism in terms of
the child's emotional reaction to the lack of the much needed
empathic parental support.

Introducing the mother: two subjects
in interaction

Indeed, all the theorists discussed above place utmost importance
on the parental (usually mother's) empathic attunement. But again,
their perspectives focus on the child's experience of the interaction.
Whilst acknowledging the need for mothering, the child/theorist
narcissistically forgets the mothering person. Yet, can the infant
emerge out of its narcissistic (en)closure without recognizing the

independent subjectivity of the (m)other? This proves to be a missing step in overcoming narcissism and establishing (inter)subjectivity within the child-mother dialectic. Here, Jessica Benjamin takes her theory one step further by pointing out that the mother has to be recognized as a subject in her own right, with a centre independent of the mothering that she carries out for her infant. This is, as Benjamin emphasises, for the infant a step as important as separation and a step that needs to be taken by the theorist as well. Indeed, she argues for a "need for a theory that understands how the capacity for mutuality evolves, a theory based on the premise that from the beginning there are always (at least) two subjects". (Benjamin, 1988, p. 23) Benjamin's 'empathic attunement' in the dialectic of mutual recognition, which is comparable to Kohut's empathic resonance, has added the focus on the experience of the mothering person in an attempt to re-establish her/his separate subjectivity. With this addition, Kohut's and Benjamin's theories can be seen as complementary. However, Benjamin's stress on maternal subjectivity not only advocates the existence of the mothering person as a human being in their own right, but also poses a question of acknowledging the maternal support. Therefore, it is even more important for understanding narcissism in the dialectic of two adults.

Kohut's two-partite dynamic that looks at the child's emotional reaction to the lack of the much needed empathic parental support partly corresponds to Benjamin's description of the domination/submission personality constellation, although she does not refer explicitly to narcissism. Alongside one favourable outcome, Benjamin distinguishes two unsuccessful ones: first, when a mother 'gives in' to the demands of the infant and therefore loses her subjectivity for him/her. This infant, Benjamin speculates, will develop into an adult who keeps assuming omnipotence for her/himself and does not recognize the subjectivity of the other.[7] However, s/he will still need the other (submissive) one to confirm his omnipotence. On the other hand, when the parent is retaliating for the infant's (limits-testing) behaviour, the baby will not believe that s/he will ever gain recognition for her/his own independent self, so s/he denies her own self and becomes compliant (Benjamin, 1988).

Despite a persistent dualism that permeates the discussion on narcissism, it is important to note that it is nonetheless not accurate to divide narcissistic behaviour into two groups or even as a continuum between two extremes. For instance, Horney (1945, p. 42) mentions three types of 'character traits' that she thinks the child develops as a tactic to operate in the environment. Besides the first two types, which she calls 'moving against' and 'moving towards' people, that can be paralleled to Benjamin's dominant and submissive type respectively, Horney introduces the third type, 'moving away' from people, which refers to a personality that is neither dominant nor submissive but stays aloof from people. Arguably, this behaviour can also be designated as originating from narcissistic injuries, perhaps the most so: while the first two types still 'struggle' to connect with people, this type represents giving up on them.[8] As such, this type both renounces the need for recognition and it declines giving it back, withdrawing thus from the reciprocity of desire. It might be due to this form of narcissistic defence that Freud believed that narcissists were un-analysable, especially since he used the term secondary narcissism originally to depict schizophrenic patients and assumed their complete withdrawal of libido from objects (Freud, 1914, p. 74).

Although both in Benjamin's and Kohut's models a huge importance falls on the responses of the mothering person, both theorists have allowed in different ways the possibility of the infant's own agency as partly influencing the dialectic of recognition/narcissistic equilibrium. Kohut (1971, p. 65 et passim), as mentioned above, has maintained that the infant's own narcissism plays a part in the modification of its rudimentary self. Benjamin is even more specific when she argues, for example, for the existence of the child's need to recognize and share emotional states of mind. Nonetheless, besides the importance of taking into account both subjects in the mother and child interaction, the most interesting point seems to be precisely that it is not clear what belongs to, or comes from, whom. Thus, an interesting comparison between the two theories arises when we consider how they both understand the psychoanalytic concept of internalization in connection to the infant's ability to soothe itself. Benjamin's interpretation of Winnicott's concept of 'facilitating' states that, rather than internalization, soothing is a capacity of the self which the other's response only helps to activate (Benjamin, 1988, p. 44). It would seem that Kohut, on the contrary, stays closer to the concept of internalization, arguing that soothing (mothering) functions are the outcome of re-integrated idealizing narcissistic libido that is released by the parents' allowing the child to see them as imperfect (Kohut, 1971, p. 41, p. 65). The integration of this libido helps to (re-)establish (secondary) narcissistic equilibrium and enables the infant to maintain it by itself.

Nonetheless, a closer examination reveals that these two views do have common grounds. In her perspective, Benjamin relates soothing to Winnicott's transitional realm and therefore to play and creativity and the interplay of fantasy and reality. If we resort to Winnicott, we find that the transitional space (transitional phenomena, transitional object) evolved as an intermediate neutral space that exists for the infant between primary creativity and objective perception (Winnicott, 1971, p. 15) and is experienced as *between* the infant and the mother. It is supported by a good-enough mother (enabling a not-too-persecutory internal object) (1971, p. 13) and by parents that do not challenge the infant in relation to the transitional object (1971, p. 18). It can be argued that Kohut's idea of parents' 'renouncing' the idealized omnipotence with which the child experiences them would support the Winnicottian position that the parents do not challenge the baby with the reality of its dependence and helplessness and help create a safe space where the baby can explore its own agency, a space that is "necessary for the initiation of a relationship between the child and the world" (Winnicott, 1971, p. 18).

Playing, for Winnicott, is a direct development from transitional phenomena and he repeats several times that it is (only) in playing that both the child and adult can be creative and discover their own selves (Winnicott, 1971, pp. 69, 71, 73). For Winnicott, "[p]laying implies trust". (1971, p. 69) A space to play is normally conceived as a neutral space where making mistakes is allowed, as it is to be open and vulnerable in front of the other. Certainly, then, the other cannot be perceived as omnipotent and over-idealized if playing is to take space. Rather, we can assume that the mother offers a space where she is not the omnipotent other but an ally, providing opportunity for illusion and then gradual, but never complete, disillusionment. Benjamin believes that this theory presumes two subjects rather than a subject and an object and it "attributes all agency neither to the subject with his innate capacities or impulses, nor to the object which stamps the blank slate of the psyche with its imprint. It argues that the other plays an active part in the struggle of the individual to creatively discover and accept reality". (Benjamin, 1988, p. 45)

Two subjects and an illusion

As the preceding discussion shows, the use of illusion is essential in the development of the infant for Winnicott. From the mother-supported illusion and transitional phenomena through playing, Winnicott proposes a further developmental step, i.e., cultural experiences. Interestingly, for Kohut, an additional function of re-incorporated idealizing narcissistic libido besides soothing is also being the " ... libidinal fuel for ... socioculturally important activities", (Kohut, 1971, p. 40). This would accord to Winnicott's concept of the infant's 'contribution' to the 'environment-mother'. As we said earlier, it is the possibility of contribution, which makes the anxiety of the love-hate emotions tolerable for the infant. Although the concept of contribution is not extensively explained by Winnicott, it implicitly underlies his understanding of the human being's relationship to and engagement with, the world. The concept seems to support Benjamin's observation of the infant's need to recognize. Furthermore, closer examination reveals important implications for understanding secondary narcissism in an adult person and consequently the importance of acknowledging the mothering person.

For Winnicott, transitional phenomena also describe a transition from primary unawareness of indebtedness to the acknowledge-ment of indebtedness (Winnicott, 1971, p. 3). If we now look at Winnicott's line of thought regarding contribution, it appears to make use of the Kleinian concepts of 'splitting' and 'reparation'. Winnicott sees the use that the infant makes of the environment-mother as different than the one it makes of the object-mother at the moment of id-tension (Winnicott, 1965/1990, pp. 75–77): the environment-mother is the one who receives affection from the infant. According to Winnicott, the capacity for concern develops at the moment when the 'two mothers' come together: this concern (anxiety) is alleviated by the infant's possibility for a contribution to the environment-mother in the form of 'giving'.

Winnicott states that contribution increases the infant's confidence. In this respect, contribution is close to the Kleinian concept of reparation: by making reparation to the mother, the infant becomes more and more autonomous in relationship to its own drives. In other words, as the mother allows the baby to make reparation, she "enables the baby to become more and more bold in the experiencing of id-drives: in other words, frees the baby's instinctual life" (Winnicott, 1965, p. 77). Winnicott contends that if the opportunity for reparation fails, it results in sadness or depressed mood of the infant. This is understandable, if we think that a failed opportunity for reparation indicates a state that does not allow for making mistakes, since it makes them irreversible and hence intolerable. Such a state is depressive because it prevents free creativity–it blocks both playing and transitional (unchallenged) phenomena. Because all actions have irreparable consequences, no illusion is allowed; no use of illusion, for Winnicott, indicates "no meaning for the human being in the idea of a relationship with an object … " (Winnicott, 1971, p. 15).

The function of reparation/contribution in the child's management of the aggressive/destructive impulses is important, since Winnicott maintains that through destruction the infant attempts to establish externality and thus the use (love) of the object (1971, pp. 120–121), which is enabled by the object's (mother's) survival of the destruction. With this, Winnicott established the importance of the link between fantasy and reality. Jessica Benjamin employs this standpoint when she argues that the infant's destruction of the (m)other in fantasy and her survival in reality allows for mutual recognition of another as a subject instead of an object, something that she believes object-relations theories, as well as intra-psychic theories, failed to address.[9] (Benjamin, 1988, p. 68 et passim, esp. p. 70) But more than that, throughout her work she develops an important extension of the concepts of fantasy and reality in connection to the sense of omnipotence and the search for the surviving other.

It is important to note here that at the same time that contribution alleviates anxiety and confirms the infant's confidence, it also exposes the infant's need for the mother, hence, its dependence. The child needs to make reparation not because it suddenly realized that what it did was wrong, but because it needs the mother that it has just "destroyed". By making reparation—by contributing—the child implicitly acknowledges its indebtedness to the mothering person, who not only survived the child's destruction, but allows for reparation. By neither 'giving in' nor 'retaliating', the mother has neither supported the child's destructive illusion that he/she does not need the mother, nor challenged the child's illusion that he/she is not completely dependent. By accepting the child's contribution, the mothering person agrees to take the child (again) as a partner in the intersubjective dialectic, to re-establish the relationship.

The link between fantasy and reality is worth following in the attempt to understand the narcissistic development of an individual. One thing that most theories on narcissism agree upon is Freud's famous statement that narcissism in an individual is never completely abandoned (Freud, 1914c, p. 97). Kohut's 'solution' to this was that narcissistic equilibrium is something that has to be constantly maintained rather than reached once and forever, which can be matched with Benjamin's ideas about constant tension between assertion of the self and recognition of the other. For Winnicott, however, this simply means that acceptance of reality is never complete. Illusion and fantasy are necessary and also creative, parts of life. Winnicott maintains that the intermediate area of experience between reality and fantasy still exists in an adult, finding expression, for instance, in art, religion, philosophy etc., hence creating an area of personal subjective phenomena for each individual. This area of the individual, when claims of its objectivity are not made upon others, is not challenged in its belonging to inner or shared reality (Winnicott, 1971, pp. 18–19) and can be understood due to its making use of illusion as an area of subjective meaning. Furthermore, this area of subjective phenomena, originating in the transitional realm and retained in the intense experiencing and imaginative living (1971, p. 19), can be said to be supported by others by the fact that it is not challenged. However, because a claim of objectivity cannot be made, this implicit support by others includes their expectation of an implicit acknowledgement by the individual that this is his/her personal *subjective* space/meaning, as if saying: "We will not challenge you with whether this certain phenomenon is objectively real, as long as you do not claim it is objectively real".

Here, the difference between the child's and the adult's use of illusion becomes clear. The infant's transitional space is supported by the parents without challenging its objectivity (without asking "Did you conceive of this or was it presented to you from without?" (Winnicott, 1971, p. 17), that is, "Have you created the breast or was it provided by the mother?") even when the infant does make the un-compromisable claim for objectivity of his/her experience. It is expected of an adult, on the contrary, to acknowledge the subjectivity of such experiences. In other words, without requiring an explicit acknowledgement of this phenomenon that would make illusion impossible, an adult is, in Winnicott's elaboration, still assumed to acknowledge (by not claiming its reality) the support by the others for maintaining his/her intermediate area. Winnicott infers that this is a paradox that has to be accepted about the space that exists between illusion and reality.

Illusion, fantasy and the maternal support

I presented Winnicott's concept of the use of illusion in the transitional phenomena at such length because I believe it provides grounds for questioning what happens when an individual is *not* able to offer this implicit acknowledgement that she/he is in need of such an 'illusion'. This seems to be the case in secondary narcissism that still retains the fantasy of omnipotence. Benjamin re-formulated the fantasy-reality paradox by arguing that, in an adult, "[t]he fantasy world of the unconscious in which self and objects can be omnipotent is balanced by the relational world in which we recognize, empathize and grasp the subjectivity of real others". (Benjamin, 2004, p. 132) Acknowledging the support of the mothering person would suggest implicitly acknowledging both the use of unconscious fantasy and the need for having the intermediate area, where, besides reality, illusion is employed unchallenged. This is a paradox which both Winnicott and Benjamin expect a mature adult to accomplish, but a (pathologically) narcissistic person cannot. In an insightful essay, *The Omnipotent Mother: A Psychoanalytic Study of*

Fantasy and Reality (2004), Benjamin emphasizes the ability to recognize "my fantasy to be a result of my feeling" in contrast to projecting it to someone else (Benjamin, 2004, p. 132) which, she thinks, would result in "world historical power struggle" (ibid, p. 133). The latter, she deems, is an attempt of domination that psychoanalytic theory has understood in terms of narcissism, "the subjective position that underpins it: the inability to recognize the other and confront difference without surrendering to or controlling the other". (Benjamin, 2004, p. 139) In a narcissistic person omnipotent control needs to be retained, therefore, neither fantasy nor reality can be acknowledged for what they are. Arguably, bearing in mind Benjamin's earlier work, this is because of the unsuccessful establishment of the externality of the subject during the infant's attempts of destruction.

From the preceding discussion, we saw how Winnicott's paradox of fantasy and reality regulates meaning and relationship with an object, a transition that is also one from primary unawareness of indebtedness to the acknowledgement of indebtedness. In Benjamin's original elaboration of his ideas, unpacking the fantasy and reality opens and allows for " … the doubleness of psychic life (Benjamin, 1990), both the fantasy of maternal omnipotence and the capacity to recognize the mother as another subject" (Benjamin, 2004, p. 132) to exist. It is precisely because she asserts the child's need to recognize the other is equally important as being recognized, that Benjamin can restore the mother as a subject rather than as an object, although the emphasis stays on the mother's responses. For example, she emphasizes the importance of the mother being the active subject of desire for the child, able to survive the rapprochement struggle when the child strives to assert his/her own agency (Benjamin, 1988, p. 122). However, it is at this point that the mother-child dialectic and that between two adults can easily be enmeshed, with the consequence of misrepresenting the latter and disregarding the important distinction between the child's and the adult's use of subjective (transitional) phenomena.

Establishing what she calls the 'burden of subjectivity' (Benjamin, 1988, 1998, p. xix), Benjamin claims that we have both to survive for the other and ask of the other to survive our destruction. However, at this point of surviving the destruction of the other, an attempt is made to transpose the dialectic between the child and the mother to that of two adult subjects, which becomes entangled with the dialectic between a man and a woman. On the one hand, Benjamin criticizes the fact that society permits the existence of a 'private refuge' supported by the split between the psychic and the social. This 'private refuge' allows for the mother, who with her holding enabled the child to discover and activate his own capacities, to become in an adult relationship the ideal wife/mother, who "protects the autonomous individual from having to admit his needs by meeting them in advance: she protects him from the shame of exposure, allowing him to appear independent and in control". (1988, p. 205) This scheme, for Benjamin, sustains the situation where "the inner core of need (...) can never be revealed" (1988, p. 205) by an adult 'autonomous' individual; a situation which, bearing our preceding discussion in mind, indicates sustaining an illusion, a narcissistic belief that the support is not needed. Consequently, the support of the wife/mother cannot be acknowledged unless the *need for support* is acknowledged by the 'autonomous' individual—thus, unless the fantasy-reality is unpacked.

On the other hand, however, Benjamin's subsequent suggestion that women should re-claim being a subject of their own desire rather than an object of desire (1988, p. 221), places once again the responsibility for the change in the dialectic of recognition on the woman/ mother, who may "thus offer men a new possibility of colliding with the outside and becoming alive in the presence of an equal other". (1988, p. 221) In this vision of recognition between equal subjects, women should be able to survive (male) destructiveness. This not only places the guilt for the inability of such male individuality to recognize the other, (which, as Benjamin points out, the psychoanalytic theories of narcissism have exposed and Oedipal theory denies (1988, p. 181)), on the woman's attitude that allows it, but also partly reinstates the dialectic of power: it implicitly states that the recognition from the other can only be achieved (earned?) by surviving the other's attempt of destruction. However, since this destruction is not anymore the infant's furious limit-testing behaviour through which the infant is establishing the externality of the 'not-me' (i.e., other), the survival of the destruction of the other cannot be the same in the mother-child dialectic as it is in the woman-man dialectic. The mother can benevolently stand up to the destructive impulses of the child without retaliating or giving in, whilst two grown-ups are both expected to assume responsibility for their own actions.[10] This somehow revised dialectic of power where recognition needs to be achieved by surviving the other's attempt of destruction undermines Benjamin's own original suggestion that mutual recognition is based on the *need to recognise* that is complementary to the need to be recognized, in other words, that one is capable of recognizing the pleasure of sharing the subjectivity by *voluntarily* offering recognition. It is of course a different question to ask how this voluntary recognition of the other could ever be reconciled with the competitive, instrumental realm of production where, as Jane Flax asserts, affective ties have to be excluded (Flax, 1990, p. 78).

In fact, Benjamin herself states that mutual recognition should not be confused with 'equal rights' policies. Recognition focuses on the particular, individual (needs of the) other (Benjamin, 1988, p. 195) and it requires empathy rather than some universal point of view that would function as a reference through which the self approaches the other. She asserts that as long as the father (man) is not as reliable for 'holding' as the mother, his is not a genuine autonomy at all: only a person who can "recognize the other or his own dependency without suffering a threat to his own identity" (Benjamin, 1988, p. 197) is an autonomous individual. Without forgetting that narcissistic injuries might be, as Freud originally suggested[11] (1914), perhaps greater in women due to their sociohistorical circumstances, responsibility for what Benjamin calls (male) narcissistic inability to recognize the other, should not be projected onto women, too.

Therefore, Benjamin's statement that women need to reclaim their subjectivity should perhaps be employed as an argument for women's rejection of the responsibility for the other's (i.e., male) narcissism and their assumption of the ownership of the support they are able to offer. In fact, something similar is suggested in Benjamin's later book *The Shadow of the Other* (1998), namely, that it is important for a woman to (actively) own her own affects and to use her own containing ability also for herself rather than just offering it to the other (Benjamin, 1998, pp. 27, 32). It is that "authorship or ownership of our desire and intention [that] is a crucial feature of subjectivity occluded by the conventional opposition between activity and passivity" (Benjamin, 1998, p. xvii). In this opposition, she implies, a man ought not to split-off his experience of being passive as this also involves a form of *containment* for the other (i.e., woman) (1998, p. 30). This, together with Benjamin's proposal that a woman should also use her containing ability for herself, allows for two possible conclusions: that passivity, if understood as a form of containment, is needed, but that the projection of passivity upon women as their sole prerogative is to be rejected. In this way, a woman using her containing ability also for herself will help her assume the position of an active subject–author, whilst it would also render it possible for her to be able to claim and receive containment from a man.

Concluding thoughts

The aforementioned theories of narcissism seem to have come a long way from Freud's original postulations, especially in the emphasis they put on the interaction with the other and the agency they assign to the self (subject). What these theories have added to Freud's relatively pessimistic postulations is the assertion of the essential and legitimate human need for empathy in support of the area of imaginative living between subjects that is neither completely shared nor challenged and that is, as already Freud observed, extended into adulthood and through the whole lifetime. With this view in mind, the dependency and vulnerability of the inner core of the self with its need never to be completely confronted with 'reality' can be seen as a necessary source of creative and playful living, providing that, as stated by Benjamin, fantasy and reality in a mature individual coexist rather than merge. This indicates that the adult world is not devoid of the need for containment and intersubjective support and although the ideal mother's/wife's support needs to be challenged precisely in its lack of an intersubjective component, what is primarily narcissistic is the denial/negation of the *need* for this support whilst using it. In fact, Benjamin claims that the social panic generated by women leaving home (thus failing to maintain such support) expresses "the fear of paying the price for individual autonomy and social rationalization, the fear that being grown up means feeling 'like *a motherless* child'". (Benjamin, 1988, p. 205, my emphasis)

Although both Winnicott and Kohut focus on this need in the child as well as on the need for empathy in the therapeutic setting and thus provide us with the potential for exploration of this intersubjective dialectic (in fact, Benjamin herself utilizes Winnicott's concepts to a large extent), their perspectives evolve around the child's (or narcissistically damaged patient's) needs and, therefore, avoid to address the need to overcome one's narcissism by recognizing the other as subject. Jessica Benjamin's theory attempts to redress this imbalance by emphasising the importance of the re-establishment of maternal subjectivity. Her theory is very powerful in raising many questions regarding the existence of the mothering person as a subject in her (or, in fact, his) own right. It points to the acknowledgement of the (m)othering support especially in its function within the social/psychic divide where the assumed 'autonomy' of the individual negates its existence together with the need for it and challenges the projections, such as the woman's alleged passivity, that are put in place to maintain this negation.

Nonetheless, Benjamin's theory does not exploit all its potential as it does not explore the differences between the child-mother and the woman-man dialectic and forgets that the latter takes place between two adult subjects responsible for their actions, placing once again the main responsibility on the woman's side. Rather, it makes sense to employ Winnicott's idea of contribution to build on Benjamin's basis that one is capable of recognizing the pleasure of sharing one's subjectivity by–voluntarily–offering recognition. The attempted 'destruction' by the other could then be recognized, since it fails to offer mutual recognition, as a narcissistic attempt for domination. The ownership of the woman's own desires and abilities, including support and containing, could then easier be assumed. Benjamin presents this supportive ability as deriving from maternal thinking, being both passive and active, when she states that "[t]he processing of other's psychic material and its integration in intersubjective expression–recognition–constitutes the active-passive reconciliation in the work of the maternal subject" (Benjamin, 1998, p. 29). This support from the other is, in a transformed form, still needed in adulthood. Narcissistic denial of both the need for it and its reception blocks the exchange of this support, whilst intersubjectivity in recognition allows for alternation in expressing and receiving it (Benjamin, 1998), where both

positions in the intersubjective couple are recognized and represented.
Perhaps, like the soothing capacity of the self that is enabled
by the other's response, this, too, is there and only needs to be
activated.

NOTES

1. Peter Gay writes, for example, that Ernest Jones called Freud's paper
'On Narcissism' (1914) 'disturbing'. (Gay, 1995, p. 545).

2. Winnicott argues that it is especially dangerous if the False self is tied up
with an intellectual approach to life, which, in other words, means if someone is
too 'conscious' or rational about themselves.

3. Perhaps we want to keep this point about the meaning of vanity in
mind when we think about its origination in the grandiose self. A thrilling
philosophical argument expanding similarly on this question from a perspective
of why a lover wants to be loved back by the beloved is offered by Sartre. (Sartre,
1943, pp. 366–372).

4. It would be pertinent here to discuss the implications of the depressive
position to the reciprocity of desire on which the society and social relationships,
including those of power, are based. Unfortunately, this cannot be addressed in
this paper.

5. Kohut repeatedly argues that the parental response is more important
than any traumatic event that might happen to the child and furthermore, that
the worst influence on the child's establishing self are the parents' own narcissistic preoccupations which in turn account for the inappropriate response.

6. Kohut maintains that the development of proper object-relations that
this recognized separateness and maturational level allows for does not replace
the development of idealizations, but rather runs parallel with it.

7. This would correspond to what Kohut calls disturbances coming from
claims of the grandiose self. While these claims are appropriate in a certain
phase, the child learns, through selective parental response, to accept its limitations and replace grandiose and exhibitionistic phantasies with pleasure in its
own activities and realistic self-esteem.

8. Neville Symington goes so far as to argue that even autism is only an
extreme form of narcissism in its 'withdrawal behaviour' type. (Symington,
1993, p. 106)

9. To survive, in Benjamin's terms, means not to retaliate. However, a nice
description of what survival represents for the child is given by Elsa First
in her paper 'Mothering, Hate and Winnicott' (2004): "This survival is not the
minimal survival of the victim, but implies resilience–that the mother or analyst

has not been damaged in her ability to be a person'. (p. 157). Ability to be a person, for First, is not to suffer change in quality, in attitude.

10. In fact, this distinction is not an absolute one either, as psychoanalysis has already exposed the repetitive infantile patterns in adult behaviour which nobody can completely avoid and which originate precisely from the same non-abandoned narcissism, turned destructive.

11. Freud later neglected his initial insight about the narcissistic injury of women due to their social circumstances and actually established his theory of sexual difference on the idea of the narcissistic injury of castration in women.

CHAPTER FIVE

Narcissism, primal seduction and the psychoanalytic search for a good life

Larry O'Carroll

Wo Es war, soll Ich werden. The maxim is at root Ptolemaic. ... But the theory of seduction imposes the reverse or complementary maxim: *Wo es war, wird ... immer noch Anderes sein.* There where there was id, there will be always and already the other. [Laplanche, 1999b, p. 83]

In his elegant essay *Narcissism, For and Against* Adam Phillips (2000) suggests that our theories of narcissism tell us more than we usually realise. As well as advising what it is to be 'narcissistic', they inform us of how major contributors to the tradition of practice and suspicion set in train by Freud have conceived of the good life. Of the sorts of lives they have found good-to-live and would prefer their patients to find and enjoy, too. In other words, psychoanalytic theories of narcissism—by the same token our conceptions of the psychic unconscious, 'stages' of development, psychic positions, defence and much else besides—cannot be decanted from the age-old ethical question of how we humans are best to live. We might say that, for Phillips, it is to the inestimable merit of psychoanalytic thought to have ignored the polarity erected between the 'is' and 'ought' by classical empiricist doctrine. Why? Because the dismissal of empiricism to quaint conceit has allowed three matters—who we are, what has made us and inquiries into the good life—to become inseparable considerations for us today.

Phillips is challenging on a number of counts, here. As we shall see, he implies that we must learn to live with the relativity of our accounts of narcissism rather than take refuge in the fantasy that some novel synthesis of opposing positions can be fashioned. And he is clear that at stake in theories of narcissism is not only whether 'relationship' is worth striving for; what 'relationship' can possibly be has always been a troublesome matter for psychoanalysis—a difficulty exacerbated by the reconstruction of Freudian thought undertaken by Jean Laplanche over the last thirty years or so (Laplanche, 1976, 1987, 1999a). We will appreciate this circumstance by comparing Kleinian thought, so ably represented by John Steiner (1993), for whom narcissism is a psychic retreat, with that of Laplanche (1999a), for whom narcissism is to be conceived as the successor to primal seduction. In question is not only the relativity of our theories, then—the fact that they propose incommensurable understandings of our human self-enraptured states. What Laplanche calls Freud's 'going astray', a disastrous shift from a Copernican to a Ptolemaic conception of the psyche, is also at stake. Suffice it to note presently that, for Laplanche, the going astray occurred when Freud replaced his early seduction theory, for which sexuality was a 'foreign body' breaking in from a source external to the infant, by a conception focusing on, amongst other matters, the primal fantasies later held to organise the 'component instincts' of infantile sexuality (Freud, 1895d, 1905d). Moreover, Freud's suppression of sexuality as an 'alien-ness' decentring the psyche led him to a Ptolemaic theory of subjectivity. The analogy is with Ptolemy, for whom the sun and planets revolved around the earth, whereas Freud's principal discovery, that sexuality is radically Other, an implanted alterity vis-à-vis the ego, constitutes the Copernican point of departure for a licit psychoanalytic understanding of subjectivity.[1] Not the least interesting point about this reformulation is that if Freud did go astray in the manner suggested by Laplanche, Steiner's Kleinian account of narcissism furnishes an exemplar of the Ptolemaism Freud failed to overcome.

The chapter has three inter-linked aims, which can be formulated as questions. Under what conceptual conditions does the category of narcissism become oppressive? How does Laplanche conceive of narcissism? And, can we infer a vision of a new kind of good life from the re-elaboration of psychoanalytic theory in the terms he proposes? To meet these aims, part one of the chapter addresses Steiner's *Psychic Retreats* (1993), as the concept of pathological defensive organisation has become influential in informing clinical work with the more anguished forms of auto-affection. However, although we may admire Steiner's achievement in writing a text replete with clinical experience and helpful clinical vignettes, of concern is not only the Ptolemaism of the conception of psychic retreat. As will be seen from the manner in which Steiner reads the myth of Narcissus, at issue is the ethical cost that must be paid when psychoanalytic thought bases its clinical practice on what is, frankly, a heterosexist conceptual apparatus. Couched in terms of projective identification, Steiner's reading indicates how a clinical category, the Kleinian variant of narcissism, secretes an ethic of exclusion.

Part two addresses the return to the early Freud constructed by Laplanche. From the perspective of primal seduction, the writing of Freud and Klein is characterised by the (conceptual) absence of the mother. This insistence is by no means new, of course. Much psychoanalytically informed feminist scholarship has proposed so. For Laplanche, however, the problem hereabouts is that the unconscious, incomprehensible significations by means of which the mother, the first ambassador of association, seduces the infant into the erotic basis of collective life have been silenced. It is as if our mothers, beloved and/or hated though they will become, were creatures who transcend a perceptible world constituted by mammals (d)riven apart by the unconscious repressed. Moreover, when the mother's psychic activity is 'disappeared', narcissism cannot but be misconceived. Laplanche follows Freud (1914c) in arguing that narcissism is an acquisition made possible by the birth of the ego. But he adds that we go astray when we reduce self-absorption to a pathological state from which only some of us suffer. First and foremost, narcissism spells the closing-in of the infant to the mother's enigmatic messages. In other words, we are all 'narcissists' by virtue of the fact that we are and will remain, de-centred subjects, hence strangers to ourselves.

The third part of the chapter returns to Phillips's essay so as to offer a number of reflections on relativism, psychoanalytic theory and 'relationship'. For Phillips, it is unsurprising that states of self-absorption have become 'abiding preoccupations' in what remains our Judaeo-Christian culture in many ways (2000, p. 200). To that sensible advice may be added the suspicion that our preoccupations *vis-à-vis* the auto-affections parachute us into worries about relativism of the epistemological and ethical kinds. Such worries not only have their point; they are augmented by the Copernican shift Laplanche has elaborated in terms of the primal seduction perpetrated on the infant by maternal unconscious activity. It is from this productive, if vertiginous, augmentation that a new vision of the good life can be inferred. It is a good life in two ways: in relation to the multi-tongued condition of psychoanalytic theory today, as well as *vis-à-vis* the temptation to pathologise those who have experienced difficulties with 'relationship'.

Narcissism as psychic retreat

We do not have to subscribe to Klein's account of early paranoid-schizoid functioning to find in her work much of lasting value to psychoanalysis. The same judgement applies to Steiner's *Psychic Retreats* (1993). Given his theory, one he does his best, like Bion's memory and desire, to leave outside the consulting room, Steiner understands that his practice would be pointless were it to serve any master except love. The sovereignty of the good object is his abiding preoccupation. Wedded to the Kleinian metapsychology of unconscious phantasy, a point of view for which all defences, as Hinshelwood (1989) has noted, are phantasies-in-action, the love Steiner serves is hard to win and maintain, so dependent is it on our often poor and tested capacities to bear loss and guilt.[2] It is a love we often scorn and despair of, too; a hard love which, even when we do win it, is threatened by quotidian times of crisis–for example, when we are grieving the loss of a loved one. As Kleinian theory thinks of this love, moreover, recognising its sovereignty depends on the registration of an external reality issuing three imperatives to the phantasising psyche. The first imperative reads: be grateful to the breast, for the source of 'goodness' comes from the outside. The second is, realise that parthenogenesis is a destructive phantasy since we owe our lives to the 'creativity' of parental intercourse. And, the third: there is no escaping death because we are not the omnipotent creatures the always-present infant in us assumes we are (Steiner, 1993).

Of principal interest here is the role the object assumes in the Kleinian account of psychic development. Consider the myth of Narcissus in this connection, a tale easily read as complementing the ethics of object-love to the fore in Klein's thought. For Steiner, the tale of Narcissus suggests that

> part of the self is split off and projected into an object, where it is attributed to the object and the fact that it belongs to the self is denied. [The] object relationship which results is not then with a person truly seen as separate, but with the self projected into another person and related to as if it were someone else. This is the position of the mythical Narcissus who fell in love with a strange youth he did not consciously connect with himself [Steiner in Phillips, 2000, p. 219].

Narcissus gazes in the pool, wherein he sees the image of a beautiful youth, with which he falls in love. The image is his own, something he does not realise at first, for he suffers from a fateful misattribution. He has split off a part of himself such that the love he seeks is but a phantasy denying sexual difference, as his reduction of Echo to death-like mimicry suggests. Already, then, we have a powerful tale, an epistemologico-affective fable, of the double-misrecognition from which Narcissus suffers, one articulated in the language of the omnipotent denial of psychic reality. Lost in monologue because he has refused the loss of the ideal part-object and the remorse conditioning access to depressive functioning, the beautiful youth does not know that it is he who has called forth his self-enraptured love. Nor does he know that the self-completion he desires, harms, in the internal world, the parental couple to whom he owes his life, in addition to harming his own development. Narcissus has fashioned a psychic retreat—a pathological defensive organisation.

That Narcissus is imprisoned in a retreat of quasi-suicide, with sustaining relations with the Other all but severed; that he inhabits an asylum on the border between paranoid-schizoid functioning and the guilt, loss and reparation definitive of the depressive struggle; that the cost of his auto-affection is death (psychically, he has murdered Echo, of course)—all renders him the saboteur of the Other and his own life. Can it be any wonder then that he, poor soul, elicits our pity and compassion, as well as our irritation and dismay—a concatenation of responses signalled by Steiner's emphasis on how 'stuck' analyses with modern-day Narcissus can become?

A qualification, a serious one, merits note. Steiner adds, in the passage cited above, that the mechanism at work in narcissistic enrapture, projective identification, applies to Leonardo as well. Leonardo "projected his infantile self into his apprentices and looked after them in the way he wished his mother had looked after him" (Steiner in Phillips, 2000, p. 219). Here, Steiner is referring to Freud's cod 'psychobiography' of the artist (Freud, 1910c). As Leonardo's homosexuality was born of identification with his mother's position, he sought to love a projected image of himself on the model of how she had loved him when he was an infant and child. Leonardo identified with his mother, with the result that his love for his apprentices was an auto-affection, a form of self-absorption at one remove. This is an unexceptional thing to advise when we assume with Freud that, in the case of some gay men, their object-choice springs from narcissistic identification. Of *some* gay men only, we should emphasise, since Freud writes, firstly, that he is far from proffering a catchall, general theory of male homosexuality by recourse to the mechanism of narcissistic identification and, secondly, that same-sex desire can be 'normal'.[3] Plainly, therefore, when Steiner (1993, p. 98) says that *all* male same-sex desire denies that "a distinction between the sexes is essential to creative intercourse", it being incontestable that the denial of such difference is the quintessence of pathology, Kleinian thought must be working with conceptions of the object and unconscious phantasy owing little to Freud.

The point is not only that the Kleinian concept of unconscious phantasy abolishes Freud's insistence on the 'normal' contingency of the erotic object by making use of the biological notion of instinct. Whereas in Freud anatomical difference comes to *figure* what psychosexual difference will be, in Klein unconscious phantasy is held to operate in such a manner that the baby enters the world with innate knowledge of the role sexual difference plays in the reproduction of our kind (Hinshelwood, 1989). Also of concern is the ethics informing Steiner's reading of Narcissus' self-absorption. Since it is only so-called heterosexuals who are to be included amongst 'us', amongst those of us who are to be counted as having managed the depressive struggle insofar as that is possible, the ethics of object-love privileged by Kleinian writing may be counted as a retreat of sorts, too. Only this time the asylum sought denies the reality of the modern world—a complex reality simultaneously political, sociological and, although it may appear odd to say so, methodological. The politico-ethical question has been canvassed: whom should we include amongst 'us'? More precisely, to whom should the hard-won, constantly threatened, civilities of liberal democratic governance be extended? Would it not be cruel to dis-enfranchise same-sex desire, as much in thought as in practice? For all, then, that we may want to be post-modern where 'truth' is concerned ('truth', that mobile army of metaphors, so Nietzsche scorned) and although theories are best adjudicated in terms of their own assumptions (see part 3), we should conclude that Kleinian thought has the duty to reflect on why it so 'hates' same-sex desire. Certainly, the imperatives that 'external reality' avowedly issues to the psyche will require thoroughgoing refor-mulation.

The sociological matter: when civil partnerships are now possible and, a complementary consideration, modern metropolitan life has undermined deference to all unaccountable authority, psychoanalytic thought will shoot itself in the proverbial foot by continuing to believe in the perverse, globally narcissistic, character of all same-sex desire. And the related methodological issue: Steiner does not cite Stoller (1975), Lewis (1989) and Stubrin (1997)—important writers who have contested the pathologisation of same-sex love by so much post-Freudian theory. In any case, that it is a *non sequitur* to think that we may extrapolate from the proposition 'his erotism is limited to bodies like his own' to 'he, that gay man, in fact all gay men, have denied sex-ual difference", is reinforced by the insistence that generalisations of the form 'all homosexuality is perverse' have been based on inevitably small, statistically unrepresentative samples of the dis-tressed gay men presenting for psychoanalysis over the years.

The foregoing suggests that the ethic of object-love privileged by Kleinian theory is predicated on a 'heterosexualisation' of ero-tism in the name of depressive functioning. When the concepts of narcissistic and projective identification are articulated, uncon-scious phantasy is already sexed and it is assumed that same-sex desire is homogeneous, an ethic of exclusion is the result.

From seduction to narcissism

That Kleinian thought implicates an exclusionary ethic is not to say that thereby it reveals its irredeemably problematic character. It has contributed too much of value to psychoanalysis for such a judgement to be other than tendentious. And it would be poor judgement of another kind to expect any theory, psychoanalytical or otherwise, to constitute a body of seamless, mutually implicative, propositions. On the other hand, that Kleinian clinical practitioners work with a vision of reality as a 'goodness' stemming from the breast, moreover with a maternal body whose phantasised contents are held to be attacked by the infant, *does* pose a problem for the Laplanchean conception of primary seduction. At stake is that, albeit in their distinctive ways, Klein and Freud 'forget' that, in the first instance, it is our mothers who, by attending to the 'zones of exchange' of our infantile bodies, implant sexuality in us (Laplanche, 1976, 1999c). What sorts of mothers are they for Laplanche? As will now be discussed, our mothers are signifying mammals marked by the possession of a repressed unconscious. And, by virtue of the 'alien-ness' (sexuality) in them, they cannot control the unconscious enigmatic significations they send their infants' way (Laplanche, 1999a & d).

Now, although Laplanche is imagining yet another myth of origin by speaking of the (m)Other who breaks into the self-preservative, 'pre'-sexual universe of infantilism, nevertheless it is plausible to ask,

> the extent to which women unconsciously and sexually cathect the breast, which appears to be a natural organ for lactation? It is inconceivable that the infant does not notice this cathexis, which might be said to be perverse in the sense the term is defined in Three Essays. It is impossible to imagine that the infant does not suspect that this cathexis is the source of a nagging question: what does the breast want from me, apart from wanting to suckle me, why does it want to suckle me? [Laplanche, 1987 in Phillips, 2000, p. 203]

Is the pre-verbal baby-in-arms, who is not to be credited with unconscious phantasies of the Kleinian kind, or with the primal fantasies central to Freud's account of the organisation of sexuality–is this infant capable of experiencing a 'nagging question?' The answer must be an unqualified 'no', when we are of a mind to pay attention to Stern (1984), for he has rightly criticised those psychoanalytic accounts which attribute an adultocentric cognitive sophistication to the infant or conceive of him as in 'total' symbiotic union with the mother. In any case, that Laplanche is ready to attribute suspicion, puzzlement and a preparatory sense of self- and other-agency to the infant re-poses what has always been a source of sizeable controversy for psychoanalytic theory. How is it to conceive of our first, post-uterine days? With a rudimentary ego in tow, though Freud demurs? with foremost emphasis placed on the baby as phantasising creature (Klein)? as a 'true self' requiring a facilitating environment to meet its potential (Winnicott)? with a tripartite distinction in place between the real, imaginary and symbolic registers of existence (Lacan)? When so many voices have to be heard, voices intolerant of petty narcissistic mortification, reflection will soon convince us that asking of our earliest days, of theoretical point zero so to speak, is not a useful strategy. What matters for my purposes here is that Laplanche has not been the first, nor will he be the last, to attribute 'inexplicable' proto-psychic capacities to the infant—capacities upon which the human subjectivity to emerge must rely. After all and as if to warn us of the *lacunae* (a poor pun: the *lacanae*) beckoned when psychic zero must be conceived, even the mirror phase, in which the ego is putatively fashioned, relies on an agency capable of recognising its own image in the mirror (Lacan, 1937). But of that prerequisite capacity nothing is said, presumably because its existence cannot be accounted for by the psycho-geography of need, demand and desire.

This noted, what is "particularly convincing", 'both evocative and instructive' in Laplanche's conception of primary seduction is that the baby's receipt of the enigmatic messages coming its way is inseparable from the circumstance that the mother makes use of perversion (Phillips, 2000, p. 201). Our mothers are perverse in cathecting their breasts or substitutes when feeding us. The notion of perversion is Freud's: cathexis of the breast in the service of such a final goal testifies to an aim stopping short of a genital union; that is to say, when sexual satisfaction is gained through an activity other than the union of the genitals, the activity is to be deemed perverse (Freud, 1905d). This emphasis on maternal perversion affords an aperture on the character of Laplanche's re-writing of Freudian theory: as we would anticipate from reversing the direction of cathexis at the start, the maternal unconscious is accorded a pivotal role in the construction of our de-centred subjectivity.

The implication is well nigh revolutionary in the annals of psychoanalytic thought. If the maternal unconscious keeps company with the infant's introduction to regimes of social relations impregnated with erotic desire, our sophisticated talk of the object, easily or hard-won, misses the point. When my first (m)Other is unconsciously motivated and when what she 'puts into me' is enigmatic, incomprehensible, psychoanalysis is to be understood as the unique method of inquiry-practice, based on the clinical situation, whose theory is obliged to revolve around the conceptual figures of *der Andere* and *das Andere*. *Der Andere:* the object, at first the mother, whose messages will render me a stranger to myself when my ego appears on the scene of action; and *das Andere:* 'the thing', sexuality, the alien, seductive thing that, upon the repression-translation of the enigmatic messages issuing from the mother, sows a veritable continent of unconscious psychic functioning in me (Laplanche, 1999c, pp. 135–6). Hence another implication: when my introduction to enculturation, to human fellowship, is conceivable as the (m)Other's implantation, we may conclude that the Kleinian ethic of the object, akin to the Freudian ethic of renunciation, purchases its explanatory power at the cost of silencing the mother's unconscious significations.

The mother as psychically differentiated being, as psychism whose functioning is continually traversed by unconscious activity is absent in the Freud who went astray and in Klein's exclusive focus on the infant's psychic activity. Roughly speaking, in Freud we meet with the libidinal organisations (oral, anal, phallic, genital) awaiting the infant, the various fixations that may beset it and the struggles that Oedipus and castration will entail for it. In Klein, the major modalities (positions) of relating to our objects, with their associated anxieties and defences, are to the fore. What is intriguing, despite the stark conceptual differences between them, is that Freud and Klein veil the seductive activity of the maternal unconscious—as has all psychoanalytic theory, Laplanche adds, since Freud went astray. That a mother is a particular psyche and, in relation to her infant, is already an internally differentiated Other whose breast is charged with erotic significance *by her*, the infant's father and the culture at large, is occluded. To Laplanche's mind, the problem here is that the 'silence' *vis-à-vis* maternal unconscious action has domesticated the early Freud's achievement by re-centring the psyche in a pre-psychoanalytical manner.

Parenthetically, we may wonder if Bion's writing provides yet another example of this going astray. The question appears absurd, given that Bion (1957) developed Klein's concept of projective identification in terms of the inter-psychic model of the container and contained. Surely, then, his work definitively foregrounds maternal unconscious activity in a manner classical Kleinian theory failed to do. Needless to say, it would be a mistake to deny that there is much in this objection if only insofar as the Bionian mother is conceived as the metaboliser of her infant's projections. Upon the infant's introjection of her care, the terrors and hostilities of early life, of paranoid-schizoid functioning, are calmed—'held', as Winnicott would say–in such a way that the birth of a human subject ensues. However, the question we should ask is this: what is the character of the Bionian container? Is it a signifying mammal or a metabolising machine? A seductive message-sender or a being whose enigmatic significations have been theoretically repressed? Formally stated, when the contained at first consists of the infant's death-like projections and the container's function is to transform the terror of fragmentation by means of reverie, the messages with which Laplanche is concerned have yet again been occulted, negated, denied.

Saying so affords an index of the scope and ambition of Laplanche's reconstruction of psychoanalytic theory. He has been hypercritical and continues to be so, of many of Freud's texts, in the attempt to keep a Copernican psychoanalysis alive; a psychoanalytic theory for which primal seduction provides the key. Focusing on four theses now will help to tease out what narcissism, from the perspective of primary seduction, could be. The first and second theses have been adumbrated: sexuality is born of maternal seduction–a 'seduction' whose vehicle is the incomprehensible message; and it is to be conceived as *das Andere*—as the alien, radically Other, implantation in me. Add the third and fourth theses now, both of which concern narcissism: self-enrapture is an acquisition whose existence depends on what Freud (1914) called 'a new psychical action' and it is a closure made possible by the ego's birth (Laplanche, 1999a, pp. 81–3).

Picture the Laplanchean infant. At first it is 'open' to the messages coming its way from the mother; so open, that the installation-
implantation of sexual desire in him or her interrupts and merges
with, the adaptive 'instinct' to survive. This opening-onto sexuality
constitutes a seduction—a seduction because, proceeding from an
external origin, the mother, more broadly from a culture of sexual
significations, it produces sexuality as something heteronomous in
the infant. As Laplanche (1987) has put it,

> The *primal* situation is one in which a new born child, an infant
> in the etymological sense of the word (*in-fans:* speechless), is con-
> fronted with the adult world. This may even mean that what we
> call the Oedipus complex is in a sense subject to contingency. ...
> I am, then, using the term *primal seduction* to describe a funda-
> mental situation in which an adult proffers to a child verbal,
> non-verbal and even behavioural signifiers which are pregnant
> with unconscious sexual significations. [pp. 89–90, 126, original
> emphasis]

Plainly it is not the sexual abuse of (older) children that is at issue
here. But neither is it what Masson (1984) has argued in respect of
Freud's supposed cowardice in abandoning his early seduction
theory—his 'neurotica'. As Fletcher (1999) has said, Masson's assault
on Freud reduces "the seduction *theory* to the mere observation or
suppression of abusive events and completely fails to grasp the presence of a distinctive if incompletely elaborated theoretical problematic" (p. 10; original emphasis) in the early notion of sexuality as a
foreign body breaking in from the outside. In question, then, are the
incomprehensible messages (the first interpellations, we could call
them) functioning to call forth infants to the erotic basis of association—messages that Freud camouflaged with the primal fantasies
of seduction, primal scene and castration and which Klein
repudiated by means of 'primitive' defence.[4]

Hopefully sufficient has been said to appreciate that Laplanche,
in addition to contesting the very basis of Kleinian theory, alights on
a dismaying Freud, a tragicomic hero too, in an all-important
respect. Far from having protected his 'fundamentals', his foundations of psychoanalysis—repression, transference resistance, infantile sexuality—by plotting with the astute Jones to keep the 'mystics'
at bay, Freud was continually beset by the temptation to deny that

sexuality is the alien bifurcating humankind. In other words, he did not live up to his promise that, like Copernicus and Darwin, he had once and for all wounded our species' narcissism by writing that the ego is not master in the house of the psyche. Consider two, related signs of this collapse, besides the evisceration of the mother's seduction. In the second topography, Freud's conception of the id designates a 'primordial' instance in the sense that, from it, all else is supposed to flow, including the ego (Freud, 1923b). Yet because that conception re-centres subjectivity as agency on the id, all it ultimately effects is a kind of transference: the agential capacity usually attributed to the ego is relocated in a clamorous 'it' operating behind our backs. Laplanche's essential point is that there has never been other than a going-astray difference that matters between holding that it is the ego that reigns supreme, as against the apparently radical proposition that it is the id that enjoys such mastery. "For if the individual is ... governed ... by the unknown drives of the unconscious, this 'id'–however strange it is supposed to be–is nonetheless not an alien. It is supposed to dwell *at the center* (sic) of the individual, whom it governs in its own way, even if it has dethroned the ego" (Laplanche, 1999c, p. 135; original emphasis). Somewhat paradoxically, then, formulations of the sort 'it is the id that thinks me' are pre-Freudian in inspiration, for the shift they avowedly accomplish stands or falls on the re-valorisation of a Ptolemaic, re-centring vision of the psychical subject.

The second sign of re-centring brings us to narcissism. The discovery of narcissism spelt a crisis for the theory with which Freud had been working until 1914, when 'On Narcissism: An Introduction' was published. Until that time he had worked with the distinction between self-preservative (ego) instincts serving the adapted survival of our kind and the sexual drives in conflict with them. In this view, the psychogenic symptom was a 'compromise formation' between self-preservative forces and a sexuality ordered by the processes of 'leaning on' the vital functions and by primal fantasy. We know the fate of that conception in Freud's later work: when the ego can be a *sexual* object, the conflict between self-preservation, the ego's task and sexuality governed by fantasy, required root-and-branch re-elaboration. The first dualism had gone.

Now, Freud's writing on narcissism in various texts, as commentators including Jones (1955, p. 340) have remarked, is often highly

condensed and elicits the impression of not inconsiderable confusion. Be that as it may, of concern is how narcissism is to be conceived as successor to primary seduction. Unsurprisingly,
Laplanche contests any conception that would picture narcissism
as a biologically ordained monadological state, as solipsistic government–a temptation to which Freud was prone on occasion.
After all, if such a state were to exist, the infant could not survive
(Laplanche, 1976). Furthermore, of especial interest is that narcissism, so Freud held, requires that a 'new psychical action", following on from the auto-erotism of infancy, has been effected:

> [W]e are bound to suppose that a unity comparable to the ego
> cannot exist in the individual from the start; the ego has to be
> developed. The auto-erotic instincts (sic), however, are there
> from the very first; so there must be something added to auto-
> erotism–a new psychical action–in order to bring about narcis-
> sism [Freud, 1914c, p. 77]

Whatever else may be said of this text, the 'new psychical action' of
which it speaks is not to be taken at its word. For there has existed
in psychoanalytic theory itself the "constant threat of narcissistic closure" (Laplanche, 1999b, p. 81), a sign of which we have come across
when Freud conceived of narcissism as a solipsistic state at the
behest of the imperative of self-preservation. At issue for Laplanche
is his tongue-in-cheek version of Haeckel's law for which ontogenesis (the development of the individual) reproduces phylogenesis
(the evolution of the species to which the individual belongs). For
Laplanchean law, "'theoretico-genesis' reproduces ontogenesis" in
the sense that "Freud's going astray is accompanied by a sort of con-
nivance with the object" (Laplanche, 1999b, p. 81). The theoretical
consequences have been momentous: the trajectory of the object of
psychoanalysis, the sexual psyche, has been mirrored by its theory's
shift from its Copernican emphasis on the implantation of sexuality
to the Ptolemaic recovery effected by Freud when he repudiated his
'neurotica'. In other words, the very notion of a psychical apparatus,
with its wishes, unconscious fantasies, compromise formations
(symptoms) and unidirectional cathexis from infant to mother, is
linked to how Freud conceived of narcissism. The new psychical
action is simultaneous with the infant's closing-in upon itself: in the
'moment' of the ego's constitution, a sort of primary defence against

the continuation of the enigmatic messages disturbing its pre-sexual state motivates the infant. Otherwise expressed, the birth of a psychical agency and the foremost illusion with which psychoanalysis deals, that the 'I' in us is all there is, have their first articulation when the baby-in-arms issues its first protest to culture. If it could speak, no doubt it would say, "no, no, no, the enigmas with which you present me are splitting 'me' apart".

Relativism (and 'relationship')

Specifying what it is to be narcissistic, even if only to a 'small' degree, relies on evoking another place, another condition, another form of life—the one occupied, realised, by the properly functioning subject. To be sure, the 'properly functioning subject' may well be a myth or ideal fiction, perhaps a psychically produced illusion too, but that does not mean that psychoanalytic theory can do without a norm of psychical comportment. If narcissism, like perversion, is to be understood as existing, therefore and considered as a monstrosity or as something less malign, we are obliged, on logical grounds alone, to elaborate some sort of psycho-developmental norm (Laplanche & Pontalis, 1983, pp. 306–9). What kind of norm could it be? Put it so: it is the norm of well-existing in any possible human world, howsoever that is to be measured. For Freud, the norm was being able to work and love without gross inhibition, for Klein something like living as well as we can with psychic reality. Yet, as we have seen from discussing the differences in our theories, it does not help at all in the endeavour to specify a norm that narcissism is always so from a perspective—from conceptual architectures calling it to a (half-)life admitting of no common measure. As we appreciate from even cursory acquaintance with the writings of Freud, Klein, Lacan, Kohut and so many others, the good life envisioned can only become 'this kind of good life", hence just one amongst many possible and, equally plausible, others.

That this is so engenders worries of relativism–worries that, we might joke, will melt into air when Laplanche's re-elaboration of the foundations of psychoanalysis commands acceptance amongst the contemporary heterogeneous psychoanalytic community. We may look forward to that day. In the meantime and on the assumption that adjudicating bodies of theory is an 'internal' affair, in other words that theories are best judged in terms of how (in)adequately they resolve the questions and problems they set themselves, relativism of the epistemological variety comes a-haunting. How are we to understand narcissism? Replying that 'all depends on the problematic in which the concept of narcissism is elaborated' makes the point. Narcissism is many things—a 'state', with its primary and secondary expressions (Freud); at its 'extreme', imprisons the subject in a psychic retreat (Steiner); is a 'need', at heart a psychological need, remaining with us throughout the life-cycle (Kohut); exhausts the character of the ego (Lacan); closes down the infant to the incomprehensible messages constituting primal seduction (Laplanche); and so forth. Furthermore, although we all 'know' people—perhaps ourselves, too!—who, as we say, are 'highly narcissistic", such practical knowledge of the everyday sort, for all that it witnesses how a psychoanalytic clinical category now lards our repertoire of responses to others and ourselves, cannot serve as an inter-theoretical critical device. To believe otherwise would be to endorse the most naïve kind of empiricism.

Ethical (moral) narcissism beckons when, with Phillips, we are not shy of thinking that the states of self-absorption signalled by the name 'narcissism' bear intimately on the sorts of lives psychoanalysts have cherished and would prefer their patients to find as well. That Freud was an indefatigable worker, what we nowadays call a 'workaholic', so much so that he penned twenty-three volumes of writing that has profoundly impacted on how we think of our kind now, is of interest in this connection. Does he not exemplify his norm of psychical comportment, working and loving without inhibition, in the ethic of stoic renunciation informing his *oeuvre*? And the courageous manner of his death, likewise? Far from implying that these circumstances render Freud's writing but the outcrop of his 'personality', for that would be to collapse into a truly pernicious and back-firing, relativism, nevertheless it is worth reflecting that there are grounds for refusing to believe that our theories are *just* architectures of interlocking concepts. Which is to say that the 'is' (the so-called facts of the matter) and the 'ought' (what some philosophers still insist has no cognitive content) cannot be discrete categories of apprehension, if ever they were, for a discourse whose overarching ethic is the relief of emotional suffering. Indeed, it may strike us, for example, that how analysts, ever since Freud, have written of the proper, clinically effective timing of interpretations has articulated the technical problem of timing and the moral problem of the patient's capacity to benefit from the intervention. That being so, the conceptual apparatus informing clinical judgement has been so intricated with the good analyst's care for his/her patient that psychoanalytic practice has always consisted in far more than the 'application' of theoretical propositions to the therapeutic *elenchus*. The therapeutic situation requires that the analyst uses him/herself well in the service of the other, a usage inseparable from the moral language of counter-transferential reaction, so that the range of human powers can be extended (MacIntyre, 1970).

What has any of this to do with epistemological and ethical relativism, as well as with what we call 'relationship'? Allow Phillips' opening remarks to orient us. If "much of the most interesting psychoanalytic theory today is sceptical of the whole notion of relationship", he writes, the 'most interesting' theorists being Freud, Lacan, Laplanche and Bersani,

> ... most of the best popular psychoanalytic theory takes relationship for granted (Klein, Winnicott, Bowlby). Either we are suffering from whatever it is that sabotages our intimacies, or we are suffering from the notions of intimacy that we have inherited. It is not clear whether better relationships are the solution to our suffering, or whether it is that very aspiration that we suffer from. Narcissism, unsurprisingly, has been a keyword in these debates and what is loosely called morality is what has been at stake. What kind of regard we are able and wanting, to have for other people and how we might distinguish between the good and bad forms of so-called self-love have become abiding preoccupations. [Phillips, 2000, p. 200]

A concern in these usefully provocative remarks is what object relations theory has made of 'relationship', particularly as "[w]hat kind of regard we are able and wanting, to have for other people" summons another consideration—how we might distinguish between 'good' and 'bad' narcissism.[5] Yet when there can be no cross-theoretical way of effecting the requisite distinction, is not one matter clear? The terms of the narcissism for-and-against debate have been enriched by the problematic of primary seduction. In what way?

Not by adding another perspective to psychoanalytic thought, although we could see it that way, if we wish, but in relocating narcissism, hence our abiding preoccupations about relationship, as born of the closing down to enigmatic signification. In other words, it will well serve psychoanalysis to 'remember' that narcissism, when conceptualised as the successor to the alien's coming, is to be construed as the psychic closure coterminous with another coming, namely, the ego's birth. To be sure, doing so will exacerbate the plurivocal character of what we read and hear and, understandably, will be resisted by many. For living with our plethora of 'parental' voices, with forms of life (theories) which invite our identification with their omniscience, is a hard-won achievement, perhaps one never finally won because it lies beyond the powers of the poor ego.

We might wonder if the architecture of primal seduction, narcissism and the (m)Other offers a new vision of the 'good life'. It does, once we are clear that the implications of primal seduction sow ruin amidst the Ptolemaic psychoanalytic theory written ever since Freud went astray. Laplanchean good life advises that we must learn to exercise a number of virtues. We must be hyper-alert to how accounts of psychic formation, their appearances notwithstanding, re-centre the psychical subject in some primordial instance or other—the id, unconscious phantasy, infantile need, true self and so on. And we must be vigilant in regard to how our theories can exclude, by use of the quasi-medical signifier 'pathology', fellow   creatures   from   the   democracy   of   'proper' psychic functioning. By no means least, when every relationship cannot but include two (or more) narcissists since narcissism *consists* in closing-down to enigmatic signification, it not only becomes mightily puzzling what a 'good' relationship could be; it is equally puzzling that the psychoanalysis of self-enraptured states has proceeded on the basis of Freud's going astray. This suggests an ethic of how to live with the Babel-like condition of our theory: respect the writing of those who have gone astray, as Freud was the first sinner; and an ethic for living: since our culture's 'obsession' with relationship is most likely the (collective ego's way of denying its de-centred condition, let us not moralise.

NOTES

1. John Fletcher's introduction (pp. 1–51) to *Essays on Otherness* (Laplanche, 1999a) has been invaluable in helping me to appreciate the wide-ranging scope of Laplanche's reconstruction of psychoanalytic (Freudian) theory. Of necessity, there has been much in that reconstruction I have been unable to address here–for example, the concept of the drive and its source-object (Ch. 3, pp. 117–32) and the re-working of *Nachtraglichkeit*, translated by Strachey as 'deferred action", in terms of 'afterwardness' (Ch. 10, pp. 260–5).

2. To respect convention, the spelling 'phantasy' is used to designate the unconscious character of the projections, idealisations, etc. with which Kleinian thought deals; otherwise the spelling 'fantasy' is used.

3. Though Freud was far from being consistent on the question of male same-sex desire, he was 'aware' of the existence of many 'homosexualities' (see Lewes, 1989; Stoller, 1975; Stubrin, 1997).

4. Laplanche discusses why he no longer subscribes to Freud's concept of primal fantasies in 'Seduction, Persecution, Revelation' (Laplanche, 1999d). The concept is Ptolemaic, as it veils the activity of the maternal unconscious in primal seduction.

5. Klein's work (not that Phillips believes otherwise) does not belong to the 'pure' object relations' tradition of psychoanalytic thought. Unlike Winnicott, Bowlby, Fairbairn, Balint and others, Klein attempts to combine a drive-discharge model of psychic functioning with the existence of object relations from the beginning of post-uterine life (Greenberg & Mitchell, 1983). Her conception of unconscious phantasy, together with the insistence that a 'rudimentary' ego capable of 'primitive' defence exists from the start, is crucial in this regard.

CHAPTER SIX

Narcissistic wounds, race and racism: a comment on Frantz Fanon's critical engagement with psychoanalysis

Julia Borossa

> The explosion will not happen today. It is too soon ... or too late.
> I do not come with timeless truths. My consciousness is not illu-
> minated with ultimate radiances. Nevertheless, in complete
> composure, I think it would be good if certain things were said
> [Fanon, 1986, p. 9].

These are the opening words of Black Skin, White Masks,
simultaneously poetic and powerful, modest and bold. As
this essay will be arguing, Frantz Fanon's insights into the
human condition, the 'certain things' he did manage to say, continue to provide psychoanalysis' theory of subjectivity with a necessary and continuing challenge on many levels. Fanon insists that the
material conditions of existence always be taken into account and
that the struggle for social justice is an ethical necessity; he reminds
us that the colour-blindness of the unconscious cannot be taken as a
given. Finally and most importantly, he argues that the universal
that does bind human beings together–this is something that Fanon
never gives up on—is always offset and indeed renewed by the particular. In this respect, Fanon wrote out of his own experience of
being a black man subjected to an othering gaze, therefore out of a
subjectivity marked by a particular social and historical situation,

113

out of which ensued particular narcissistic wounds. Inasmuch as Fanon's thought encompasses a view of the human that is extendible to all, psychoanalytic theory serves it well. In turn, Fanon challenges psychoanalysis to face up to history and his insights show how subjectivity is fashioned by narcissistic wounds. Fanon's writings directly interpellate us, his readers, black and white, male and female and as they do, they demand of us that we inhabit our positions as subjects and objects of desire with a little less certainty and a little more compassion.

The outlines of Fanon's life are well known. Born in Martinique, he trained in medicine and psychiatry in the French provincial city of Lyon. Subsequently, he took up a posting in France's troubled colony of Algeria, soon became deeply involved with the cause of the Algerian independence movement and died young. Meanwhile, his writings inspired national liberation movements across Africa as well as the civil rights movement in the US and remain central texts in Postcolonial Studies Departments. Their place in the psychoanalytic cannon, however, is less clear. It is true that Fanon never underwent a psychoanalytic training and practiced in the context of colonial psychiatry (Vergès, 1996). However, he explicitly took on the persona of a *psychoanalyst* as he unfolded his theories of subjectivity, race and racism. As a writer, he situated himself within the discourse of the discipline of psychoanalysis and, as we shall see, the clinical interventions he recounted are offered more as critiques of psychoanalysis than of psychiatry, in as much as they are specifically engaged with the possibilities and limitations of psychoanalysis' remit and with a therapeutic relationship that recognises transference and unconscious motivations. "Beside phylogeny and ontogeny stands sociogeny" (Fanon, 1986, p.13), Fanon affirms loud and clear, setting out his project, therefore not only echoing but completing Freud's often stated belief that ontogeny recapitulates phylogeny.

Whilst Fanon's later writings in *The Wretched of the Earth* (1990), *Towards the African Revolution* (1988) and elsewhere, strike the reader as more overtly political and activist texts, his first book, *Black Skin, White Masks* (1986), published in 1952 as *Peau Noire, Masques Blancs*, is explicitly marked by his youthful engagement with literature, philosophy and psychoanalysis. He wrote it during his training and had been intending to submit it as his medical degree dissertation, but was forced by his advisors to write an alternative, organicist piece concerning a case of Friedrich's ataxia, a disease of the central nervous system. The medical faculty of the university of Lyon was by no means an innovative establishment and its teaching staff could not see what relation such a literary book, whose lines of argumentation were derived from hybrid sources, could have with what they considered to be the object of their own discourse and ministrations, the suffering human subject (Macey, 2000, pp. 138–139). However, it is precisely such a human subject which directly preoccupies Fanon here, a human subject, however, always inflected by history and society, by the 'fact' or 'lived condition' of being black.[1]

And so Fanon starts off with his demand to state certain things, within the possibilities offered by a hesitant dialectic between 'too soon' and 'too late', but he finds himself bound to an uncertain present that might preclude these things being heard. In the fifty years since he wrote the book, the political landscape of the world has changed massively, as it moved into a state of post-and/or neo-colonialism and globalisation. However, Fanon describes a psychic landscape, one in which "the white man is sealed in his whiteness [and t]he black man in his blackness" (Fanon, 1986, p. 11) in ways that remain completely pertinent. He goes on to state his aim: "We shall seek to ascertain the directions of this dual narcissism and the motivations that inspire it" (Fanon, 1986, p. 12). Indeed, a central concern throughout is the workings of identification, as it occurs across a materially and historically constituted racial divide and how this reinforces division, mistrust, envy and shame instead of connectedness. Whiteness and blackness clearly do not function here as hermetic containers and to a large extent are dependent on each other. Crucially, in Fanon's elaboration of the processes at play, *both* psychic and social facts are relevant and their interaction undermines any easy solutions. In an essay that treats, among other things, the place of Fanon's thought in the humanist tradition, Max Silverman brings out the ways in which *Black Skin, White Masks* is a text that resists any easy opposition between the universal and the particular:

> One of the many fascinations of *Peau noire* lies in the way in which the conscious and unconscious demands of the phenomenology of lived experience coupled with the teleology of dialectical thinking establish an overdetermined text in which the concepts of humanity and freedom are never clearly defined. [...]

Rather than assume that Fanon opts ultimately for difference over sameness, particularism over universalism, or vice versa, we might instead read the contradictions in the text as an unconscious symptom of a search beyond the constraining logic of the binary itself. [Silverman, 2005, p. 123]

In this respect, the insights and methods of psychoanalysis seem to suit Fanon's project well, for a key characteristic of psychoanalysis lies precisely in putting into question apparent certainties and in reminding us of the inherent deceptiveness of apparent truths. A second characteristic of psychoanalysis, its reliance on universalising psychic structures which rest on Western social patterns, such as the Oedipus complex and its overwhelmingly Western institutional presence (Derrida, 1998) is more problematic for Fanon's project, as it bears all the hallmarks of a colonialism of the psyche. However, this very universalism becomes necessary in order to offset the political dangers inherent in a view of the human subject rooted in cultural relativism. For it is precisely the notion of cultural relativism as implying the implicit assumption of the superiority of white, colonising cultures–human beings are products of different cultures and some cultures are definitely superior to others—which underpins the entire profession of colonial psychiatry.

The problem of the workings of 'the primitive mind', was a practical one for colonial administrators who needed to identify and define abnormal behaviour within a culture that was to remain 'alien' to them and which they considered as being essentially 'imperfectible' (McCulloch, 1995; Vaughn, 1991). Clinical illustrations of this attitude, some of which are inflected by the language of psychoanalysis are easy to find; they are strikingly similar even though they originate in very different colonial contexts. For example, in a 1921 article, "The Anal-Erotic Factor in the Religion, Philosophy and Character of the Hindus" Owen Berkeley-Hill argues how the Indian subject is arrested at the anal stage of development and he goes on to develop a parallel between the general psychology of the Hindu and that of European patients suffering from obsessive-neurotic compulsion (Berkely-Hill, 1921). B.J.F. Laubscher, working in Southern Africa in the 1930s and 40s, argues in his book *Sex, Custom and Psychopathology: A Study of South African Pagan Natives*, that there was an affinity between the psychotic European and the 'normal' African (McCulloch, 1995, pp. 84–86), thus clearly pathologising the latter in comparison with an ideal norm of psychic health based on Western subjectivity. Octave Mannoni, whose book *Prospero and Caliban: The Psychology of Colonialism* Fanon subjects to a devastating critique in the central section of *Black Skin, White Masks,* claimed to offer a critique of just such pathologisation of the 'native', a process with which Mannoni became familiar during his extended stay in Madagascar where he worked as a teacher and representative of colonial France. In his analysis of the colonial encounter, Mannoni posits two complementary personality types and complexes originating in childhood. The colonised allegedly possesses a depend-ency complex which he transfers from his dead ancestors whom he worships onto the European invader. The invader, in turn, interprets this dependency complex as inferiority and projects onto the colonised his own fears and feelings of inferiority (Mannoni, 1984). In other words, the coloniser is portrayed as making use of the colonised in order to shore up his narcissism and the colonised is portrayed as taking the coloniser as his ego-ideal. It is clear that Mannoni recognises the fantasmatic underpinnings of the colonial enterprise, but posits them as pre-dating colonialism itself, existing in the collective psyche and therefore imbuing colonialism with a kind of inevitability.

But as Fanon points out, "the Malagasy 'dependency complex', at least in the only form that we can reach it and analyze it, [...] proceeds from the arrival of white colonizers on the island". (Fanon, 1986, p. 108) "The landing of the white man on Madagascar inflicted injury without measure. The consequences of that irruption of Europeans onto Madagascar were not psychological alone. ..." (Fanon, 1986, p. 97), he writes and proceeds to show the extent and the violence of the economic and social consequences of colonial exploitation. Fanon had been fortunate to meet and train with the Catalan psychiatrist Francois Tosquelles, a committed Marxist, well-read in philosophy and psychoanalysis, who ran the St. Albans psychiatric hospital on radical experimental lines which Fanon subsequently tried to integrate into his own practice in North Africa. The patient was understood as alienated from his social environment, his/her symptoms a direct result of this alienation. Any therapeutic intervention therefore needed to take into account, to involve and to act upon social structures. At St. Albans, patients and staff were seen as forming part of an integrated social network and the aim of treatment, much of which was practical and social, was to encourage patients to take up their rightful place within it. Treatment took the form, for example, of theatre presentations in which everyone was invited to participate, thus fostering a sense of social agency and inclusion in the patient, who, just as all staff, from psychiatrists to cleaners, was considered to be an integral part of the symbolic universe of the hospital. Everyone was perceived as participating in a system of symbolic exchange which was in turn subject to analysis (Vergès, 1996; Macey, 2000, pp. 143–153). In a recent lecture about the institutional psychiatry movement and the St Alban project, Jean Oury recalled how the cleaning staff at St Albans, aware of their very essential place within the particular social system of the hospital, described what they did in the following way: "*nous ramassons les poussières et les paroles*. We pick up dust and words". (Oury, 2005, original emphasis) Fanon learned much from this therapeutic and philosophical context, which provides an implicit ammunition to his critique of Mannoni, particularly at the point when he affirms that social and economic factors are inseparable from psychological ones and should never be separated out and bracketed off during treatment. Commenting on a series of dreams of Malagasys, recounted in Mannoni's book, all manifesting a form of identification with the white coloniser, Fanon writes "As a psychoanalyst, I should help my patient become conscious of his unconscious and abandon his attempts at a hallucinatory whitening, but also to act in the direction of a change in the social structures" (Fanon, 1986, p. 100).

But does effecting a change in social structures belong to the remit of the psychoanalyst? Or is it the role of the activist and the revolutionary? Can the two positions be reconciled? Fanon writes:

> If society makes difficulties [for the black man] because of his color, if in his dreams I establish the expression of an unconscious desire to change color, my objective [. ...], once his motivations have been brought into consciousness, will be to put him in a position to *choose* action (or passivity) with respect to the real sources of the conflict-that is, toward the social structures. [Fanon, 1986, p. 100]

Fanon's concern here is with the healing of an individual suffering patient through the restitution of a sense of agency, but this process is of limited use unless social conditions—colonial domination, in this case—are addressed. In subsequent years, Fanon came to identify with the cause of Algerian rebels (the *Front de Libération Nationale* or *FLN*) who were engaged in a violent struggle against French rule, a struggle which was in turn violently repressed. Forced to flee Algeria, he continued his psychiatric work in Tunisia, while also travelling widely as a representative of the FLN. In *Wretched of the Earth*, he notoriously advocates the necessity of violent change, the violent overturning of existing social structures being the only possible response of those who have been denied agency through the double violence—symbolic, actual—of colonial rule. To the man denied access to subjectivity and agency, violence remains the only means to reach towards a transformed conception of the human that includes him as well. But Fanon also recognises that although violence certainly constitutes action, by its nature it also precludes thought. "The armed struggle mobilizes the people; that is to say, it throws them in one way and in one direction". (Fanon, 1990, p. 73) This is ultimately problematic for it carries the risk of running into an impasse. As Nigel Gibson notes in his analysis of that text,

> Violence alone cannot win the revolution. It is not enough to move the protagonist from reaction to becoming a thinking, actional being. Action is, of course, the key to reaction, but reaction is still an action determined by the Other. Only 'enlightened action' (which cannot be furnished by violence alone) proves once and for all that the native no longer exists within the Manichean world developed by colonialism. [Gibson, 2003, p. 123]

In the final chapter of *Wretched of the Earth* Fanon presents a series of clinical vignettes of individuals, both French and Algerian, affected by violence in varying ways and bearing within them as a result, a traumatic kernel that resists thought, that resists interpretation. In one striking case, he presents two Algerian boys, aged thirteen and fourteen, who had decided to kill a French boy their own age, a boy who had been their playmate until that point. Asked why they had acted in this way, the older boy invokes a massacre in the village of Rivet, committed by the French militia.

> "Well, nobody at all was arrested. I wanted to take to the mountains, but I was too young. So X—and I said we'd kill a European".
> "Why?"
> "In your opinion, what should we have done?"
> "I don't know. But you are a child and what is happening concerns grown-up people".
> "But they kill children too ... "

"That is no reason for killing your friend".
"Well, kill him I did. Now you can do what you like".
"Had your friend done anything to harm you?"
"Not a thing".
"Well?"
"Well, there you are. ... " [Fanon, 1990, p. 219]

The violence of these boys, although presented as inevitable under these conditions, is not a means to an end, it is not a way of acceding to subjectivity, for social violence already inhabits them and puts a stop to any possibility of understanding: "Well, there you are. ..."

It is in *Black Skin, White Masks* that Fanon first lays out the problem of the violence of racism. In one of the most famous passages of that text, the author describes his first experience of being identified as 'other', a potentially dangerous other. In a park in Lyon, a little white boy sees a black man, Fanon and speaks out:

"Look, a Negro!" It was an external stimulus that flicked over me as I passed by. I made a tight smile.
"Look, a Negro!" It was true. It amused me.
"Look, a Negro!" The circle was drawing a bit tighter. I made not secret of my amusement.
"Mama, see the Negro! I'm frightened!" Frightened! Frightened! Now they were beginning to be afraid of me. I made up my mind to laugh myself to tears, but it had become impossible.
I could no longer laugh, because I already knew that there were legends, stories, history [...] Then, assailed at various points, the corporeal schema crumbled, its place taken by a racial epidermal schema. [...] On that day, completely dislocated, unable to be abroad with the other, the white man, who unmercifully imprisoned me, I took myself far off from my own presence, far indeed and made myself an object. [Fanon, 1986, pp. 111–112]

It is a striking *mise-en-scène*, with far reaching effects. Significantly, it is the white child who is made to inflict a shattering narcissistic wound on the black man. As Vicky Lebeau points out, it is the child whose

fright echoes through *Peau noire*, breaking through to Fanon, breaking into him. Letting that fear speak through his writing, Fanon brings his readers up against the question that drives *Peau noire,* the origins of racist hatred, its role as a destructive force in collective life. Slavery, lynching, segregation: with a child's looking and pointing, Fanon associates some of the most virulent expressions of that hatred, as if discovering the foundations of racism—its passions, its politics—in the figure of the child [Lebeau, 2005, p. 131].

But it is important to insist that the little boy in the park is not a wise innocent who speaks the truth of a natural difference that cannot be denied—out of the mouth of babes. Neither is that child guilty. Fanon knows that the child sees what he has already been made to see. He is accompanied by his mother, who in the process of trying to reassure him, reinforces, even creates his fear, as she reveals her own anxious, sexualised fear of the black man. The danger of miscegenation inherent in the coupling of the white woman with the black man is one of the most persistent racist cultural fantasies, as well as one key cause of racist violence, of the lynchings in the American South for example and Fanon returns to this theme throughout this book. The child and the man are both already caught up in structures that bind them to each other and the mother is made to stand as a representative of cultural ideas to which she herself had surrendered. And had she any choice in the matter? As Freud writes in "On Narcissism—An Introduction", "we never mean that the individual in question has a merely intellectual knowledge of the existence of such ideas; we always mean that he recognizes them as a standard for himself and submits to the claims they make on him". (Freud, 1914c, p. 93) The strength of the scene in the park lies precisely in the fact that it concentrates and dramatises the effect and hold of those claims and shows them to be products of the violence of the dominant culture. The anxious gaze of the child punctures the man's ego, his narcissism, but more than that, it undoes his subjectivity. Alice Cherki suggestively discusses this scene in terms of an encounter with the real (Cherki, 2001, pp. 304–305). Undone by the gaze of a white child who speaks, necessarily, in the register of the symbolic, the black man realises that his own place is not subject but other. In the very moment where he is seen not as a man, but as a black man, he is created *as other* by the cultural ideas of white society.

In this respect, *the white man is sealed in his whiteness and the black man in his blackness.* The frightened French boy in the park who speaks out; the frightened Algerian boys who know that their brothers are being killed, who act because the very condition of subjectivity, of choice and thought has been denied them. It is a chilling juxtaposition that the logic of Fanon's thought invites us to make, but in order to move on from it, towards a new conception of the human. In order precisely to come to the point where thought and choice become possible. He points out the violence of social structures, repeatedly points to their effects, to be sure, but in the conclusion of *Black Skin, White Masks,* he also affirms the following: "I do not have the right to allow myself to be mired in what the past has determined" (Fanon, 1986, p. 230), going on to state that "it is through the effort to recapture the self and to scrutinize the self, it is through the lasting tension of their freedom that men will be able to create the ideal conditions of existence for a human world" (Fanon, 1986, p. 231). As he had been suggesting throughout, Fanon aims for nothing less than a shift in social structures, a shift in the symbolic structures. He aims for those who have been othered and denied their status as fully fledged subjects to be able to intervene at the level of the symbolic and not be condemned by history to resort to action without thought or words. Does such a conclusion to the project of *Black Skin, White Masks* imply that psychoanalysis serves its purpose up to a point and needs to be left behind? Perhaps. But perhaps not. Fanon never gives up on the concept of the human and it is the psychoanalytic concepts of trauma and the narcissistic wound which can, as we shall see, provide a means to render an understanding of subjectivity which, marked by history, becomes more ambivalent and more open to difference.

The question of trauma and symptom, at the very origins of the invention of psychoanalysis, has never ceased to inhabit its discourse. In one paper Freud asks, "But what should we think of a Londoner who [...] shed tears before the Monument that commemorates the reduction of his beloved metropolis to ashes although it has long since risen again in far greater brilliance? [Hysterics and neurotics] remember painful experiences of the remote past, but they still cling to them emotionally; they cannot get free of the past and for its sake they neglect what is real and immediate". (Freud, 1910, pp. 16–17) The key of course does not lie either in a simple 'forgetting' as in eliminating from consciousness, from the present moment in time, because that would constitute 'repression' and would lead to the past returning to haunt the present in all kinds of unforeseeable, indeed unbearable ways. Conversely, the key does not lie either in a monumental 'preservation' of the past, which 'deadens' memory, confines it to split off parts of the ego, the psychic equivalent to museums and mausoleums. For these stand in danger of becoming a space outside history and this kind of preservation of a wound would leave us psychically impoverished and worse, split off from precisely that which would allow us to work towards a conception of the human that is potentially inclusive because it recognises the way in which our histories have shaped, structured and flawed us.

In one of his later essays, Ferenczi described the development of subjectivity through our growing ability *to live with* the wounds to our narcissism and thus accept difference and even love it:

> [The] things which do not yield unconditionally to our desires, which we love because they bring us satisfaction and hate because they do not submit to us in everything, we attach special mental marks, memory-traces with the quality of objectivity and we are glad when we find them again in reality, i.e., when we are able to find them once more [Ferenczi, 1926].

The ability to work through ambivalence, therefore, is what would make us human in this account. Tellingly, when he wrote those lines in 1926, Ferenczi, sparked by his work with shell-shocked soldiers during the Great War, had been interested in the role of trauma in the shaping of human subjectivity for a number of years. In a reflection arising initially from close work with patients who had suffered immense physical hardship during trench warfare, soldiers who had both committed violent acts and had been subject to them, Ferenczi elaborated the idea of trauma in terms of an unassimilated psychic wound. This began to serve as a kind of organising principle in his thought. "I have no hesitation in regarding even memory-traces as scars, so to speak, of traumatic impressions", (Ferenczi, 1926) he wrote. Significantly, Alice Cherki, who worked alongside Fanon in Tunis, recalls his fascinated reading of Ferenczi's work on trauma in the late 1950s. (Cherki, 2001, pp. 305–306) Indeed, as pointed out earlier, the effects of colonial violence on the subjectivity of the colonised was one key aspect of Fanon's clinical practice.

In an article called 'The North African Syndrome', Fanon describes his consultation with an Algerian patient whose inarticulate physical pain points to a traumatic kernel within him, a diffuse, inarticulate symptom which invites, as we have seen, a different kind of listening, a broader explanatory scheme:

> The North African Syndrome. The North African today who goes to see a doctor bears the dead weight of all his compatriots. Of all of those who had only symptoms, of all of those about whom the doctors said, 'nothing you can put your teeth into' (meaning no lesion). But the patient who is here, in front of me, this body which I am forced to assume to be swept by a consciousness, this body which is no longer altogether a body or rather which is doubly a body since it is beside itself with terror—this body which asks me to listen to it without however paying too much heed to it—fills me with exasp–eration.
>
> "Where do you hurt?"
>
> "In my stomach" (he points to his liver).
> I lose my patience. I tell him that the stomach is to the left, that what he is pointing to is the location of the liver. He is not put out, he passes the palm over that mysterious belly.
> "It all hurts" [Fanon, 1988, pp. 8–9].

The pain of this iconic patient, his scar, if one likes, is both particular and universal, symbolic and real. "It all hurts", he says. All, meaning his body, all, meaning his situation in the world. The diffuse inarticulacy of his pain is a symptom that involves not only the patient, but also his doctor/psychoanalyst, the hospital where they both find themselves, the histories that brought them to that space in time. How can the real of that suffering body start mattering and mattering for all humanity? That is what is at stake here. The final chapter of Foucault's *The Order of Things* (1970), a history of the human sciences, a text which ends with the chilling image of the concept of the human itself being as ephemeral as a profile traced in the sand by the sea, offers a reading of psychoanalysis, alongside ethnography, which stresses its subversive aspects, whilst it also criticises it for being an authoritarian, totalising discourse. According to Foucault, both psychoanalysis and ethnography call into question the very idea of a science of man, because they are constituted by "a perpetual principle of dissatisfaction, of calling into question, of criticism and contestation of what may seem, in other respects to be established". (Foucault, 1977, p. 373) These disciplines cannot do without the concept of man, but neither can they ever hope to master it because it is they who mark it as perpetually beyond their grasp. Perpetually beyond their grasp, it can be undone and redone and undone once more.

Tzvetan Todorov has explored similar issues as he researched the philosophical and historical underpinnings of totalitarianism. Unlike Foucault and less critically than Fanon, he is led to the possible areas of positive resistance that humanism might offer. He starts one of his latest books, *The Imperfect Garden: The Legacy of Humanism* (2002), with a little parable. This concerns a pact that humanity makes with the devil in order to succeed in the pursuit of knowledge. The devil says, "You will [believe] you have knowledge, but you will pay a triple price: first by separating yourself from your god, then from your neighbour and finally from yourself". (Todorov, 2002, p. 3) Although little explicit mention of psychoanalysis is made in the book, this story resonates perfectly with Freud's account of the three blows to mankind's self esteem. In that story, Copernicus informs man that he is not master of the universe, Darwin informs him that he is not master of creation and finally, psychoanalysis, *aka* Freud himself, informs him that he is not master of his psyche. Tellingly, Todorov presents an account of humanism in which the devil of the parable can be defeated, but only by accepting a wager, not as in Pascal's case, that god exists, but rather that both ambivalence and compassion exist.

> Men are free, it says; they are capable of the best and the worst. Better to wager hat they are capable of acting willfully, loving purely and treating one another as equals than the contrary (...) God owes us nothing neither does providence or nature. Human happiness is always in suspension. We can, however, prefer the imperfect garden of humankind to any other realm, not as a blind alley, but because this is what allows us to live in truth. [Todorov, 2002, p. 236]

Edward Said is another thinker who never gave up on the concept of humanism, on its inclusiveness, despite the worse kind of violence, the seemingly most intransigent hatred and fear. One of his last publications was a reading of Freud's *Moses and Monotheism* in which, among other issues, he explored the ambivalence at the origin of identification. He writes:

> Freud's symbol of those limits [of identity] was that the founder of Jewish identity was himself a non-European Egyptian. In other words, identity cannot be thought or worked through itself alone; it cannot constitute or even imagine itself without that radical originary break or flaw which will not be repressed, because Moses was Egyptian and therefore always outside the identity inside which so many have stood and suffered—and later, perhaps even triumphed. The strength of this thought is, I believe, that it can be articulated in and speak to other besieged identities as well—not through dispensing palliatives such as tolerance and compassion but, rather, by attending to it as a troubling, disabling, destabilizing secular wound—the essence of the cosmopolitan, from which there can be no recovery, no state of resolved or Stoic calm and no utopian reconciliation even within itself. [Said, 2002, p. 54]

In Said's reading of Freud, identity is troubled and contradictory for it incorporates a radical originary flaw—the stranger within the group, within the self. He describes this as a "disabling, destabilizing secular wound—the essence of the cosmopolitan". It is stunning and moving to realise the implication: it is precisely this wound that provides subjectivity with a resistance to closure and allows for the continuation of the process of man's refashioning. This is also what Fanon repeatedly argues. In his insistence on the 'fact' of race and racism, he opens up the universals of psychoanalysis to the demands of the particular. In his terms, the wound therefore remains and it is constitutive of subjectivity. The pain remains, but it need not shut down the possibility for thought for ever. Let us end with Fanon's hopeful, secular prayer at the end of *Black Skin, White Masks*, "Oh my body, make of me always a man who questions!" (Fanon, 1986, p. 232)

NOTE

1. In the French original the title of chapter five of Fanon's book reads: '*L'expérience vécue de l'homme noir*' (the black man's lived experience), but the English translation renders this as 'the fact of blackness'. However, this may not be contradictory, for Fanon argues that if there is any 'fact', as opposed to 'fantasy' in the psychoanalytic sense, it is to be found in lived experience.

CHAPTER SEVEN

The culture(s) of narcissism: simultaneity and the psychedelic sixties

Justin Lorentzen

In our tele-visual culture it is perhaps a commonplace to announce self absorption as a founding motif in any discussion of contemporary popular cultural activity. It is not necessary for academics to emphasise the triumph of simulation and surveillance in popular media forms, rather the television schedules will reveal, in the most basic commonsense forms, the prominence of reality-based celebrity and the ubiquity of programming that has created an instant index of fame. These shows need little introduction and they are not easily dismissed, except by the most conservative of critics (Murdoch, 2004).

Likewise, a consensus appears to exist in many diverse media forms that 'fame' is an inevitable logic that both fascinates and repels large audiences within a wider mass culture. There is a growing body of cultural criticism that recognises and contributes to the logic of celebrity culture. Dissecting and analysing the traits of fame and celebrity are perhaps the inevitable by-product of a of a contemporary cultural studies that privileges the popular.

There is, of course, a well-worn path that highlights the endless engagements between the high culture low/popular culture binary opposition in British and Continental Cultural Studies. A debate that continues to amuse many critics and writers in the post World War II era who, like it or not, have been shaped and emotionally marked by the Anglo-Americanised popular culture of the last fifty years. This culture has always had its critics and a lively debate continues to emphasise the recurrent motifs of manipulation and vulgarization *versus* popular emotional pleasures.

From a psychoanalytic perspective, however, we can see that there have been only a few meetings of 'socius' and 'psyche' that are worth recounting. Clearly, the history of the Frankfurt School is one such case in point. Here, the celebrated School of Social Critique addressed the rise of consumer culture and the dominant logic of entertainment that so infused culture and psyche in a post-war/holocaust society. A mindless popular mentality was the product of a ruthless capitalist system that obliterated all points of resistance and critical distance. Contemporary culture was threadbare and lacking even the space for examined self-reflection. A popular cultural triumph of narcissistic pleasure that crushed the last vestiges of European high modernism was now the basic reality of everyday life.

It is, of course, interesting to note that the Frankfurt School position was powerfully influenced by the success of the Fascist revolutions in Europe, particularly Nazi Germany. This success was, of course, a terrible problem for a European Left convinced of its own fundamental truths–class, power, revolution. It appeared that Nazi culture was able to infuse political power with libidinal energies, producing a cultural stage of dark neo-classical designs of spectacles and uniformity. The Frankfurt School writers, Adorno and Horkheimer (1944), argued that post-war culture had taken a lead from Nazi culture and placed libidinal manipulation at the centre of an empty popular culture dominated by fantasy and manufactured desires. In short, here was the recipe for cultural decline writ large.

Christopher Lasch presented a similar critique of American popular culture in the aftermath of the 1960s. Here, of course, the 1960s should not be understood as a decade *per se* but as a state of mind and critical sensibility. New forms of lifestyle and individual expression emerged during this historical period, along with original and innovatory forms of social regulation. Lasch is a radical critic of the more excessive experimental fictions that this tumultuous decade produced.

The Culture of Narcissism (1979) has a sub-title: *American Life in an Age of Diminishing Expectations*. With its broad analytical sweep and its bold theoretical concerns, it was nothing less than a 'state of the union' address. A book written by a cultural critic at the height of his powers. A text that brims with big ideas, intellectual swagger and penetrating criticism. In short, a book that by contemporary standards of cultural theory is deeply unfashionable.

Long before the advent of debates about modernity and its aftermath, Lasch articulates endings and decline. He proposed to examine contemporary social processes, politics and cultural forms from the perspective of collapse and impending catastrophe. In this regard, he was self-referential to a poetic tradition of elite pessimism and doom and aware that modernity's avant-garde had preached the coming 'wasteland'. The difference for Lasch is that in the 1960s and 70s this cultural pessimism had entered the popular imagination. As he states:

> The Nazi holocaust, the threat of nuclear annihilation, the depletion of natural resources, well- founded predictions of ecological disaster have fulfilled poetic prophecy, giving concrete historical substance to the nightmares or death wish, that avant-garde artists were the first to express. [Lasch, 1979, p. 5]

There is a strong existential dimension to this argument. For Lasch the contemporary culture of consumption has placed at centre stage a new form of individual. Shaped by the logic of consumption and driven to experience new realms of self-realisation, a narcissistic self, distinct from the individual that represented industrialization and modernity, had replaced the traditional self of industrious spirit and self-imposed restraint. The new self of consumption had emerged, Lasch argued, because of the erosion of traditional certainties grounded in class, family, community and religion. A variety of post-war cultural forces had radically changed the relationship between the present and the traditional historical past. Social upheaval and dynamic change, in short, had destabilized the social fabrics of meaning and reliability that were fundamental to traditional world views.

Lasch goes on to argue that this process of change has resulted in alienation and anomie that have reached psychological and social levels of pathology. Consequently, a compelling question is asked of each individual and posed collectively: how do we make sense of (our)selves in this climate of dynamic change and uncertainty? Today, we could perhaps also add the presence of 'terror' as an unavoidable risk to stability and continuity.

For Lasch, there was a new post-war sensibility of despair which had resulted in the evolution of new strategies, new regimes of living (ideals for living) that he sees as attempts to counteract and engage with the meaninglessness and helplessness that characterise these contemporary pathologies. Lasch coins the phrase 'void within' to communicate a vacuum of feeling, a sense of being frozen and lacking emotional sustenance and psychic invigoration. These, of course, are familiar sociological themes and, in a sense, are constantly played out and repeated particularly during periods of rapid social, cultural and technological change. From Durkheimian anomic insecurity to the notion of the 'risk society' (Beck, 1992), 'the void' has always been invoked by social theorists as a psychic and social reality. Lasch, nevertheless, is a persistent critic of his time and clearly dreads the formal and informal attempts to locate and pacify collective existential terror. He offers five major arguments that contribute to the post-war landscape of cultural decline.

Firstly, in the post 1960s United States, Lasch detects a retreat from politics. There is an overriding sense of cynicism with regards to conventional political processes. Lasch highlights the fact that 50% of the American electorate do not vote in Presidential elections. This retreat is based on a political sensibility that 'nothing can be done' or that 'nothing changes'. There is a similar theme in Martin Amis's *Einstein's Monsters* (1989). It is not that the political institutions are simply seen as corrupt and lacking in imagination and vigour; it is rather that the politics of nuclear blocs itself leads to an overwhelming sense of despair. We live collectively in the shadow of catastrophe. This leaden weight of despair has entered the unconscious. Collectively we have normalized the fear of mass annihilation. Amis in his fictional approach to this doomsday scenario speculates on how this impossible fear, internalized as it is, may influence our moral sensibilities and inform the micro world of relationships and behaviour. Random acts of violence may have a deeper resonance within wider international political power blocs. Lasch, of course, emphasises the retreat from politics as a rejection of collective ideals and social solidarity and as a sign of the individual's retreat to a more internalized space that is disconnected from the civic world of debate and political action.

Secondly, Lasch turns his attention to what he sees as a sharp, post-war increase in mental illness, from schizophrenia to neurosis. Again, this is an issue that is symptomatic of a modern malaise. Not only are there more people diagnosed as mentally ill, there is a clear and steadily increasing trend that sees individuals actively seeking professional psychiatric help. This is a crucial feature of our contemporary culture's obsession with individual self-realisation. Of course, many have recognised the central role psychiatric discourses have played in defining modern therapeutic regimes. There is a long history, including the works of writers such as Thomas Szasz (1962), R.D. Laing (1964) and Michel Foucault (1979), that have identified the role of psychiatric discourses in defining, producing and controlling the psychic landscape. More recently, Beck (1992) has emphasised the process of 'individualisation', the desire to 'live my own life", as being a contemporary form of religious desire. Individualisation is a goal that so many people set themselves in order to feel fully realised in their lives and relationships and clearly the argument here is that an established therapeutic culture helps define and meet the demands of such self-awareness and emotional fulfilment. This, of course, is the goal, but the sociological reality might be somewhat different.

Lasch is clearly contemptuous of this therapeutic culture. For him, the pursuit of professional support and help is just one more example of the contemporary culture's embracing of narcissistic self-absorption. The continual surveying of emotional landscapes (interiors) appears to promise a fundamental release from traditional forms of authority and obligations, plus a possibility of finding a 'happiness' that defies collective moral sanction. For Lasch, this is clearly corrosive of social solidarity, as it emphasises a perpetual state of adolescent petulance that the culture mirrors and reflects. The seekers of therapeutic release are simply feeding a utopian desire for ease of emotional commitment and profound sense of 'well-being'. These are just 'myths' of narcissistic indulgence and avoid the 'true' maturity of obligation and responsibility that characterises a fully integrated social fabric. A social fabric that may never have existed but which Lasch laments the passing of.

Thirdly, for Lasch the post-Sixties culture exhibits the turn away from external social concerns and inwards towards a world of self-examination. This is most notably expressed by the dramatic increase in drug and alcohol use. What were once the pleasures of the avant-garde experimentalists, from Charles Baudelaire to William Burroughs, the free form realms of elitist transgression, are today mainstream and mundane features of the life world. Lasch sees this once more as a retreat from the external world of relationships, work and politics, to a celebration of the internal, hedonistic satisfactions and quests for altered states and oblivion. Here, pleasure and terror mix in a matrix of chemical 'suicide'. Once again, Lasch perceives these desires, however individual, as also part of a wider mass culture and deeply embedded in a culture of narcissistic self-expressive desire. Libido unbound is not a cause for celebration or radical elevation; rather, it is one more indicator of cultural collapse, fragmentation of the social and individual dissolution.

Fourthly, the rise of a materialistic consumer society in the post World War II American economy, i.e., the construction of false needs and desires and deep commitment to a materialistic lifestyle and self aggrandisement, is another target for Lasch's critique. Others, such as Featherstone (1995), have also pinpointed narcissistic cultural traits as being decisive in the centrality of the body and its presentation in contemporary consumer culture. How diet, exercise, cosmetic re-drawing and surgery have focused on the physical self in relation to well-being and self-gratification. Featherstone uses Lasch to show how a global media network of industries and televisual cultures have galvanised audiences and consumer sensitivities to body making our social selves more vulnerable to body maintenance and notions of beauty and self-regard.

Intimately linked with these notions of consumption and narcissistic personality comes the accompanying tyranny of 'fame' and 'celebrity'. For Lasch, modern media (films, TV, popular music, advertising) directly pander to notoriety. A desire for recognition that is a dominant source of pleasure and envy in contemporary popular culture defines a modern spiritual ethos. For Lasch, fame satisfies the craving for self-recognition. Without recognition there is only isolation, rejection and misery. The self is only a self if it is reflected, reproduced and then projected back to its point of origin.

Celebrity, therefore, creates a mediated space that intersects the fragile connections that link psychic identity with social self.

There is also here a link to writers and concerns that come after Lasch. Baudrillard (1983) has documented and theorised the rise of a mediated consumer culture that celebrates lifestyle and sign fetish, while simultaneously destroying the popular link to the past. Fame, celebrity and consumption are ultimately concerned, in their industrial process, with the present. Contemporary mass media landscapes are not suitable environments in which to approach or engage with history. Rather, in the absence of history the media industries engage with recycled, retro versions of the past, which are fetishised as nostalgia. Not a complex, detailed past, but a commodified and codified selective history that presents a purely ideological present past. Baudrillard's (1983) skilful analysis of Hollywood Vietnam cinema is a case in point. The undoubted emotional impact of films (particularly like *Apocalypse Now*) undermines the complexity of the historical reasons for the United State's involvement in Vietnam. The ideological grasp these films maintain for the viewer represents a sentimentalised, patriotic narcissism that consoles but does not inform.

More recently, Slavoj Žižek (2003) has applied a similar reading to the events of September 11th. Catastrophe is, as we already know, what awaits the narcissist and the Hollywood film industries have, from the 1930s onwards, produced a series of catastrophic urban nightmares that predicted the appalling disasters of collapsing new buildings. *King Kong, The Day the Earth Stood Still, Towering Inferno, Independence Day,* all attest to the strange desire for demolition spectacle that so enthrals the blockbuster audience.

The process not only degrades history but also formulates a future that blends Eros with its intimate sleeping partner Thanatos. This is a logic that Nazi spectacle knows so very well (Lorentzen, 1995) and it is troubling to note that an audience for mass spectacle is very much alive in our contemporary cultural climate. Lasch makes a very telling moral point. Using traditional (Freudian) psychoanalytic insights, he argues that an important resource for balanced maturity springs from a well of loving memories. In a popular culture that eulogises and fetishises terror, simulated cultural memories clearly lack a key component in developing a sense of social and subjective continuity.

Lasch, then, is clearly a critic of what he sees as a Sixties sensibility. However, the upheavals of Sixties cultural politics are not some sudden 'break', but they are part of a wider historical process of industrialization, secularization and rationality. Clearly, these are key elements in any valid definition of modernity and its symptoms. Central to the articulation of his arguments is the decline of the family. Drawing heavily on Freud and Freudian speculation, Lasch maintains the distinction made by Freud between primary and secondary narcissism. Primary narcissism demarcates the moment of loss the child experiences when the unitary bliss of the womb is broken by birth. Learning to accept the bitter realisation of the separation from the mother's body and the recognition that a singular desire is always thwarted, are the key elements in the individual's psychic development. Lasch points to the role families have played in this formative process of personality construction. To put it very simply, Lasch sees the family as a foundational site of social continuity, a place where children learn to recognise the limitations of their own desire and become familiar with the desires of others. This is a classic sociological cliché in the development of a metaphorical social solidarity. There is of course a profound pessimism at work here. Lasch, like Freud, recognised the implicit violence in the formation of the human personality, but he believes that this violence was a prerequisite for producing collective social stability. In the 1990 'Afterword' to the reprinted *Culture of Narcissism*, Lasch emphasises the following:

> Psychoanalysis confirms the ancient religious insight that the only way to achieve happiness is to accept limitations in the spirit of gratitude and contrition instead of attempting to annul those limitations or bitterly resenting them: [Lasch, 1990, p. 242]

The clear focus of this argument is to communicate that the culture of narcissism is much more than a critique of self-absorption. In the three decades since the publication of the book, money, power, greed and excess have become clichéd journalisms to describe the dynamic vibrancy of materialistic popular culture and the hallmarks of celebrity. However, the warning and moral message of Lasch's critique is that the desires for these external objects of self-recognition is driven by a deadening emptiness. This is a return to the 'void within', posing the question: how should we live now? The answer seems to promote a therapeutic sensibility:

> The contemporary climate is therapeutic, not religious. People today hunger not for perpetual salvation, let alone for the restoration of an earlier golden age, but for the feeling, the momentary illusion of personal well being, health and psychic serenity. [Lasch, 1979, p. 7]

Let it be very clear, however, that Lasch is not valorising or indeed sympathizing with the professionalisation of psychoanalytic discourse. It is slightly ironic to recognise that Lasch, whilst very much an admirer of Freud's theoretical and philosophical insights, appears to have very little affinity with psychoanalytic practice. On the contrary, professional therapists are seen as part of the wider cultural process of narcissism. Therapeutic regimes validate self-absorption while simultaneously appearing to offer no solution to the freezing 'void within'. Lasch, however, should not be seen as a reactionary critic of the 'new age'. Conservative with a small 'c' would be a more accurate description. He is equally contemptuous of the arguments put forward by the American Right, with their systematic attacks on the 'young' and their rigid adherence to 'traditional values'. This clearly appears to be a major contradiction in Lasch's position, as he most obviously reserves his most radical critiques for the legacy of the 1960s revolt. He dismisses the radicalism most readily associated with mid-sixties counter-culture and demands for political change as having no lasting significance, except in the destructive self-centredness that a culture of narcissism signifies.

The social ills highlighted by Lasch's critique emanate from a very particular source of American ideology. The rugged individualism that, arguably, is foundational to national identity in the United States, has produced in a later twentieth century context a rampant egoism that triumphs self-realisation. Lasch sees the impact of this individualism in so many aspects of American life— health, food and diet, jogging, Eastern Mysticism, radical politics, conspiracy theory and occultisms—that all signal a culture in retreat from the shared communal values of inclusiveness, to be replaced by a shallow longing for personal growth at all costs. This is the very centre of Lasch's theory of cultural narcissism. Lasch recognises the importance of 'self-love' but, as it has been argued, the sociology of narcissism is more complicated.

Narcissus, in the myth, falls in love (in a Lacanian fashion) with an image that is external to his being. So enamoured is Narcissus with the reflection that confronts him, he appears captivated by an image he does not recognise as himself and falls in love. This is mis-recognition with tragic consequences. Echo attempts to save him but her words are simply repetitions of his own utterances. The defining features of this classic metaphor are alienation, detachment and the aestheticisation of a human being's representation.

For Lasch, however, cultural narcissism is articulated by a rela-tionship of dependence. As he puts it: "The narcissist depends on others to validate his self-esteem–he cannot live without an admir-ing audience". (Lasch, 1990, p. 10) Here Lasch is defining the modern narcissist as a product of unrestrained 'individuality'. This, then, is the secondary narcissism that Lasch sees as the culturally corrosive process.

It is remarkably clear from Lasch's perspective that the 1960s represented a naive, excessive and self-absorbed break with tradi-tional social structures and forms of cultural organisation. The great casualty of this era of social change was the increasingly atomised self, cut off from social ties, communities and moral responsibilities. However, although Lasch makes a series of very strong arguments that resonate profoundly some three decades since the publication of the book, his cultural and political pessimism fails to recognise that the same narcissistic culture he identifies also produced new forms of individual freedom and personal transformation.

I would like, therefore, to emphasise a series of neglected areas of cultural life that Lasch ignores. I am not suggesting that the sen-sibilities of the 1960s are to be politically admired wholesale; rather, I would prefer to highlight the transformative impulses that, for a brief period of time, surfaced to ask difficult and complex questions about how our societies are organised and experienced. If we can agree that the decade marked off by the 1960s *label* can be under-stood as a period of transgression and rule breaking, then why must these processes of questioning and transformation be simply recorded in a negative light?

Sociologically, decades become convenient cultural markers, to order and simplify history. Decades shore up the narrative of time into easily accessible historical data. What is most fascinating about this process is that it helps to construct not only a gloss of coherence, as we glance back at recent historical events, but also sustains and fulfils our fantasies about the past. The Sixties do maintain a strange mysterious hold on the cultural imaginations of the West. It is clearly seen as an ambivalent area of attraction and repulsion. It has become a sacred moment in time, a sacred entity, capable of destabilizing and confusing in equal measures. (see Bataille, 1986). If 'events' have passed into history (Baudrillard, 1983), what remains of the 1960s is an ever-present re-running of the images and iconography that represents and replaces the complex reality of that decade. The Sixties are the most simulated decade of all-a repertoire of powerful newsreel, photographic and film archived screen memories. I do not think that it is possible to represent the truth of the Sixties, but I do feel there are 'true' representations. These representations construct a mediated landscape that continues to fascinate, disturb and exhilarate in equal measures. Our obsession with the mediated events of that decade is in part explained by the present cultural anxieties we project on to the iconography that remains; youth, rebellion, war, poverty, race, drugs, gender identities all play in the shadow of the Sixties enduring legacy. As Green (1997) states:

> The idea that no-one had done this before, is central to the impact of the Sixties. Taken individually, most of the Cultural Revolution had to be carved out before. One had been able to procure an abortion, to utilize contraception, to take recreational drugs, to read illicit literature, to divorce and to indulge in same sex relationships. But one had not been able to do any of it very openly. [Green, 1997, p. xi]

The transformative impulses that I would like to discuss are intimately linked to the very processes of cultural narcissism that Lasch so vividly highlights. The radical challenges to authority and social status that the Civil Rights movements and youth rebellion articulated clearly indicated the limits of established political power. They also proposed, particularly in the case of youth, a categorical rejection of fixed identities and ideological conditioning. Many of these identities put on display a radical concern for appearance and style. The 'dandified' youth of the Sixties used the body and dress as

forms of political resistance that helped draw clear lines of demar-
cation between the generations, at best expressed by the student
slogan: *"You're either with us or against us"*. These emphatic words
paradoxically helped create spaces where genuine forms of experi-
ments in lifestyle could take place. The radical movements of the
decade fused, in many cases, a popular cultural revolt with serious
social critique. Most notable were the Situationists whose critique of
consumer culture coined the term *Society of Spectacle* (Debord, 1994)
emphasising the world of images that had constructed a sinister
new media-scape.

The popular music of the Sixties also played a galvanizing role in
turning display and narcissism into a new and compelling art form.
The notion that this music and the artists who produced it are merely
outcomes of a spectacular consumer logic, loses credibility when one
considers the startling impact of performers like *Jimi Hendrix, The
Beatles and The Rolling Stones*. Using the strange visceral medium of
rock music, these artists constructed personas whilst cultivating sexuality and self-love as a medium and message and communicated complex social messages concerning the desirability of social change
through counter-cultural activity. The profoundly emotional nature of
the popular music of the period is perhaps best exemplified by Jimi
Hendrix's powerful and unsettling performance of the *Star-Spangled
Banner* at Woodstock (1969). So deeply committed and yet so open to
interpretation, this piece best illustrates what I would like to call
mimetic narcissism, that is to say, this piece is a spectacle of a dandified,
libidinal narcissistic display which incites each individual member of
the audience through shock emotional impact to believe that *"I am he
as you are he and you are me and we are all together"*.

More specifically, mimetic narcissism can be understood as the
compelling need to imitate that is a fundamental feature of human
desire. Gerard (1970) argues that individuals always desire something that they lack and more strikingly, often desire the object that
those they desire, desire. Mimetic narcissism implies then the desire
to become or assimilate someone else's persona. A process of merg-
ing of identities that can, by the ambivalent nature of the process,
both confuse and liberate (McCabe, 1998). A love of another's
persona is clearly a projected desire for self-love. It asks, "Just think
what I could become!" It all, nevertheless, reveals the strange interconnectivity between subjects. A desire that can, on occasion, reveal

itself to be a simultaneous recognition of one-ness disguised as other-ness.

This brings me to another feature of the mid-1960s counter-culture. Much has been made of the experimental nature of drug taking during this period. Drugs plainly have very complex histories that often obscure the variety of uses to which they are part. In the middle years of the 20th century, there appears to be a generalized assumption that drugs entered the popular culture and the collective imagination of youth purely on recreational terms. The history of LSD resists such simple explanations. Examining various sources, memoirs and commentaries we can recognise that the history of LSD is a compelling indicator of ambivalent (sacred) cultural conflict. Most informed histories (Green, 1997; Black, 2001) have noted the strange cohabitation between secret government agencies (i.e., CIA) and the counter-culture. Both sides of the political fence saw the potential of LSD to deconstruct the human personality. For the counter-culture this meant that, via the path of LSD, a new modern spiritualism could be born. The 'trip' promised a process of self-realisation and revelation that could not be contained or controlled by government authorities.

For the security forces and secret services the potential offered by hallucinogenic experience was related to the ability (it was argued) of LSD to control minds and provide useful new tools of interrogation. The sacred status of LSD was assured (Green, 1997, p. 106). It is perhaps no accident that LSD attracted bohemians, celebrities, government officials and political figures, ironically demonstrating how the drug, as claimed by the counter-culture, could create a sense of unity and interconnectivity.

There are a number of points to be made here in relation to Christopher Lasch's arguments. To begin with, I would like to take issue with the simple notion that narcissistic personality traits are necessarily negative in effect and ultimately destructive of human personality. There have been moments in post-war popular culture where the narcissistic processes outlined in Lasch's critique have become radicalized to subvert and invert this narcissistic effect. The period we call the 1960s is one such moment.

The narcissistic display of rock and pop music culture fused with the disorientation experience of hallucinogenic drugs to produce radical insights, most notably the revelations of consciousness and the profound recognition that the barriers and cultural divides between individuals were politically spurious and without foundation. Ultimately, this clash of style, display and chemical travel revealed a profound *simultaneity* of experience that the Sixties and the early forms of global communication allowed and predicted.

For many, the overlapping layers and channels of communication celebrated by Marshall McLuhan (1967), the conflicting meanings and messages documented by competing electronic media, mirrored exactly the deep emotional experience of the psychedelic. McLuhan referred to this as the *'simultaneity'* of electronic media experience. Iain Macdonald (1997), in his moving and insightful study of the *The Beatles* music and its connections to Sixties culture, articulates the central significance of *simultaneity*:

> Briefly a buzz-word among Parisian poets and Cubists before 1914, simultaneity was revived in the early Sixties by Marshall McLuhan in texts hailing society's liberation from the 'tyranny' of print by electronic media (of which of which the most dominant was and is, television). Deploring linear thought and fixed points of view, which he saw as a sources of conflict and tension in the Western min, McLuhan welcomed the chaotic 'flow' of media simultaneity, communal exchange and amplified sensory experience. Little read today, he was a prophet of modern fragmentation-of multi channel TV, multiculturalism, multimedia, multipolar politics, polymorphous sexuality and the extreme critical relativism of Deconstruction. In their characters, collective and individual, The Beatles were perfect McLuhanites. More importantly, their work showed them to be prophets on their own terms: pioneers of the new 'simultaneous art'. [MacDonald, 1997, p. 20]

Communicating this experience is an almost impossible task and it is interesting to note that the artists of the era were more likely to articulate an expression through recourse to music. Sounds provided the signifiers by which the complexity of psychedelic experiences were recorded and communicated (see *The Beatles* albums *Revolver* and *Tomorrow Never Knows* 1966).

Lasch is recognisably right when he focuses his critique on internal self-absorption and the cultural conditions that validate that experience. However, I would like to argue that the psychedelic experience does not belong to a particular period of history; rather it is like a door that is occasionally opened but, more often than not, shut. I use this metaphor in homage to Aldous Huxley and *The Doors of Perception*. If the door opened in the years 1965–1967, then the secret was let out, never to be put back. LSD is perhaps a mythical Pandora's Box that haunts the popular imaginations of the West, a common course in psychiatrics that offered revelation through its reversal of standard narcissist experience.

I feel that it is important to emphasise that I am not advocating a glamorisation or indeed a promotion of drug experience. This would not only be naïve, it would also be deceitful not to recognise the dangers and limitations of hallucinogenic experimentation and would fail to recognise the clear dangers inherent in uncontrolled drug experiences in relation to transpersonal consciousness. However, as MacDonald points out:

> Yet for the mass of LSD users (which during the late Sixties numbered several million of the brightest young men and women of their generation) the effects of this potent hallucinogen were more benign, if in the long term more insidious. [MacDonald, 1997, p. 15]

What can be advocated, however, is the notion that the very processes of narcissism and self-absorption that Lasch considers corrosive of more traditional cultural forms, can in fact be re-examined as a powerful and sensuous exploration the inner renditions of self in conjunction with the recognition of new forms of interpersonal connection and community. This is best expressed by the exhortation coined by the Student Movement: *"Get out of your head and into your senses!"* (Capra, 2002)

The Sixties counter-culture as documented by Green (1997) was a complex mix of romanticism (in the true 19th Century tradition of poetic romanticism) modernism and revolutionary politics. Green considers the era not as a cohesive political movement but as an internationally interconnected network of people and ideas, which emphasised *cultural* rather than direct political change. Political change would be a desirable side effect of the counter-culture strategy, but the focus was changing awareness by celebrating non-ordinary modes of experience (Capra, 2002). This then was a radical challenge to commonsense and everyday ideology that had its antecedents in the modernist traditions of art intervention, best illustrated and authorised by Dada, Surrealist and Situationist movements. The connecting principle between these groups was the belief in the power of disruption and subversion of the common-sense life world. It is, therefore, understandable that the recourse to hallucinogenic drugs that so many of the counter-culture groups championed and pioneered, would fit a consciousness expanding game plan. *"The revolution in the head"*, so celebrated by the Sixties pop celebrity, best illuminates this political option:

> The first expansion of consciousness, then, was a moment beyond materialism and toward a new spirituality, beyond ordinary reality via meditative and psychedelic experiences and beyond rationality through expanded sensory awareness. The combined effect was a continual sense of magic, awe and wonder that for many of us will forever by associated with the Sixties. [Capra, 2002, p. 1]

In concluding the connections I have made between Lasch and the sixties counter-culture, I would like to draw on the work Charles S. Grob (2002) and his colleagues Ralph Metzer and Andrew Weil. All three writers have indicated the potential of psychedelics to support and offer profound insight into psychiatric research. All three have located the 'golden age' of experimentation that existed in psychiatry and psychoanalytic research during the 1950s and 1960s, before the legal embargos on the use of LSD and associated hallucinogens.

Grob (2002), in particular, outlines a broad historical arc of perspectives that are useful in considering the social and cultural impact of psychotropic substances. He carefully considers the Shamanistic/Aboriginal roots of hallucinogens in non-Western collective traditions. Here the emphasis is on the central role played by mysterious plant knowledge in the carefully administered sacramental use of sacred substances that were at the core of collective experience and individual transformation. More specifically, Grob draws our attention to the work of ethno-botanists who have produced well-researched investigations of Ancient Greek civilizations (e.g., the Eleusinian Mysteries) and Aztec societies where hallucinogens were widely used for religious and healing purposes. (Grob, 2002, p. 264) Although there maybe a clear temptation to romanticize the 'non-Western other", for Grob the important connection between non-Western and European-American traditions of ecstatic substance use has been the Occidental suppression of psychedelics characterizing a long and problematic history concerning the social role of mind-expanding drugs. Grob argues convincingly that there is an ingrained cultural resistance to the revelations of psychedelic experience. From the 17th century onwards, morning glory seeds, peyote, psilocybin mushrooms were all considered dangerous and corrupting of official dogmas of either religious doctrine or the instrumental reason of governments. An obvious paradox, however, is manifest in relation to contemporary debates about drug use and abuse. Western societies have only understood psychoactive drugs as being used and pursued decadently or hedonistically without appreciating the potential for ritual and collective expression. The argument is clear, if not somewhat contentious: rather than produce social disorganization and corruption, perhaps the hidden mystery is the ability of hallucinogens to bring enlightenment, social solidarity and empathy.

More contemporary models of analytic interest coalesce around the intimate relationship, explored in the middle years of the 20th century, between the discovery of LSD and its critical use in the treatment of psychosis. Grob calls this emphasis on utility, the 'psychotomimetic model'. Albert Hofman's discovery in April 1943 led immediately to the marketing of LSD to clinical practitioners and researchers. Qualified professionals were actively encouraged to self-administer the drug to acquire the requisite insight into psychotic experience. There was genuine belief in the power of LSD to mimic exactly psychotic states.

However, a period of experimentation quickly supplanted the psychotomimetic model with a more radical approach that saw LSD as having therapeutic potential and a positive contribution to psychotherapies. This he calls the 'psycholytic model'. Grob's states:

> In subjects given a relatively low dose of LSD, there appeared to occur a release of repressed psychic material, particularly in anxiety states and obsessional neuroses. By allowing this otherwise repressed and threatening material to flow effortlessly into consciousness, investigators surmised that low dose LSD treatments could facilitate the psychotherapy process. [Grob, 2002, p. 273]

Grob clearly outlines the limitations of the psycholytic approach particularly in relation to the Freudian and Jungian therapeutic orientations that may have influenced the outcome and interpretation these clinical encounters. However, a case is convincingly made for low dose treatment.

> Application of the low dose model in Europe as well as the United States ascertained the psycholytic treatment had particular value with patients with rigid defence mechanisms and excessively strict superego structures. [Grob, 2002, p. 273]

The implied procedural 'advances' contained within the above quote for psychoanalytic paradigms are profound and the full implications of these early encounters between psychedelics and psychotherapy have still to be fully addressed and contemplated. The ethical and philosophical repercussions are of intense interest, if only on theoretical levels of enquiry.

Perhaps there are points of intersection in the dialogue I have selected to facilitate between Lasch's *The Culture of Narcissism*, the counter-culture themes I have singled out to represent the experimental 1960s and the implications for contemporary psychoanalytic thinking. As Grob (2002) clearly reveals, there has been an institutional suppression of psychedelic research since the late 1960s. A climate of fear and ridicule has marginalized any imaginative reappraisal of the experimental vigour that 1960's popular culture might have produced. What makes psychedelics and simultaneity so compellingly neglected is the nexus of their embrace, which bought together technology, science, popular culture and psychic expansion. Psychoanalytic thinking has gifted and bequeathed many fecund ideas and concepts to charge the poetic imaginations of the West. The *unconscious*, the *collective unconscious*, the *imaginary, fantasy* and the *real, soul* and *archetype*, all provide ways of addressing problematic areas of human experience that encounter ambivalence, transcendence and numinosity. These are exactly the forms of experience that the popular counter-culture of the 1960s restlessly articulated. Paradoxically, they are also the very experiences that Christopher Lasch felt were so detrimental to the contemporary crisis of culture. The cultures of narcissism are paradoxical and contradictory, shallow and excessive, fragmented and uniform, banal and terrifying. Nevertheless, they compel us to seriously and openly discuss human potentials. A return to these extraordinary experimental moments in time is long overdue.

CHAPTER EIGHT

The psychoanalytic framing of the art object as narcissistic agency

Tessa Adams

It is recognised that Freud formulated his theory of 'narcissistic personality' through his psychopathography of Leonardo da Vinci and that psychoanalytic approaches to art practice have been much influenced by this text. Nevertheless, concerns can be raised as to the relationship between pathological analyses of creative practices and historical representations of the aesthetic. This chapter takes up this problematic by addressing the position that Freud holds in establishing Leonardo's work as both compensatory and sublimatory with the focus on Freud's presumptions regarding Leonardo's infancy and his assertion that Leonardo's paintings trace his attempt to re-create the 'boy adored and desired' by his mother. From this position, the incorporation of Freud's analysis of Leonardo will be examined as well as the way in which certain psychoanalytic theorists have conceived analyses which promote a contrast between creative practices, casting that which is seen to derive from narcissistic investment as subordinate to that which is seen to derive from the sublimative ambitions of Oedipal resolution.

The question of 'artistic authenticity' is raised by profiling the work of Kristeva who lays emphasis on categories of creative expression. Her analysis offers an opposition between works which speak of 'maternal *jouissance*' and works which strive for 'symbolic coherence' in search for the 'maternal phallus'; the latter is determined as the product of narcissistic reinforcement. This analysis of Kristeva's position is followed by the profiling of what could be seen to be a contentious contribution to this topic: the work of Janine Chasseguet-Smirgel. A critique is given in relation to Smirgel's leading text *Creativity and Perversion* (1984) in which she proposes that certain art works (dominated by the ego ideal) derive from what she terms, 'the anal universe'. What is interesting is that Smirgel discredits works that are thus dominated by claiming that the nature of narcissistic investment renders them fundamentally inauthentic.

Furthermore, attention will be paid to the work of Hanna Segal whose concerns for artistic authenticity parallel those of Chasseguet-Smirgel in that certain art work is seen to fail in terms of the artist's pathological ambitions. Here the pathological position is perceived again in terms of the artist's presumed psychological immaturity couched as narcissistically fixated. Finally, the status of artistic practice will be investigated more generally in terms of the question as to whether artistic endeavour inevitably serves narcissistic aims.

The work of Leonardo—sublimation or narcissistic substitution?

Freud's essay on Leonardo provides an analysis that frames certain acts of creativity as the agency of sublimation or substitution. Typical of the 'art historical' analyses of Leonardo's works is the view that his exploratory attention to painting, on the one hand and science, on the other, were less in opposition but more the product of his innovatory capacity. Yet Freud became concerned with the unconscious subjective nature of Leonardo's paintings in contrast to the objective nature of his scientific investigations.

While Freud claims that Leonardo had an "extraordinary capacity for sublimating the primitive instincts" he also suggests that Leonardo had a "quite special tendency towards instinctual repressions". (Freud, 1910c, p. 136) But what Freud culls from his

investigation of Leonardo (in what has been termed a 'pathography') is his theory of narcissistic object choice. That is to say,
notwithstanding certain criticism in respect of Freud's interpretation
of Leonardo's texts, it is clear that Freud's analysis of Leonardo's
paintings affords Freud the prospect of locating narcissistic investment in terms of Leonardo's repressed homo-erotic pre-occupations.
The question to be raised is: how does Freud come to these conclusions simply by attending to certain of Leonardo's works?

Freud builds up his clinical picture by establishing the dynamic
of Leonardo's childhood from his study of the artist's writings and
biographical details. This investigation is furthered by the interpretation of certain paintings and drawings that are used to furnish his
hypothesis. The core of Freud's thesis maintains that Leonardo had
significant homosexual inclinations engendered by his feelings
about his illegitimate birth, the absence of a father during infancy
and the 'tender seductions' of his natural mother. Freud enhances
his thesis by taking up a position in respect of Leonardo's masterly
painting of The Virgin and Child with St. Anne and the Lamb (circa,
1510). This painting portrays St. Anne and the Virgin intertwined in
an unusual combination of drapery and form. In fact this painting
has interested many art critics in that the configuration of the two
figures strangely implies that the Virgin is virtually sitting on the lap
of St. Anne. Amidst this implied intimacy we find the Christ Child
portrayed as the centre of attention as if the subject of a double
mothering held in a dual gaze of blissful adoration.

A primary factor which led to Freud's conclusions about
Leonardo's narcissistic aim was a passage from Leonardo's scientific
notebooks that recorded a childhood memory of a vulture's tail
striking the lips of the infant Leonardo in the cradle. Within this passage Freud had incorporated a crucial mistranslation which was
later exposed (the vulture was in fact a kite). The content of this
memory in Freud's view is interpreted as a symbol of Leonardo's
infant experience of maternal seduction. Freud justifies his analysis
by suggesting that there is configuration of this moment subliminally
located in the form of the painting of the 'Virgin and St. Anne'. That
is to say, we are told that a vulture can be discerned by the nature of
Leonardo's treatment of the folds of the drapery of the Virgin. So
convinced was Freud of Leonardo's unconscious portrayal of his

cradle experience within this painting that his contemporary, Oscar Pfister, chose to superimpose a delineation of the form of the vulture on a reproduction of the painting in order to demonstrate that there could be, indeed, a tail appearing to touch the lips of the Christ Child held in the maternal gaze. Freud subsequently used the Pfister drawing in order to validate his hypothesis (Freud, 1910c, p. 116). But the fact that Freud had used a mistranslation, could potentially invalidate Pfister's drawing (since the tail of a kite is far less elaborate than that of a vulture) and thereby render questionable Freud's interpretation of Leonardo's recall of maternal seduction.

Yet, notwithstanding the anomaly raised in the defining of the structure of these different bird's tails and Freud's interest (enhanced by Pfister) to account for Leonardo's narcissistic aims, it is clear that the Leonardo essay offers insight into Freud's theoretical position in relation to narcissistic object choice. Fundamental to Freud's analysis of Leonardo is that he sees much of Leonardo's work as representing the boy who is gazed at and adored: the boy mirrored by the mother's need of him. In this light Freud deems the androgynous nature of the figures characteristic of Leonardo's paintings as no less than the representation of Narcissus gazing into the pool at his own reflection. That is to say, Freud casts Leonardo's extraordinary capacity to configure beautiful youths as servicing Leonardo's need to sublimate his homosexual aims which are identified as the product of 'precocious arousal' in infancy. The essential feature of this speculation depends on Freud's introduction of the concept of narcissism which is used to explain Leonardo's choice of the ideal homosexual love object. Freud maintains that the outcome of the precocious sexual arousal within infancy inhibited Leonardo's conscious development of love for his mother and consequently this love suffered repression. Thus the boy's solution to this dilemma, Freud tells us, was to identify with the mother and thereby with the narcissistic love object—young boys who in phantasy become the child loved by the mother. Freud states his position unequivocally within the following passage:

> The boy represses his love for his mother: he puts himself in her place, identifies with her and takes his own person as a model in whose likeness he chooses the new objects of his love. In this way he has become a homosexual. What he has in fact done is

to slip back to auto-eroticism: for the boys whom he now loves as he grows up are after all only substitute figures and revivals of himself in childhood—boys whom he loves in the way in which his mother loved *him* when he was a child. [Freud, 1910c, p. 100]

Thus, Freud interprets the content of Leonardo's early paintings as embodying both the repressed desire for his mother and the narcissistic love object, thereby proclaiming that artistic products can become the vehicle of repressed sexual desire. The following passage emphasises how certain Freud felt about this hypothesis:

We must be content to emphasise the fact—which is hardly any longer possible to doubt—that what an artist creates provides at the same time an outlet for his sexual desire; in Leonardo's case we can point to the information that comes form Vasari, that the heads of laughing women and beautiful boys—in other words, representations of his sexual objects—were notable among his first artistic endeavours. [Freud, 1910c, pp. 132–3]

It may well be argued that Freud's pathography of Leonardo's work is simply designed to advance Freud's concern to frame the dynamic of narcissistic investment as a vehicle for opening up the question of homo-erotic attachment. Certainly Freud's intention for this essay was not to venture towards aesthetic evaluation, since Freud implied that aesthetic judgements stood beyond the range of the psychoanalytic project declaring that, "Before the problem of the creative artist analysis must, alas, lay down its arms". (Freud, 1928, p. 177) As we can observe Freud appears to be quite determined to state the basis of Leonardo's preoccupations within his paintings, on the one hand, while appearing to mourn the limitations of psychoanalytic explanation, on the other. Perhaps Freud's poignant 'alas' masks a level of questioning that he experienced in studying Leonardo so closely.

Yet what is obviously lacking in Freud's evaluation of Leonardo's artistic production is the absence of any critical historical positioning of his work. For example, at the time of Leonardo's apprenticeship the employment of boys as young as six years old meant that they learnt their skills and approach from the teaching of their masters. Thus it must be remembered that from boyhood Leonardo had predictably served the Renaissance aesthetic. Since

Leonardo's subject matter was bound to subscribe to the genre of the time, it could be argued from a broader social/cultural perspective that Freud's hasty assumptions as to the narcissistic revelations within Leonardo's work appear to be crudely fashioned. This is especially relevant when we consider other artists of the period who promote depictions of the Nativity which equally portray the adored Christ Child captivated by the maternal gaze. Notwithstanding this obvious concern for the lack of context in Freud's speculations it is significant that within the field of psychoanalysis Freud's pathography (despite the vulture/kite dichotomy) appears to have taken root.

The search for the 'maternal phallus'

Not least among those who have built upon Freud's analysis of Leonardo is the work of the French psychoanalyst Julia Kristeva, whose seminal text, *Desire in Language: A Semiotic Approach to Literature and Art* (1980), outlines a distinction between the works of Leonardo da Vinci and Giovanni Bellini in terms of narcissistic aim. Kristeva claims that there are 'two destinies' that have dominated Western Culture in terms of artistic practice. Her concern is to demonstrate that much of post-Renaissance painting has derived its impetus from the prospect of shoring up the patriarchal dominance of the primary signifier—the phallus—at the expense of repudiating the maternal discourse. This is a complex argument that is based upon Kristeva's appropriation of the Lacanian perspective which proposes language as the foundation of social oppression. In her terms we are repressed by our entry into language, the 'symbolic order' and as 'speaking and writing subjects' are required thereafter to survive the psychological cleavage which has been bought about by the ensuing enculturation.

That is to say, Kristeva conceives two processes of communicative interaction: the *semiotic* which pertains to the "organisation, or disposition, within the body of instinctual drives as they affect language and its practice"; and the *symbolic*, the realm of judgement, "sign and syntax, paternal function, grammatical and social constraints, symbolic law". (Kristeva, 1980, p. 7) It is her view that artistic practice operates to either subvert or to reinforce this symbolic law. In the case where the artist is seen to shore up the symbolic order (the law), Kristeva attributes the ambition as that of a secondary narcissistic investment, which inevitably will deny the primary infant experience of symbiotic maternal engagement. Kristeva indicates that the outcome of this transposition from the semiotic realm to symbolic coherence is the construction of a compensatory phantasy, the 'phallic mother", the purpose of which is to retrieve symbolically the loss of the maternal body. Thus, the conceptualisation of motherhood, through the dominance of symbolic signification, is seen by Kristeva to have been irreversibly canalised and the principle of the emergence of the fiction of the phallic mother compensates the reality that renders the 'maternal realm' permanently subversive. It is from this position that Kristeva's marks out the contrast between Leonardo and Bellini in their treatment of the Virgin and Child. Her claim is that Leonardo's work serves his narcissistic longing in portraying Virgins in states of pleasurable absorption with their infants as an attempt to represent his phantasy of maternal seduction. Defining Leonardo's mother as the primordial seducer unconsciously dominating his work she claims that:

> His was the forbidden mother because she was the primordial seducer. ... She established the child's diffident narcissism and cult of the masculine body which he ceaselessly painted.

Such a stance, we are warned, renders the work unsatisfying since it remains the "fetishistic search for the maternal phallus" offering an "abundance of objects and bodies which ceaselessly excite and disappoint". (Kristeva, 1980, pp. 245–6) Kristeva concludes that Leonardo "eclipses maternal imprint by his own symbolic power", which enables her to cast Leonardo's work as simply a portrayal of narcissistic infant omnipotence. From this position she asserts that his work will inevitably fail to reach its full potential, namely, fail to offer the viewer a representation of 'maternal jouissance'.

By means of a contrast, Kristeva presents the work of Giovanni Bellini as exemplar in its non-narcissistic aims. She argues that in Leonardo's case the characteristic depiction of the Virgin's solicitous gesture and smile convinces us that her infant is the centre of her universe in which the "maternal figure is completely absorbed with her baby". (Kristeva, 1980, p. 245) Bellini, in constrast, is seen to present a very different analysis of maternal engagement for it is

Kristeva's claim that he shocks us by the mother's apparent distance which, although intimate in terms of the body contact, draws us to question the object of the Virgin's distraction. From this position, Kristeva asserts that Bellini appears to rob the infant of the narcissistic joy of the intimacy of the maternal gaze. That is to say, typically Bellini's Madonnas, rather than gazing adoringly at the Christ Child (as in the case of those of Leonardo) appear to look outwardly and beyond the child. This element of otherness within the apparent distraction draws Kristeva to conclude that Bellini's Madonnas speak of an unreachable 'maternal jouissance' that cannot be fully signified. She furthers her hypothesis by referring to the architectonics of (Fig. 1) Bellini's paintings suggesting that it is within the clashes and resonances of the colours and forms that this fugitive jouissance becomes manifest.

Significantly, Kristeva positions her argument as to the inferior nature of Leonardo's work (in failing to reference the unsignifiable maternal jouissance) as the result of his lack of fathering throughout his infancy. This is set in contrast to Bellini whose father was present throughout his childhood and we are led to believe that

Fig.1.Giovanni Bellini, *The Virgin and Child*, workshop of probably 1480–1490. Copyright © National Gallery, London.

thispaternal presence mitigated the prospect of Bellini forming a homo-erotic narcissistic attachment to his mother. Kristeva declares Leonardo's fixation virtually in polemical terms when she states:

> Thus, we have the typical configuration of a homosexual structure. Persuaded by precocious seduction and double motherhood of the existence of the maternal phallus, [Leonardo] never stopped looking for fetish equivalents in the bodies of young people, in his friendships with them, in his miserly worship of objects and money and in his avoidance of all contact with and access to the feminine body. [Kristeva, 1980, p. 344–5]

What is apparent here in the term 'double motherhood' is a direct reference to the painting of 'the Virgin and St. Anne' confirming that Kristeva has taken up Freud's interpretation of Leonardo's work as the product of the repressed narcissistic longing (the longing to be in the place of the boy adored by the mother) which led to homoeroticisation of desire. As it has already been mentioned, in contrast, Kristeva promotes the work of Bellini as addressing that of which the mother cannot speak, "the ineffable jouissance", deriving from her claim that Bellini was able to relinquish narcissistic attachment to the mother through his identification with the father. What is more important is that the works of each artist are seen equally to be in contrast in terms of affect, i.e., Leonardo's work is deemed to 'excite and disappoint' while Bellini's work is seen to offer an enduring engagement with the non-configurable maternal realm. Of Giovanni Bellini we are told that, through his identification with his father (Jacopo) who was an established artist, there was the prospect of "penetrating through the being and language of the father to position himself in the place where the mother could have been reached". (Kristeva, 1980, p. 249) It has been stated above that Kristeva asserts that within Bellini's paintings the paradoxical absence of the Virgin's gaze toward her infant becomes highly evocative, coupled with the attention to the body contact through the hands. These are the crucial factors that Kristeva draws upon to demonstrate that Bellini was in touch with the maternal function through the transposition of narcissistic attachment. The following passage sets out Kristeva's determination to locate an oppositional psychological basis of the work of these two esteemed Renaissance artists:

... let us also behold the distance, if not hostility, separating the bodies of infant and mother in [Bellini's] paintings. Maternal space is there, nevertheless—fascinating, attracting and puzzling. But we have no direct access to it. As if it were a maternal function that, unlike the mother's solicitude in Leonardo's painting toward the baby-object of all desire, was merely ineffable jouissance, beyond discourse, beyond narrative, beyond psychology, beyond lived experience and biography—in short, beyond figuration. [Kristeva, 1980, p. 247]

As we can see Kristeva has not only reinforced Freud's analysis of Leonardo's narcissistic engagement with his work, but she has indicated that certain artists (exemplified by Bellini) can go beyond subjectivity to seek that which cannot be reached. This position, as already mentioned, casts Leonardo's complex narratives as seductive but disappointing, since it is her view that the fugitive maternal *function* (ineffable jouissance) heralds the sublime. Again, from an 'art historical' perspective, Kristeva's contrast can appear to be limited by the fact that she does not fully address the influences and demands on Leonardo and Bellini at that time. What is lacking is a full exposition of the relationship between genres, specifically the aesthetic contrast of Florence and Venice.

Authentic versus factitious creation

In order to demonstrate further the psychoanalytic tendency to attribute certain art products to narcissistic aims, I will now turn to the influential writings of Janine Chasseguet-Smirgel who equally holds that artistic creation can be engendered either to facilitate psychological development or, on the contrary, to play a role in reinforcing the ego's defences. Smirgel suggests that at root the creative enterprise is primarily concerned with the restoration and maintenance of self-esteem which marks the end of primary narcissism. In studying Smirgel's position, it is relevant to acknowledge that although Smirgel has not directly addressed Freud's pathographic essay on Leonardo, she appears to be in no doubt about the prospect of the narcissistic investment of certain artistic practice. That is to say, Smirgel's intention is to demonstrate that certain artistic practice suffers from a lack of objectification in its purposes since the primary aim is compensatory rather than sublimatory. Clearly from this perspective, the influence of Freud's analysis of the fetishistic nature of narcissistic attachment is in evidence.

Smirgel's position borders on the polemic since she suggests that there are those art works that achieve 'authenticity', while others remain 'factitious'. When she uses the term factitious, she is not referring to deliberate imitation or counterfeit: rather she draws assumptions from what she considers to be the level of the artist's psychological maturity. Authentic works in Smirgel's terms are seen to be solely the product of those artists who recognise 'the difference between the sexes and the generations'; in other words, the work of an individual who has resolved the Oedipal conflict and secured maturity in terms of genitality. (Smirgel, 1984) A key factor of this proposition is Smirgel's analysis of the dynamic of the 'ego ideal' which she determines as thwarting the prospect of the Oedipal resolution in the case of the individual whom she cites as producing factitious work. A fundamental question that Smirgel attempts to solve is how to distinguish between a work of art and a neurotic symptom. What Smirgel emphasises is one of the positions that has dominated psychoanalytic preoccupations with artistic creation, namely, that a work of art can be limited by the fact that it serves narcissistic ambition. Significantly, both Smirgel and Kristeva concern themselves with this form of aesthetic evaluation by locating the psychological capacity of the artist; simply put, mature psyches are seen to produce superior work. This approach to aesthetics marks a shift away from the traditional view that it is the artist who is imbued with a creative capacity to a greater or lesser degree (often referred to as talent) which is seen to be independent of the individual's psychological maturity. Smirgel not only claims that a work that is narcissistically dominated will fail to gratify the viewer, since it will appear to lack depth, but she offers a description of the affect of those works which are seen to reach the optimum, namely, authenticity.

Let us consider the means by which Smirgel identifies factitious creation. Fundamental to Smirgel's analysis is the role of the pre-genital ego ideal which is seen to carry the artist's narcissistic projections. In her analyses of the ego ideal, Smirgel critically reads Freud's earlier writings in which he discusses the role of the ego ideal in mitigating the loss of omnipotence as the infant grows to understand that he is not the sole object of his mother's love. That is to say, the ego ideal is seen as the agency that allows the infant to relinquish the primary narcissistic longing to be 'all that the mother desires' by offering a compensatory secondary narcissistic alliance that is also to be eventually given up. As Freud states,

> [man] is not willing to forgo the narcissistic perfection of his childhood..[and] seeks to recover it in a new form of an ego ideal. What he projects before him as his ideal is the substitute for the lost narcissism of his childhood in which he was his own ideal. [Freud, 1914c, p. 94]

Smirgel's intention is to reinforce the contrast between the pre-Oedipal compensatory institution of the ego ideal (as a necessary transitional narcissistic construction to which Freud's earlier writings refer) to that of his later writings which indicate the ego ideal as the agency for the resolution of the Oedipal conflict. Utilising this contrast, namely, the pre-Oedipal attachment to the projection of the self as ideal and the post-Oedipal resolution of this ideal as an aspect of the superego, Smirgel offers two scenarios for the creative individual and for the art work produced. There are those works which are dominated by the pre-Oedipal ego ideal (which she terms 'perverse') and those works which are situated within the social contract of law and order which embrace the ego ideal of the Oedipal resolution. Smirgel's position is as follows: On the one hand, artistic creation is part of the natural order of 'universal law' (the world of truth) which depends on the difference between the sexes and the generations; on the other hand, artistic creation is seen to stand as an artificial dynamic: an inauthentic ornament adorning the 'anal universe' (the world of falsity) which derives its impetus from the agency of the pre-genital ego ideal. The passage below emphasises Smirgel's perception of the problematic of factitious creation.

> It seems to me that the pervert's creation represents the proto-type of these creations of the anal phallus, a factitious penis whose kinship with the fetish is undeniable. Certainly the pervert does not have the monopoly of these factitious creations, but the process involved is similar to his. [Smirgel, 1984, p. 69]

Fundamentally, Smirgel holds that the narcissistic aims of the pre-genital ego ideal are a limiting factor as far as authentic creativity is concerned. Yet what is surprising, in contrast to what seems to be a reactionary analysis, is that Smirgel frames the dynamic of 'genius' in broader terms. As if she has taken up Freud's position in relation to Leonardo, she indicates that the 'gifted individual' draws inspiration from both the narcissistic investment of pre-Oedipal grandiosity and the resolution of the post-Oedipal social contract with the law. As she puts it:

> A characterological analysis of a highly gifted individual and in particular in one with an artistic disposition, may reveal a mixture in every proportion of efficiency, perversion and neurosis. [Smirgel, 1984, p. 90]

What is implied here is that the gifted individual has the capacity to exhibit narcissistic 'perverted' responses while at the same time is able to sustain a neurotic part of the personality, thus leaving the 'door open' for a degree of libidinal energy to be diverted towards sublimative aims. As we have seen this reflects the paradox that Freud presents in relation to Leonardo, since Freud both refers to Leonardo's work as exhibiting fetishistic narcissistic ambitions while claiming that Leonardo demonstrated an 'extraordinary capacity for sublimation'. But the question to raise is how does Smirgel identify the constituents of 'authentic creation'. As already stated, she locates 'factitious creation' as that which lacks depth and it is evident that she determines the affect of the work as indicating the psychological capacity of the artist producing it. But how is the affect of an authentic work to be assessed? Authenticity in Smirgel's view has no glittering facade, rather she emphasises the 'plainness and truth' of the authentic artefact. This is exemplified by her use of an excerpt from Troilus speaking to Cressida when the latter warns of the prospect of being seduced by the 'dazzling' quality which reflects the over-aestheticisation of idealisation that characterises factitious works:

> "Whilst others fish with craft for great opinion
> I with great truth catch mere simplicity:
> Whilst some with cunning gild their copper crowns,
> With truth and plainness I do wear mine bare."
>
> [Smirgel, 1984, p. 100]

Furthermore, Smirgel proposes that the depth of authentic aesthetic experience depends on the artist offering a trajectory to the "very exposure of primary processes, which relies on the economy of means", a quality that is unachievable through any creation governed by the ego ideal. This exposure of primary processes is identified as the dynamic which affects the viewer when contemplating the authentic work. Smirgel explains this concept by reference to the phrase "[l]ong, backward-looking incline" which she promotes in an attempt to encapsulate the depth of experience, namely, the transformation of primitive instinct through sublimation. (Smirgel, 1975, p. 115) Smirgel holds that it is only possible in cases where the work benefits from the intermediary of sublimation that the viewer can enjoy his/her own equivalent instinct through the contemplation of the authentic work. She contrasts works which inhibit access to this trajectory as the repression of primary process and a limitation of affect, claiming that where narcissistic identifications ensure the supremacy of the pre-genital ego ideal the work will inevitably remain inadequate. Thus, Smirgel emphasises that it is only when primary processes are utilised and transformed through sublimation, that creative expression is allowed to explore "the wealth and multiplicity of emotions, effects and images lying along the whole length of that '[l]ong, backward-looking incline'". (Smirgel, 1975, p. 115) So convinced is Smirgel of her analysis of the affect of authentic creation that she confidently explains how certain works facilitate our capacity to experience primitive instinct:

> A verse of Ulahume, any Paul Klee or Nicholas de Stael drawing, a few chords by Bach take us at an instant through the vast areas of the psyche and leave us marvelling at the wealth of emotion poured out through a whole series of condensed images that are spread before us, all issuing from primitive instinct. Like a deep-sea diver discovering a lost kingdom, the work suddenly illuminates the unconscious and its light spreads right to the surface. [Smirgel, 1975, p. 115]

As we can see Smirgel offers an aesthetic evaluation in terms of the simplicity and truth of authenticity and appears to shun the prospect that creativity can reward with excess. From this perspective the exuberance of the Baroque period of painting, for example, would be interpreted as serving both the narcissistic desires of the viewer and certainly the narcissistic ambitions of its creators. Again, it is clearly the case (as with Freud and Kristeva) that Smirgel's analysis pays scant attention to the social/historical influences that equally forge the co-ordinates of the art object as those of the psychopathology of the creator. For example, in suggesting that 'any Paul Klee' offers the illumination that depends upon the accessibility of the depth of 'primitive instinct' demonstrates that Smirgel is simply choosing a European artist that could be easily assimilated (with his subtle decorative representative abstract narratives) without providing us with the historical positioning of Klee's documented ambitions (see Klee's Pedagogical Sketchbooks).

As we have seen, it is obvious that both Smirgel and Kristeva cast the narcissistic aim within the art work as that which limits affect. Clearly there are aesthetic implications in the kind of oppositions that they each provide. Both writers claim that the most effective work is that which reaches the mystery of primary experience: for Kristeva, this is the fugitive realm of 'maternal jouissance"; for Smirgel, it is the 'lost kingdom' of primitive instinct. Each writer implies that the viewer will gain from the art work that does not aim to seduce, rather they deify the artist whom they present as exhibiting the capacity to access the essential meaning of early experience and who thereby signifies the affect of the necessary transformative aesthetic. But in each case the accountability of this aesthetic is problematised, since it is the resolution of the Oedipal conflict that is seen to be generative of authentic creativity.

What this tendency suggests is that psychoanalysts find it difficult to bear the vagaries of creativity, not least in their understanding of the processes of sublimation. Clearly, this is in part due to the difficulty of Freud's original thesis on Leonardo and also due to Freud's lack of resolution of the essential nature of sublimation. As Laplanche and Pontalis point out:

> In the psycho-analytic literature the concept of sublimation is frequently called upon; the idea indeed answers a basic need of Freudian doctrine and it is hard to see how it could be dispensed with. The lack of coherent theory of sublimation remains one of the lacunae in psychoanalytic thought. [Laplanche & Pontalis, 1967, p. 433]

'Beauty and ugliness'

Notwithstanding the legacy of these theoretical complications, it is important to include the work of Hanna Segal which becomes equally relevant to this discussion. Central to Segal's analysis of creative practice is her involvement with Klein, on the one hand and, on the other, her significant contribution to the *Imago Group* that focussed primarily on the viewer's experience of the artefact in respect of aesthetic evaluation. It is interesting that the *Imago Group* included not only psychoanalysts whom had a specific interest in creativity, but also leading art theorists of the day whom were intent upon defining aesthetic criteria in relation to various aspects of artistic practice. That is to say, leading psychoanalysts, such as Segal, engaged with the analysis of art process with, for example, established art historians, such as Adrian Stokes and Richard Wollheim, both of whom were in turn fascinated by psychoanalytic interpretations of artefacts. From this position Segal wrote a seminal article for the *Times Literary Supplement* in 1975, titled *Art and the Inner World* which provided a further example of the view that narcissistic gain could impair creative practice.

Segal sets up an opposition that is far more outspoken than either Kristeva or Smirgel in that she uses discriminatory terms that are commonly understood, namely, 'beauty' and 'ugliness'. Significantly, for Segal, the basis of this opposition is not seen to solely reflect the artist's literal creative ability in terms of competence: rather, it is deemed to indicate the status of the stability of the artist's 'inner world'. What this means is that work that is seen to be sufficient in gratifying the viewer is attributed to the harmonious internal resolution of the 'depressive position' (in Kleinian terms) that bids for reparation, set in opposition to works that offer no resolution. The latter are cast as unsatisfying in bearing the scars of subliminal psychotic manifestation. For work that owes its affects to the congruence of the inner world Segal institutes 'beauty', that is, all that will satisfy (in terms of a sense of wholeness), while work which speaks of narcissistic engagement is identified as overwhelmed with discord, namely 'ugliness', that is seen to destroy not only the inner world, but the prospect of the aesthetic. The following passage demonstrates Segal's proposition:

... the ugly corresponds to the destroyed, to the fragmented, lacking in rhythm and wholeness and harmony. I would say the ugly signifies the destruction of the internal world and its results; the beautiful is usually seen as rhythmical, the harmonious, the whole—corresponding to the experience of a loved, whole good object and self. [Segal, 1975, T.L.S]

The question that now arises is: how does Segal validate such stark distinctions? Central to Segal's position is her conviction that the problematic of psychotic processing will, through narcissistic investment, inevitably impair creative potential and thereby aesthetic judgement. The means by which she discriminates is through her analyses of symbolic functioning which are associated with Klein's phases of infant development, namely, the paranoid-schizoid and the depressive position. Her claim is that the symbolic process within the paranoid-schizoid position is very different in function to that of the depressive position. In the paranoid-schizoid position the mode is seen to be a 'primitive function' identified as 'symbolic equation' constituting the concretisation of bodily experiences, while in the depressive position, it is understood to have matured into a transformative modality (sublimation) and is described as 'symbolic representation'. That is to say, in the first case the object is experienced as interchangeable with its bodily counterpart, while in the second, the object is experienced as divorced from the affects of its original impetus to become the medium for transformation. What is significant in the context of art practice is Segal's view that the capacity for symbolic representation is seen to be the critical feature of mature creative expression. Furthermore, ironically, Segal emphasises that aesthetic achievement (beauty) partakes of some aspect of symbolic equation to give the mature work its 'punch' without which it would be mere decoration. As she states:

Any art, in particular, does embody concrete symbolic elements that give the work its immediate punch; it has a concrete impact on our experience provided it is included in an otherwise more evolved type of symbolism [symbolic representation], without which it would be no more than a meaningless bombardment. [Segal, 1991, p. 43]

If it can be argued that valued artistic expression is seen inevitably to involve a synthesis of concrete symbolic elements and symbolic representations, the issue here again is that of the artist's psychological maturity. Segal has implied that a 'truly' creative individual is someone who has developed sufficiently to be capable of readily accessing primitive schizoid phantasies which are transformed and transmuted for depressive purposes within artistic production. In this light, Segal's understanding of the dynamic of successful artistic practice is that it should harness paranoid-schizoid phantasy yet not find itself thus dominated. What this means is that (as with Smirgel and Kristeva) the resolution of the Oedipal conflict is seen to be the necessary condition that will ensure that the artist will gain the capacity to provide the desired affect. Thus, Segal offers yet another example of the narcissistically fixated artist who is unable to touch upon the sublime.

The artist as affective

It is evident from the positions of psychoanalytic thinking outlined above that there remains a view that psychological maturity provides/produces the aesthetic. Successful art has been named as that which will inevitably gain the desired level of affect that a narcissistically dominated work will fail to achieve. What this conclusio nraises is the problematic of art practice in that there is no doubt that many leading artists have suffered psychologically, to the extent that they have been identified as regressed, yet can be seen to have produced mature works (we only have to think of Van Gogh as one example). Furthermore, it was Anthony Storr in his seminal text of 1972 *Dynamics of Creation and* his later work in the Eighties (where he discusses genius) who indicated that more often than not it is the narcissistic personality that becomes the crucible for creative inspiration. In a paper titled *Creative Solitude,* he emphasises that many leading thinkers and artists preferred a solitary life and unconventional relationships, stating:

> When I was in a conference in Germany, one of the participants drew my attention to the fact that nearly all the great philosphers

of the Western World since the Greeks lacked a normal family life. This is true of Descartes, Locke, Hume, Pascal, Spinoza, Kant, Leibniz, Shopenhauer, Nietzsche, Kierkegaard and Wittgenstein. Some of these men of genius had transient sexual affairs with either men or women; but none of them married and most lived alone most of their lives.... I think that contemporary psycho-analytic wisdom is mistaken in thinking that satisfactory object-relationships are the sole source of human happiness. [Storr, 1987, p. 43]

Storr may well have added that 'contemporary psychoanalytic wisdom' could also be mistaken in attributing the capacity of the artist as directly relevant to the capacity of psychological maturity. Furthermore, as we have seen, he claims that a considerable access to narcissistic aim can be the necessary catalyst for artistic achievement, rather than, as indicated by the writers above, cited as the impediment to sublime affect.

Thus, we have a paradox: on the one hand, psychological maturity is seen to be related to the capacity for authentic creation, while, on the other, at least a level of narcissistic ambition is seen to be effectively furnishing original thinking. What seems to be the case is that Freud's original thesis on Leonardo has borne fruit, since although Freud indicated that it was Leonardo's narcissistic fetishistic attachment that led to his seductive engagement with his work, he also marvelled at what he termed Leonardo's "extraordinary capacity for sublimating the primitive instinct". (Freud, 1910c, p. 136) It is interesting that Klein frames the question that Freud did not solve when she asks, "how did Leonardo escape hysteria?" From her reading of Freud's analysis of Leonardo's 'precocious arousal' in infancy, she determines that the predictable outcome for Leonardo would be fixation and that this route was avoided by the fact that, first, Leonardo had the capacity in infancy to make "far-reaching identifications with the objects in the world around him", second, that he had the "ability to hold libido in a state of suspension" and the third capacity Klein describes as "the ease with which an ego-activity or tendency takes on libidinal cathexis". (Klein, 1921–45, p. 87) What this means is that Klein identifies Leonardo's extraordinary capacity for sublimation as fundamentally dispositional without which the outcome of his experience of 'precocious arousal' would not have offered so rich a harvest. Perhaps the apparent combination of such discreet dispositional capacities that Klein locates in relation to Leonardo mark out the constituents of 'talent'.

CHAPTER NINE

Narcissism, individuation and old age

Rob Mawdsley

Whatever the 21st century brings, one characteristic seems, on present trends, to be certain and needs to be taken on board by therapeutic practitioners: there will be a greatly increased population of older people, resulting from the 'baby boom' period of the immediate post war years–what has been termed, perhaps pejoratively, 'the demographic time bomb'. Alongside this, we see in North America and Western Europe at least a decline in the birth rate over the past twenty years or so, so that—whatever the consequences of immigration from the new members of the European Union–the number of old people will have increased quite dramatically and will be all the more notice-able as the younger population declines. Latest forecasts suggest for example that by 2013 the number of pensioners will exceed the number of children under sixteen (ONS/The Guardian, 22.03.05). People are also living longer and are for the most part physically healthier, so that it is estimated for example that by 2050 one per-son in five in the UK (12 million) will be over seventy and that there will be a further 8 million in their sixties (Bakewell in The Guardian, 31.01.04). Retirement from full-time work will mean perhaps twenty or more years of life for many and possibly those years will imply a search for a new role in life and a search for meaning beyond that offered by occupation. Society in general will need to re-evaluate its own attitudes towards older people; for example the ambivalence currently felt between the notion of 'old people as a burden' (hence the 'demographic time bomb' beloved of leader-writers) and the rather idealized images of old people as 'cuddly' or 'sweet' (in a sense, infantilising old people).

One can see this deep ambivalence in the following example. In the exceptionally hot summer of 2003, more than 15,000 old people died in France as a direct consequence of the heat (The Guardian, 23.12.2003). In the resulting enquiry it was said that the major cause was that the regular 'flight to the south' in August by most French families almost invariably left behind elderly parents, many of whom suffered as a consequence. However, following these dreadful events, a kind of collective denial took place in that country about what had happened and it certainly never became the enduring scandal that might have been expected. A similar story also emerged in several other European countries during that time and lest the British reader be complacent about such matters, a report by the WRVS (BBC Radio 4 News–08.03.2004) estimated that over 12,000 old people die alone each year in Britain, having had no contact with friends or relatives during the period leading up to their deaths.

What I am suggesting here is that there has been a tendency to somehow turn our faces away from older people *as people*. It is far easier to stereotype or to ignore completely than to accept the fact that old age does not mean the removal of individuality or humanity. To the question of why this might be so, I further suggest that it has to do with an unwillingness to face our own process of ageing and inevitable death; thus when gazing into the face of an old person, one sees one's own–and as in Wilde's *A Picture of Dorian Gray*–and one might become horrified at the realization that 'old age' is within us all and, literally, 'is only a matter of time'. I place this in the above social context, simply because there will be many more older people around–visible, probably more active and likely to be more vocal and politically powerful. This I believe will have consequences not only for older people themselves, who will have more time to reflect on their lives, but also on the younger population whose attitudes toward their own lives, towards the ageing process and a search for meaning, is likely to be challenged by this new *demographic reality*. As Bakewell (2004), clearly optimistic about this trend, has written:

> There will be a new generation of sprightly old people, many still working, plenty of them around and about, hell-bent on having a good time and being useful and vocal in their communities. [Bakewell in The Guardian, 31.01.2004]

Equally, however, there will be considerable numbers of those older people coming to terms with a life characterized by a significant sense of loss, regrets about their lives and unable to come to terms with themselves in old age. Just as it may be said that the roots of racism (Fanon, 1968) and homophobia lie in the fears within darker recesses of our psyche and confront us with unpalatable truths about ourselves, I suggest here that our feelings about older people are characterized by deep ambivalence. As one consultant psychiatrist who specializes in working with older people has pithily written:

> The congratulations given to people seeming younger than their years reflects the negative view of old age that permeates our culture. [Garner, 2002, p. 128]

Given the inevitability, in my view, that the client list of therapists will reflect the demographic shift described above, a readiness to address the specific issues relating to older people appears vital.

In this paper, I will try to explore some of these issues, focusing on the concept of *narcissism* as it may apply to older clients and shall attempt to show the link between this and the notion of *individuation*. Although it will be noted that I adopt a largely Jungian perspective to underpin my argument, I shall also be drawing on the work of Kohut and Erikson and other theorists. Finally, I will include some examples from my own therapeutic work and that of other practitioners, in order to make the link between theory and practice.

Psychoanalytic views on older people

In my definition of 'old/older' I do not intend to be prescriptive and, indeed, I shall work from the premise that we are concerned here as much with the *process of ageing* as with the reaching of an arbitrary age when one is considered to be 'old'. Whatever their obvious differences, Freud and Jung, for example, were very conscious that 'mid-life' represented a significant shift in the psyche, so perhaps it can be agreed at least that this is the point when an individual's concerns about ageing begin. Whether this occurs in one's forties or fifties is a moot point and, of course, when reading psychoanalytic literature one must always be aware of the era in which these texts were written. So that in 1933, when Jung referred to forty as the 'noon of life' and a 'zenith' (Colarusso & Demiroff, 1981), I believe one cannot be too rigid about this today, given the great increases in longevity referred to in this introduction as well as the changes in social mores (e.g., later marriage and procreation).

Nevertheless, what can be said is that a significant strand of psychoanalytic thought regarded working with people over fifty as an impossible task. It was suggested that anyone over this age was too psychologically rigid and that there was too vast an amount of material to be covered (Bateman & Holmes, 1995). The former point does seem rather ironic, however, when one considers that Sophocles was over seventy when he wrote Oedipus Tyrannus and that both Freud and Jung were likewise both productive in their later years.

Therefore, it can be observed that differing views about the 'second half of life' exist in the psychoanalytic field and although I do not intend to focus on the precise distinctions (for example, between Freud and Jung) in this paper, it is worth noting that these differences very much reflect society's own ambivalence towards old age.

Nevertheless, any discussion of old age unavoidably concentrates on how an individual deals with his/her *mortality*, with the inevitability of his/her death. Death can be seen as the ultimate 'narcissistic wound' the prospect of which, for many, is quite literally 'unbearable'. As Yalom (1989) writes:

> We know about death, intellectually we know the facts, but we–that is, the unconscious portion of the mind that protects us from overwhelming anxiety–have split off, or dissociated, the terror of death. [Yalom, 1989, p. 5]

From my own clinical experience of a 68-year-old woman, beset by depression and anxiety, the subject of her own death was never mentioned, until one day she told me of a dream that her dog had died. It emerged after some time that her earliest memories of love, in the absence of familial affection, was that of curling up beside the family dog. She also told me she had felt 'alive' only when this happened. From this we began to work around the central issue which was deeply disturbing her, that is, the fear of dying alone–as her mother had done. In her case, interestingly, she had had in childhood a 'crisis of faith' which had led her to reject religious belief entirely. Now in her later years and faced with physical and emotional stresses and the prospect of death, she is in the process of a kind of 'spiritual re-awakening' which seems to be, as it were, proceeding alongside the therapeutic process.

Thus, it is how one faces death, how individuals deal with–on a deeper, non-intellectual level–their own mortality that I believe is central to psychotherapeutic work with older people. It is not that the issues of relationships, sexual conflicts, feelings about one's childhood experience are irrelevant to older people; clearly they are not. What is the case, however, is that in later life all of these issues tend to be seen in the context of what I can only term a *life-evaluation*, asking the question "how did I get here and how can I incorporate the experience of 'good' or 'bad' into a meaningful whole to help me live successfully now, but also meet the end of my life 'gracefully', as it were?" A reply to these questions will be attempted by approaching the specific phenomenon of *narcissism* as it applies to the ageing process.

Narcissism and ageing

In writing about narcissism, I feel that from the outset I should acknowledge that this is an area of considerable controversy in psychoanalysis and its very existence is open to debate. For example, the Kleinians speak of 'pathological defensive organisations' rather than narcissism, implying, as Steiner (1997) has suggested, a kind of *'psychic retreat"*, born out of an innate hostility to relationship. Aside from debates over the existence of narcissism, there is the belief by some that the very word has "inescapable disparaging overtones". (see Rycroft, 1995) However, this is an accusation which applies to the majority of psychoanalytic terminology and therefore I think it is something that just has to be 'lived with", though always recognizing that it is the person, not the label, with whom therapists are concerned in their practice.

Thus, in the following—which is not an analysis of narcissism as such, but more of a reflection on the insights the concept of narcissism can offer as it applies to psychotherapeutic work with older people–I am aware of the existing controversy, but have nevertheless accepted the value of the concept. What should be made clear from the outset, however, is that in employing the term 'narcissism', the reader should understand that I am referring to 'unhealthy narcissism", rather than a more normative state which can be seen as in many ways desirable, for example, a strong sense of self and positive self-image. Conversely, 'unhealthy narcissism' is fundamentally a *defence mechanism* with pathological implications. In this context, this is a defence against ageing itself and all that seems to represent for many (loss of autonomy, physical decline and the constant fear of dying). Rather than employ specific adjectives with which to prefix the word, then, I have tended to use the accepted convention and simply used the word 'narcissism'. I shall however clarify the distinction later in the chapter.

For the narcissistic person, the ageing process almost inevitably brings about crisis. As Jacobs (1998) writes:

> Since a narcissistic person has a fragile sense of self, which constantly needs boosting, there may well be real difficulties for the self-absorbed person in mid-life, when physical well-being begins to wane, illness becomes more common and the signs of ageing are more apparent. [Jacobs, 1998, p. 64]

Jacobs goes on to refer to an article by Chessick (1983) in which a client in her late forties, a successful musician who had very much relied upon her achievements and the acclaim of others, came into therapy because she found she could no longer rely on past achievements to sustain her, now that she was becoming arthritic and was performing less well. She had also become depressed by the death of some friends and relatives, so that Chessick concluded she was "what we might call a 'successful narcissist' until the second half of her life". (Chessick in Jacobs, 1998, p. 65) It was also concluded, Jacobs writes, that the woman "had to face weakness and limitations in the immediate future and *mortality* in the long term". (Chessick in Jacobs, 1998, p. 65, my emphasis)

For Colarusso and Nemiroff (1981) the issue for such a patient would be that of *authenticity* (from the Greek authentikos–"one who does things for oneself"). They go on to say that the mature adult self, the *authentic* self,

> ... conveys a sense that one is singular (separated psychologically from parents, yet interdependent with important people in the present and capable of *making and accepting a realistic appraisal of life, including suffering, limitation and personal death ... regardless of the narcissistic injury involved.* [Colaruso & Nemiroff, 1981, p. 86, my emphasis]

For these authors, it is not enough to resolve the narcissistic issues of childhood, but they contend that adulthood and the ageing process *per se* can bring about new ones. Garner (2002), for example, suggests that ageing can be viewed as a "narcissistic wound from which there is no recovery". (Garner, 2002, p. 3) This is open to dispute, of course, given Chessick's contention that the patient was a "successful narcissist" until her crisis, rather than believing merely that 'new' narcissistic issues can be thrown up as one gets older. Personally, I would not wish to get bogged down with this debate here, save to say that, given its very nature, narcissism (both 'healthy' and 'unhealthy') surely has its roots in early infancy. Thus, Kohut (1971, 1977) maintained that, as it were 'unhealthy', secondary narcissism stems from deficiencies in the early bonding experience and leads to what has been called "a withdrawal into the self in the face of a hostile environment" (Bateman & Holmes, 1995, pp. 58–9) or what Winnicott regarded as 'a false self protecting a true self' (see Abram, 1996). Kohut is essentially saying that where an infant does not experience the positive parental responses necessary for the development of the self, this clearly has negative consequences in later life. For instance, severe disapproval or constantly 'letting down' the child carry with them the potential to create narcissistic disturbances into adulthood. One example of this, particularly relevant to this discussion, is Kohut's concept of the *'grandiose self'*. Kohut's view, in essence, is that an individual attempts to retain the all-encompassing narcissism of infanthood via a concentration of perfection upon the self. Such people–like the 'successful narcissist' described above–typically equate personal achievement (often exaggerated) with maturity and fulfilment. As Jacobs (1998) notes:

Where there is narcissistic injury, the child may grow into a grandiose person, as if they are always struggling to feel grand, but never succeed in this, *whatever their external achievements*. [Jacobs, 1998, p. 64, my emphasis]

Thus in later life, a narcissistic individual confronted with the distressing reality that his 'achievements' (and perhaps personal wealth and the acquisition of 'grand' material possessions) have failed to stave off profound emptiness and ultimate disappointment, can only regard his life as worthless and the thought of death terrifying. Jacoby (1989), in a discussion on Kohut's theories, refers to a kind of bipolarity between "a pole of ambitious initiative that strives for admiration and, on the other, a pole consisting of meaningful ideals". This type of 'self' is considered to be fundamentally healthy, having emerged from a transformation of the "archaic grandiose self" and where the bipolar tension is regulated by an individual's talents and skills. Where this fails, however, Jacoby concludes that a sense of "inner emptiness" ensues (Jacoby, 1989, p. 145). Conversely, an otherwise 'well-integrated' individual may in late adulthood display the return of aspects of the grandiose self as a narcissistic defence against ageing and the prospect of death. (Colarusso & Nemiroff, 1981, p. 99)

In any event, the re-emergence of narcissistic defences in later life as well as the realisation that a lifetime of narcissistic defence mechanisms must inevitably disappoint can lead ultimately to a point of despair. Kernberg (1977), for example, suggests that the narcissistic patient exhibits a painfully-felt 'envy' of herself as she was 'in the past'. (Kernberg in Colaruso & Nemiroff, 1981, p. 97) Incidentally, both Kohut and Kernberg have observed that in many cases "acute narcissistic disturbances break out from mid-life onwards". (Jacoby, 1990, p. 98)

This state of narcissism in later years implies an overwhelming sense of *disappointment*. Not in the normative, everyday use of that word, but in a far deeper, more profound sense, all the admiration one has sought–and may indeed have experienced—and the achievements, the accumulation of material wealth and so on, have in the end amounted to nothing. Lasch (1979) suggested that feelings of infantile grandiosity somehow alternate with an experience of anomie, of deep emptiness and inferiority, within the narcissistic personality. Further to this, he states that to be in a narcissistic state inevitably leads to a separation from other people, in any true sense of intimacy and meaningful personal relationships. In fact, Lasch posits that narcissistic self-organization is essentially a defence against infantile rage, which "focuses on a complete inability to accept reality itself". (Lasch in Elliot, 2002, p. 64) One can relate this to Winnicott's contention that primary narcissism is in fact a defence against a 'loss of sense of (what is) real'. (Winnicott, 1963)

Lasch essentially and rather pessimistically, also seems to imply that the modern world *per se* has created the narcissistic personality and that in fact we live in a narcissistic culture. Given the example in France quoted in my introduction, one can see that he has a point. For here we see an older, 'pre-modern' familial structure, (several generations living together), somehow disrupted by a consumerist 'flight to the South' for the August holidays–a very modern phenomenon which one can say represents a kind of *narcissistic greed* (my phrase) on which, one can argue, modern societies are built. It is instructive to note that in 2005 the French government's attempt to 'make amends' for the tragedy by asking the nation to work a bank holiday and donate the proceeds to 'the old", was met by a resounding *'Non'*. Very few workers took up the suggestion, which led to a comment from the French daily 'Le Figaro' that:

> The French prefer to take refuge in egoism and individualism … what reigns here is each for himself, a cult of the self. [The Guardian, 2005, p. 17].

Whether one accepts Lasch's wider criticism of narcissism and modern society or not, his description of this narcissistic 'modern' self, then, seems difficult to argue with:

> … [it is] unappeasably hungry for emotional experiences with which to fill an inner void; terrified of ageing and death. [Lasch, 1979, p. 82].

At this point, it is perhaps worth remembering the tragic *denouement* of Ovid's tale that Narcissus literally 'pines away'. Reflecting on this, Ledermann (1989) noted how her narcissistic patients often spoke of being in a 'living death", or belonging to 'the undead dead", concluding that such patients psychologically 'pine away' until they get help. Likewise, Symington (1993) refers to the 'internal saboteur' of the narcissist, which has led to a kind of 'living death' of non-relationship to others, rather than contending with the disappointments which 'true' relationships create. He seems to be saying here that the narcissist literally 'cannot bear' being seen for *who she really is*, beyond, as it were, the elaborate artifice of the carefully constructed narcissistic defence. Moreover, Jacques (1965) suggested that unconsciously we have our own 'private meaning' of death, the phantasy being essentially that of immobilisation and the fragmentation of the self. He further suggests that awareness of mortality in middle age is essentially a 'reworking' of the paranoid-schizoid/depressive conflict, which leads either to rage or to acceptance of one's limitations (the ultimate 'limitation' being death).

From all of this one can thus perhaps say that Narcissus failed to live *authentically* (see Fromm, 1991), to accept 'things as they really are' and this was the source of his undoing. It is this sense of, as it were, 're-connecting' with reality, or perhaps finding one's 'true self", that provides us with the central task of living authentically through old age towards the end of life.

Toward individuation and integration: the final task?

I now wish to go on to discuss the process of moving away from what Kernberg (1975) calls 'pathological' narcissism, with its implications of self-absorption (and self-delusion), towards what may be considered a psychologically healthy state of personal integration and individuation. Here I shall be drawing largely on the work of Erikson and Jung.

The rather pessimistic views of Lasch need in my view to be modified somewhat, inasmuch as we need to draw a distinction between 'healthy narcissism"–which Marcuse (1956) regarded as an essential condition for a "creative and autonomous engagement with self, others and the outside world" (Marcuse, 1956, p. 258)–and the idea of narcissistic disorder. Such a distinction is a source of some confusion in psychoanalysis, but one can perhaps simply say that narcissistic disorder is, essentially, an 'over-valuation of the ego", as opposed to the 'proper self-respect' afforded by healthy narcissism. (see Rycroft, 1995) In other words, in this as in all of life, in my view 'nothing is inevitable, but death'. This being the case, the road from the damaging dimensions of narcissism in old age towards integration and individuation is not somehow blocked forever by the nature of modern life, or the prevailing *zeitgeist* (which is itself, after all, merely fleeting). It is through the 'examined life' of ancient philosophy, by means of spirituality and religious experience in general and (in the context of this paper) by therapeutic intervention in particular, that 'the living death' experienced by some (perhaps many) in old age can be transformed into a positive experience.

The 'inevitability' (as seen by some) of decline and disappointment in old age has been challenged by the work of Erikson (1968, 1977). Reminding us that Erikson, far from denigrating Freud's legacy, actually built on it and that indeed Anna Freud was his 'psychoanalytic mentor'', Colarusso & Demiroff (1981) go on to contend that

> Erik Erikson provided the first psychosocially integrated view of how an individual develops *throughout* the life-cycle. [Colaruso & Nemiroff, 1981, p. 28, original emphasis]

From my perspective, I have discovered that Erikson's most helpful contribution to psychotherapeutic work with older people lies in his use of the little word *'versus'*! For in this can be seen that, indeed, 'nothing in life is inevitable' and that we as human beings are faced with choices at various times in our lives. It is true that such choices are often buried within the unconscious and need help to be 'excavated', as it were, but nevertheless even that process implies the choice of exploring oneself and one's psyche. The very act of entering into the therapy room is itself a choice and one thing I have learned in my practice is never to underestimate how profound and courageous such a choice is for the client. Indeed, I was awakened to this quite recently when a forty year old female client entered the room, sat down and began to weep uncontrollably for the entire session–a mixture of sadness and relief that she had finally decided to "come clean" with herself (her words) and face reality. For Margaret (not her real name) "time" (she felt) was "running out". She told me that if she did not face her problems now, she would carry the burden forever and could not face that prospect. Thus, Margaret was "looking ahead" at herself in the future, imagining what she would look like and was filled with dread. None of her successes–she is a book editor–any longer had *meaning and* she had been so wrapped up in a version of herself which was at some fundamental level *false,* that she instinctively knew that something felt 'wrong'. Yes, Margaret was distressed when she sat down and wept during that first meeting. But through her distress there was what Symington (1993) has called "an essential spark of goodness" which counter-balances the "internal saboteur of the narcissist" and it is this which creates a "push towards health".(Symington in Bateman & Holmes, 1995, p. 152)

Erikson in a sense 'codifies' such times of choice which he sug-gests appear at certain stages throughout the life-cycle:

> ... psychosocial development proceeds by critical steps–'critical' being a characteristic of turning points, of moments of decision between progress and regression, integration and retardation. [Erikson, 1977, pp. 243–44]

In terms of mid-life and old age, Erikson's *'epigenetic chart'* states that the critical choices are those between *'generativity versus stagnation'* and *'ego integrity versus despair"*, the former occurring, Erikson sug-gests, from one's forties and fifties. (Erikson, 1977, p. 245) What he means by *'generativity'* is an interesting idea which seems to imply the care and nurturing of the younger generation, the generation 'coming up behind"*, as it were. For many this will mean that by the age of fifty or so one's own children will have grown up to be, or are approaching, adulthood and that where the person in mid-life feels this has been done 'successfully', then stagnation does not occur.

Erikson goes on to say that the having of children is not a pre-requisite for *generativity,* but that this might include other forms of 'taking care of' the next generation: for example, in meaningful work related to the community. This theory is expanded on by Vaillant who suggests the further stage of *'the keeper of the meaning versus rigidity'* (Vaillant in Whitbourne, 2001, original emphasis). An example given of this might be the sports coach who, in later life, goes on to be a senior administrator concerned with the particular game as a whole, in essence, the guardian of a large group or the preserver of some aspect of a particular culture (in this case North American). Vaillant suggests that such actions assist an older indi-vidual to successfully manage the losses and disappointments of ageing–essentially by creating more adaptable, age-appropriate, ego defences to replace those which only served well at an earlier stage in development.

Both Erikson and Vaillant, therefore, seem concerned with the moving away from what is essentially a narcissistic, self-absorbed position towards the position that one has responsibility for the coming generation. The moving away, as Erikson (1973) puts it, from a position of 'who you care to be' towards the state of 'whom you can take care of'. He goes on to write:

> ... as a principle it corresponds to what in Hinduism is called the maintenance of the world, that middle period of the life cycle when existence permits you and demands you to consider death as peripheral. The only happiness that is lasting (is to) increase the good will and the higher order in your sector of the world. [Erikson in Colarusso & Nemiroff, 1981, p. 33]

The above encapsulates what Erikson regards to be the ultimate state one achieves in life, the state he terms *'ego integrity'*. Having in some way *taken care* of others, whether one's own offspring or others in the wider community during midlife, one is more able to 'ripen the fruit' of the seven stages. Of course what he is saying here is *not* that the achievement of generativity *by itself* is sufficient for ego integrity, but it, along with the resolution of the other conflicts (i.e., identity versus role confusion, intimacy versus isolation, etc), means that such ego integrity is possible. Indeed, from my earlier example of the 68-year-old woman, generativity *per se* is certainly 'not enough'. This person not only had a child, but was caring for him at home even now (her son is 28 years old); she is very active–almost hyperactive one could say–within her community, doing any amount of voluntary work and yet because she had not addressed earlier conflicts, this activity was essentially unfruitful and she was laden with guilt, anxiety and despair. In her case, the activity of what we might call *pseudo-generativity* may have been *preventing* her from addressing those earlier conflicts, by 'filling her up' with distractions which make her forget–almost literally–'her-self'. In this sense, it could be argued that, paradoxically, her continuing to care for her son in such an intensive way is of itself an act of narcissism.

Erikson himself describes the state of ego integrity as *post-narcissistic and* goes on not really to *define* what he means by ego integrity, but to describe what one can only regard as a *state of being or an attitude of mind*. Using phrases such as "the ego's accrued assurance of its proclivity for order and meaning", he paints a picture of an individual who has been reconciled with the world around him and with his own death, which he faces with equanimity. Conversely—or as Erikson puts it, *versus!*—lacking ego integrity in the latter stage of one's life is simply characterized by a fear of death. Thus *despair* is the ego state in which such a person must be, having failed or not attempted to resolve the various crises of life and this state " ... expresses the feeling that time is now short, too short for the attempt to start another life and to try alternate roads to integrity". (Erikson, 1977, p. 242)

For all its attractiveness in its presentation of a coherent 'chart', as it were, of human psychosocial development, Erikson is not without his critics and although space does not permit a full exposition of such criticisms here, it is perhaps sufficient to say that they tend to centre on his focus on the process of *adaptation*. In this respect, he makes what Elliott (2002) calls "an uncritical linkage of self and society". Moreover, Elliott suggests that Erikson essentially "sidesteps" important issues in psychoanalytic theory, those *internal divisions* such as projecting and splitting, in favour of the belief that

> ... contemporary social conditions provide an all-inclusive framework for affirmative identity, an ideological vision which is at one with much contemporary multinational advertising, such as the projected world unity of 'The United Colours of Benneton'. [Elliott, 2002, p. 71]

In short, Elliott accuses Erikson of superficiality and although some of the aforementioned quotes from Erikson can sound somewhat esoteric—elsewhere, for example, he writes of ego integrity as 'conveying some world order and spiritual sense"—I do believe that Elliott's criticisms are too harsh. As I have noted above, Erikson was the first to consider the entire life cycle and to codify this into a meaningful whole and whatever one might say about this, in terms of clinical practice this represents a useful and *practical* insight into the task of the therapist. After all, Erikson, working from an (American) object relations perspective essentially, recognizes that internal conflicts occur throughout life and that these must be resolved for growth and change to take place. Unlike Elliott and others, I cannot perceive this as a superficial or trite exercise. On the contrary, where Elliott has accused Erikson of 'sidestepping', I see the exact opposite. Put simply, Erikson seems to be saying "If you don't resolve the conflicts appropriate to your given stage of life, you have to go back to deal with them somehow, or you will never reach the final state of *ego integrity*".

There may be an argument about the validity of Erikson's psychoanalytic perspective, as indeed there is about any other psychoanalytic perspective, but his critics fall short off the mark by attacking it on largely political grounds. In fact, Kohut has been subject to the identical criticism of 'espousing conformity' (a criticism rebutted, in my view most eloquently, by Jacoby 1990, p. 110).

Although at first glance Erikson's notion of *ego integrity* seems similar–at least in terms of the language Erikson uses to describe this state—to Jung's concept of *individuation,* in fact Jung's ideas go further and do not really imply *adaptation,* but are fundamentally concerned with *self realisation.* As Jung himself writes in the first lines of his autobiography: "My life is the story of the self-realization of the unconscious". (Jung in Stevens, 2001, p. 38)

To this extent, it may be said that on Erikson's epigenetic chart, *individuation* would be placed above *ego integrity.* Samuels et al. (1986) leave it an open question as to whether integration is a necessary precursor to individuation, though they do go as far as to say that " ... obviously, the chances are better for the ego that is strong (integrated) enough to withstand individuation". (Samuels et al. 1986, p. 79)

Thus we can see that the concept of *individuation* implies a deeper and more significant state of being, the summation, if you will, of the active confrontation of one's unconscious from mid-life towards old age and death itself. Another way of putting this, in the context of this chapter, might be that Individuation is the *opposite* of Narcissism (can one even use the word *versus,* again?). That is to say that narcissism as a defence mechanism against the inevitability of ageing and death is, by its very nature, *bound to fail.* What Jung is suggesting is an altogether higher goal, a more profound quest to achieve *meaning* in one's life beyond those things that may temporarily 'shore up' a fragile ego. For Jung, narcissistic needs are fundamentally illusory and self-knowledge is the way through, what he termed, the prison of "the petty, oversensitive, personal world of the ego". (Jung in Jacoby, 1985, p. 154) Further to this and replying to the somewhat paradoxical claim that the quest for individuation is itself a 'self-absorbed' preoccupation, Jung wrote that "individuation does not shut out the world, but gathers the world to oneself". (Jung in Samuels et al. 1986, p. 79)

Stevens (1990) offers a thoughtful consideration of Jung's ideas in a very sensitive and practical way. Recognizing that there are indeed 'tasks' of old age, he appreciated that Jung was not prescriptive in the way in which individuation might be achieved, but he insisted that we had to "come to terms with the notion of death and to experience our co-existence with creation" in our own unique way. Stevens, echoing Jung, calls this "coming to Selfhood" and highlights the fact that this is more than just "a cultural commitment to becoming a good citizen" (which seems to be the preoccupation of Vaillant, Erikson et al.), but from the second half of life, this refers to making what he calls an "ethical choice" to "transcend one's fear of death". (Stevens, 1990, p. 190)

Stevens goes on to suggest that individuation ultimately implies some kind of spiritual and religious dimension–though not a prescriptive one. If death, as has been said earlier in this paper, is regarded by Jung as 'the last step in the individuation process, then a coming to terms with this reality and facing it with equanimity requires some kind of 'belief-system'"; though not necessarily one which embraces an after-life or personal redemption. Rather, one can say that a minimum requirement is the belief that one is part of an order of things, linked with all of creation and that one's own unique life has had meaning—and will end.

To this extent, I find the idea of constant development, even to the point of death, a very useful and heartening idea to take into my professional practice. Both as a therapist and a mental health social worker, I see distress and confusion about the ageing process; feelings of loss of meaning and identity on retirement; bewilderment and abandonment when friends or loved ones are dying; people reflecting on their lives and questioning what it has amounted to; and frustration at the loss of this or that bodily function.

As someone who is in his mid-fifties and having endured major illness some years back, I can readily identify the issues of mortality and life's ultimate meaning. At fifty I took up running and ran the

New York marathon. Two months after 9/11, matters of life and death still seemed to hang in the atmosphere like a damp grey blanket and it seemed everyone in the city had woken up to the fact that one day they were going to die. And there was I, pounding the streets of Manhattan island–"running through" my fiftieth year, as it were. Was this an act of *narcissism*, or rather, as I now hope, a stage in my journey towards *individuation*, happy to have clung on to life all those years ago and fully aware of time passing, yet seeing this as an opportunity: "a blessing, not a curse?"

Narcissism and the problem of ambivalence: reflections on a case study

'Jane', a fifty-two year old fashion designer, came to therapy following the death of her mother and the ending of an intense, erotic relationship, after which she had fallen into a deep depression. Whilst in therapy, her father also died. These losses became unbearable for her and she began quite frantically to take on responsibility for the welfare of an elderly aunt, an eighty-year-old woman at her church and a neighbour in her seventies who had been suffering from a range of physical problems. However, Jane's attitude towards these women was highly ambivalent. She would nurture them, visit frequently and generally "take care" of them, often at the expense of her own work. At the same time, she would, in therapy, become enraged by them, resentful at the "time they were taking up". She was often in debt and had to work to make ends meet; yet, she felt driven to see these old people, quite literally "at her own expense". Thus at one and the same time Jane felt compelled to somehow keep her charges alive, whilst in therapy frequently expressing powerfully the wish that they would "die soon".

As the therapy progressed, it became clear that Jane's obsession with the women represented her own growing fear of ageing, which was something she had been denying for several years. The nature of her work involved good eyesight and nimble fingers, both of which faculties she felt had been fading since her mid-forties. She told me that she felt intensely envious of younger people whom she had taught and encouraged in the fashion industry, who had now "overtaken" her.

She was always a person who had required praise and critical acclaim. At the beginning of her therapy, she harboured a grandiose image of herself, telling me that she had "very high standards" and felt impatient when these were not met. She told me of her background, which included musicians, artists and actors (on her mother's side, she stressed) and with whom she identified. After several months, though, Jane told me that at twenty-one she had won a scholarship to study fashion in Milan, but after just two weeks she had returned to England–fearful of failure, she told me and afraid of losing all the praise she had received at home–"I felt I was just a little fish in a big pond". When I suggested to her that she might have feared "drowning", Jane wept uncontrollably, expressing both deep disappointment at how her life had turned out and profound terror of what the future might hold. From that point on, the issue of her own ageing process and death became the focus of the therapeutic work. Faced with the death of her parents, abandonment by her lover and fearing the loss of those abilities which had brought her the admiration of the world, Jane was in a sense *forced* to acknowledge her own mortality and the reality of the ageing process. This reality was initially met by a fascination with older people and a need to keep their company–alongside an equally powerful rage and even disgust with them. Through the process of therapy, however, the *narcissistic edifice* began to crumble and, it is hoped, a resolution to this destructive ambivalence may be reached.

Concluding thoughts

At the beginning of this chapter, I noted the ambivalence of society towards its older citizens. This very much reflects the attitude of the narcissistic individual towards their own ageing process and mortality. The playwright Henrik Ibsen represents this in his essay 'A Letter in Rhyme' (1875): a ship sets sail and all seems well, when suddenly, in mid-ocean, a blackness descends upon her. Ibsen refers to the sailor's phrase when this happens as 'the corpse in the cargo'. The depressive feeling, the 'opening of the narcissistic wound' which can emerge in mid-life is fundamentally the realization that we carry within us this 'corpse in the cargo'.

Viewed in this light, it is perhaps unsurprising that individual dread of old age and dying permeates through to the attitudes of wider society. One wonders whether the cases, not so uncommon, whereby some health professionals and other carers of old people become so fascinated with, yet repelled by, old people that this can sometimes turn to abuse–or in some cases even murder. Whilst not wishing to minimize the genuine repugnance towards the mass murderer, the GP Harold Shipman, were a doctor to be found guilty of murdering more than two hundred children, or even younger adults, I feel that the sense of outrage and incomprehension would have been far greater than was the case with these older patients. Indeed, I feel sure that in any other age group such deaths would have been investigated earlier and many lives saved.

In case this all seems too far-fetched, we have been reminded over the years of 'health rationing' that has resulted in age discrimination for life-saving surgery. In mental health, the severe limitations of services for over-65s was exposed in a major study (MIND, 2005). These include: age discrimination by GP's, including lack of drugs choice and information; lack of any suicide prevention policy, despite the very high suicide rate of over 55's (over a third of the UK total); and the doubling of the rate of electro–convulsive therapies for this age group. Interestingly, the report mentions that many older people are 'too old' for 'talking therapies'.

What seems to be the case, then, is that this feeling of turning away from old age is an attempt to turn away from the inescapable and this is the cause of deep-rooted anxiety and ambivalence. Within the narcissistic individual this can precipitate a 'crisis of being'. If one accepts that modern society itself is fundamentally narcissistic, then ambivalent attitudes towards older citizens are the product of a similar crisis.

In this chapter, I have also attempted to address what I believe to be some of the core issues of psychotherapeutic work with older people. Recognizing the new demographic realities and suggesting this will inevitably impact on our practice, I have suggested that many of the problems and sources of personal distress which older clients may bring will tend to be narcissistic ones. Moreover, the growing awareness of the limitations of life itself must almost inevitably bring about a crisis point where an individual is faced with the choice to continue living with the defensive self-organisation s/he has maintained for so long, or choose to live 'authentically' by, to use Jung's phrase quoted earlier, 'confronting the unconscious'.

In essence, one can live with despair and profound regret, as Thomas Hardy writes in the poem

"SHUT OUT THAT MOON:

Too fragrant was life's early bloom,
Too tart the fruit it bought."

Hardy [1990]

Or else, one can follow the way of Jung's older patients who have chosen a different path. As he puts it:

They came to themselves, they could accept themselves and were thus reconciled to adverse circumstances and events ... [they have] made their peace with God. [Jung in Stevens, p. 227]

These two polarities seem to me to represent the central task of psychotherapeutic practice with older people and, when one thinks about it, with clients of any age.

CHAPTER TEN

"I'm not in my own skin. I want to be in my own skin": revaluing fragmentation and narcissism

Christopher Hauke

This chapter offers a re-take on two areas of theory: the development of the self (from a post-Jungian perspective) and the development of self-representation, framed as the theory of narcissism, from a post-Freudian position. In this I am concerned with ideas of fragmentation and wholeness—for reasons I will detail shortly—and the relationship of these to self-representation and narcissistic damage. My thesis involves linking Jungian ideas concerning the self and individuation (as developed by Fordham 1957, 1973 and Neumann, 1973, amongst others) with psychoanalytic ideas on narcissism (notably Kohut, 1971, 1977, 1978). Important work has already been achieved in this area (Jacoby, 1991, Schwartz-Salant, 1982) but what I intend to deliver here is a particular revaluation of the negative overtones of the terms 'fragmentation' and 'narcissistic' and an indication of their place in the process of individuation. Along the way I will show how classical Jungian and Object Relations notions of 'wholeness' are not sustainable and need to be replaced by an emphasis on the communication between 'parts' (or fragments or complexes) so that the term 'whole' may be re-interpreted by an alternative, pluralistic concept: the healthy communication or linkage between all the parts or fragments.

When I come to relate these theories to practice using a particular case example, I emphasise the analyst's healing role through mirroring or reflecting and embodiment or incarnating. Both of these are forms of holding of the patient but there are important differences. Mirroring is more active on the part of the analyst, in that it consists of a more or less conscious reflecting back of what the patient brings. 'More or less' conscious would have to include the degree of processing that goes on in the analyst needed to reflect the self as opposed to distorted or fragmented ego-parts on their own. I discuss this aspect of mirroring later.

Embodiment or incarnating, in my usage, is a 'passive' holding. It 'happens to' the analyst who can suddenly find him or herself being attacked for something or treated as someone not yet known. It can also happen as a countertransference experience which can supply knowledge of a patient's unconscious state. Either way something is being carried for the patient, a split-off projected part that needs holding for it to serve in a healing dialogue with the patient. What is carried may refer to historical material or to the current dynamics both within the consulting room and those reported from the patient's life. Sustaining of both these modes, even when the analyst is confused or is feeling attacked, provides the atmosphere in which healing, linking and growth can take place. This sustaining depends on the capacity of the analyst, a capacity partly enhanced by a buoyant and enriching theoretical position which supports a flexible analytic attitude.

Self and ego

I would like to insert a word here on my use of the terms 'self' and 'ego'. Briefly, until Kohut, psychoanalysis preferred 'ego' to denote the person. Kohut's use of the term 'self' is closer to the Jungian use in that he describes the need for "two approaches: a psychology in which the self is seen as the centre of the psychological universe and a psychology in which the self is seen as a content of a mental apparatus". (Kohut, 1977, p. xv) But while Kohut's self is created during development, post-Jungian analyst Michael Fordham's more archetypal approach designates an *a priori* primary self. Important for this present paper is Jung's image of the self as both the centre and the circumference of the psyche and of the ego as a 'content of the self' that is in relation to it (see Jung, CW7, para. 399–405).

But none of this should contradict the notion of self as 'self-representation"—the subjective sense of oneself we all experience. Although partial and determined by an individual's degree of conscious self-knowledge, the 'sense of oneself' is an expanding experience dependent at first on 'good enough' early conditions but later on an ongoing awareness of unconscious contents as encouraged and discovered through an analysis. Such discoveries are, from the Jungian perspective, the gradual unfolding of the larger personality, Jung's notion of the self, as it comes into conscious (ego-) awareness.

This is the self I have had in mind when developing my own views. However, although I have chosen not to focus specifically on the distinction between 'self' and 'ego', this should be acknowledged as an important area of debate especially in relation to ideas of 'wholeness'. This is because from the position of the self, the ego is only a small part and in need of ongoing enrichment via the 'ego-self axis"—a term which refers to the optimal health achieved through ongoing communication between conscious ego and the unconscious self. Similarly, self cannot be known at all unless it is realized in ego-consciousness. Thus the idea of 'wholeness' of the psyche or personality is seen nowadays as referring not to 'completeness' but rather to the fuller communication between parts of the personality and especially the conscious and unconscious mind in what is very much a two-way street.

Fragmentation and wholeness

We would do well to begin with a recap of models of the mind and personality that postulate an original wholeness, or non-dual state, which then 'develops' by differentiation into parts through contact with the environment (which for most theories means the mother).

Common assumptions or postulates seem to be:

(a) The existence of an original psychological wholeness, an undifferentiated unity, as the initial state of being for the human neonate or foetus.

(b) The existence of differentiated phenomena. These are the bits or parts that are suggested by different behavioural phenomena in the developing infant and the aspects of personality revealed in the adult.

(c) The process by which the original state is required to differentiate (moving from a. to b.) which, depending on the theoretical emphasis, involves internal drives and instincts seeking satisfaction; the function of frustration and defences against this in the encounter with the environment; or, the facilitating qualities of the early relationship between infant and mother; or, psychological 'readiness' or 'triggering' and the activation of archetypes, or a combination of these. The Jungian view is that humans are born with an archetypal expectation to have typically human experiences and images which produce typically human behaviour. Thus humans develop human minds in adulthood just as the human skeleton will mature into its typical adult form. But although this potential is present in everyone, environmental factors—nutrition in the case of the skeleton and interpersonal and intrapersonal dynamics and events for the mind—provide the conditions under which the archetypal potential succeeds, or is prevented from expression or is distorted. In this way a deformed skeleton or a damaged personality can result from initially poor environmental conditions limiting our inherited archetypal potential.

(d) The function or aim of this process of differentiation. This teleological perspective is a distinctively Jungian idea where the focus is on the the *aim* of mental phenomena rather than its *cause*. This can be posed in the form of a question: what psychological satisfaction is being aimed at (even temporarily) by this fragmentation? Is it something defensive or protective of the individual, or part of an inevitable trajectory of growth? Is it the development of consciousness from unconsciousness, for example, the growth of the ego with its knowledge of the other? Or is it the management of id passions requiring repression and the abandonment of desires left unconscious?

(e) Secondary phenomena and processes that arise leading to questions of what is a normal, or successful, outcome and what is seen as a pathological result or failure for the maturing personality. The differentiated parts may regroup to sub-wholes. Various nuclei are formed and bits get left behind, stranded and unlinked. These are known as 'the Complexes' in Jungian theory where, indeed, the ego itself is regarded as a complex vital to managing the perception of reality and orientation in the world. Perhaps emergency structures are formed too early and persist inflexibly—which is a way of describing Winnicott's 'False Self' (which is nothing to do with Jung's self as such, but is a complex more like the Persona and thus masks the self).

Many of these ideas and questions constitute both the theories of the development of self and ego and psychoanalytic theories of narcissism. We could weight these along a continuum that illustrates a preference for biological theorising at one end and a preference for ethological theorising at the other. The first preference is exemplified by a dependence on the notion of drives or instincts which is retained to various degrees in the theories of Freud, Klein & Kernberg. The second preference emphasises the importance of the interpersonal relationship the infant experiences initially with the mother (Balint, Bowlby, Mahler, Kohut, Winnicott & Stern). This continuum is dichotomised elsewhere as Instinct or Drive Theory and Object Relations Theory (see Rycroft, 1985, p. 74) and holds vital implications for the different technique and analytic attitude that arise from absorbing different theoretical positions.

Finally, when it comes to analytic work that rests on an image of a psyche that proceeds from unity to differentiation, a useful question to ask may be: What is being held in the analytic work? Is it an undifferentiated uroboric self (Neumann, 1973) which needs holding, insufficiently supplied by others in the past, to begin a more successful individuation? There may be implications in this view for the analysis of very early defences (in a Kleinian sense) that have arisen from poor integration of early drives. Or are we dealing with a potentially, fairly cohesive self-structure (Kohut, 1977) that needs help to integrate a range of part-selves, at present split off? There are implications for mirroring in this conception (Winnicott, 1971). How does the analyst decide what should be mirrored and accepted and what should be challenged and interpreted; which mirroring is therapeutic and which is a collusion with a part-self? Narcissistic patients, the patient discussed here especially, tend to make a great many demands for mirroring many of which seek reassurance of self (-esteem) in the context of possessing little knowledge of the self and its range. This results in a radical uncertainty about whom (in the sense of which part-self) the analyst might be in dialogue with at different times and an obscuring for both analyst and patient of the need for acceptance and linking of the part-selves that have been, for the moment, rejected and are thus unexpressed and unrecognized.

Primary narcissism

In expounding his theories of the formation of the ego through dein-tegrative processes in the 'original self", Michael Fordham makes the link with Freudian views when he states, "Primary narcissism is an analogue of my ideas". (Fordham, 1973, p. 84) A Jungian 'whole-and-part' model is linked with ideas of narcissism via a mixture of biological and ethological theorising. For example, Fordham speaks of the original self deintegrating spontaneously as a "release phe-nomenon comparable to that discovered from the study of instinct" in animals (Fordham, 1957, p. 127). The deintegrates only constitute a readiness for experience, perception etc., however and require a fit with the environment (primarily through the relationship with the mother). Fordham's words are important here:

> While there is a perfect fit between the two [a bit of ego and a bit of environment] there can clearly be no differentiation between them. The separation must therefore occur as a consequence of failure by the environment to fit the deintegrate (1957, p. 129).

So awareness of the separateness of ego and other is seen to arise out of the meeting of the 'original self' with an antagonistic envi-ronment (the 'failure to fit' with its affective correlate, frustration).

With Klein's infant it is the mechanisms of 'primitive' defence that construct the inner world. Victoria Hamilton writes of theories of primary and secondary narcissistic states, contrasting the Kleinian position:

> The negativity (Klein) describes does not take the form of a passive withdrawal or even of a homeostatic organisation in

order to reproduce the lost intra-uterine state; it takes an active form as the infant projects his pain and anxiety into the mother (Hamilton, 1982, p. 56).

When developed by Kernberg and Rosenfeld, this theorization of narcissism (narcissistic withdrawal as a defence) suggests that what is being defended against is separateness. I challenge this conclusion and see it as deriving from a negatively-toned theoretical attitude towards the infant's dependence. Realisation of this dependence by the infant is thought to arouse feelings of anxiety and hostility in the infant which are then retreated from by a return to a narcissistic omnipotence. But why should dependence necessarily entail anxiety? As Winnicott points out, the infant only becomes aware of holding when holding *fails* (Winnicott, 1960, p. 52). There is nothing intrinsically anxiety-provoking about dependence *itself*. It is failures in the infant-mother relationship, the interactive to-and-fro, that result in narcissistic pathology, not the attacks made by the infant upon the link between the mother and himself that Kleinian writers suggest. Such failures may typically be seen to arise from interruptions caused by a non-supportive father or demands arising from other siblings, as we shall see in the case example below. My point, here, is that the 'environment' is more than the mother. Indeed, the rest of the environment constructs the particular mother the infant gets and, let us not forget, this eventually includes each mother's particular cultural and historical location.

So a question hovering over this area of theory might be: What is being defended against and what is being attacked? The implication for the analyst on the receiving end can be put in terms of his ability to sustain attacks arising from archaic grandiosity and demands arising from archaic idealisations. Kohut is the source here. He posits two kinds of self-objects (i.e., mother in relationship with her infant)—the mirroring self-object and the 'idealised parent imago' (Kohut & Wolf, 1978, p. 414) or idealised self-object. Kohut emphasises the importance of empathic response, the reflection by the parent (and later the analyst) of the infant's grandiosity—his or her "innate sense of vigour, greatness and perfection" (1978, p. 414). For Kohut, the bi-polar 'nuclear self' is formed with the poles of archaic grandiosity and archaic idealisations being transformed into, respectively, the poles of goals and ambitions on the one hand and inner ideals and values on the other.

The clinical material will show how my patient, 'Peg', produced attacks and demands of this nature in the analysis, which required my understanding and tolerating of how I was embodied or incarnated in many roles by her fragmented relating. Hindsight provides the luxury of defining the source of her attacks and demands (failure of the erotic relationship with father or loss of mother's attentive holding due to the demands of her disabled sister, for example) but in our sessions I was compelled to engage with them in the immediacy of the moment. Sometimes I was driving blind, gripping the wheel and bumping from moment to moment as I tried to keep my eyes on the horizon that was Peg's self and her individuation journey. I know we got somewhere in the end but it was never easy and, with Peg's kind permission, I offer the following material to illustrate aspects of our struggle.

The case history

When I considered writing about Peg (not her real name, of course) several years ago, I found myself confronted with notes upon notes, nothing but a mass of fragments, pieces of a personality—the unrelated population of her inner world. In the analytic work any attempt to interpret this material tended to fall between the fragments, my comments just seemed to drop through the gaps and they did not seem to catch or connect with anything in Peg. I was traveling off-road with no clue as to the right direction. Some sessions were so fragmented that I became lost in the hinterland of Peg's borderline, or, more accurately, border*less* state.

For example, in just one session, she smelt cigarette smoke outside the consulting room and told me she had stopped smoking with the help of Alan Carr's book. Then she told me that "Freud tried to stop" and the method was "quite psychological"; "it's my main project at the moment, all my concentration is on it", she said. We then explored how she felt let down by me and the analysis. She was giving and I was taking, she said. She was giving up smoking but not with my help—she had to use a do-it-yourself book. Next she told me that if she gets on a Shiatsu course she will leave the analysis. She then said that she was "getting into E.S.P". (extrasensory perception—telepathy and distant viewing) and gave me an example of correctly guessing when a friend of hers was going away. This was followed by: "My mother thinks Marlon Brando is going to die ... and she wants to meet him ... and I want to help her to meet him. ... I nearly worked with him on a film once ... because he is the ultimate actor".

I think you get the idea. It seems that, unconsciously, Peg let such a series of fragments serve to break up the session. Perhaps the process was a defensive move on her part to help her feel in control and to render me powerless. Her more direct statements on the uselessness of analysis and threatening to leave certainly had such an impact. Peg's far-ranging grandiosity (couched in the form of unconnected plans and ambitions) masked her emptiness as she moved from talking about giving up smoking, to achieving psychic powers and on to arranging a meeting between her mother and Marlon Brando.

In one session Peg came out with the statement: "I could be a bag-lady now". The image is one of her carrying her fragmented parts in separate bags within bags. The fragments are placed outside as the mess within is too hard to bear. There is also a distressing sense of having to hold onto all this baggage for fear of experiencing a nothingness, painful inner emptiness, without it. In an effort to structure and focus such disorganised material, I have chosen three areas of Peg's past and present psychodynamics—both within her and between her and others. All of these can be seen to involve poor opportunities for mirroring early in life, with a consequent lack of a sense of identity and self-knowledge and a fragmented, unconnected psyche.

First, I will attempt to convey the abusive atmosphere of Peg's home life, her sadomasochistic relation to me and her predator-victim attitude to men. Secondly, using pronounced bodily imagery, I will discuss material involving Peg's disabled sister—a self-image of internal damage echoed in images of scars, plastic surgery and dismemberment. Tramps, the bag lady and the socially damaged, provided an extension of this self-image. Lastly, I would like to say something about our transference/countertransference processes, how compelling a presence Peg could be and how images of babies appeared in the material offering positive hope for healing and which reminded me of Peg's potential for 'bringing herself together'.

The way in which we are seen and known during our early years contributes a good deal to an individual's sense of self. Accurate empathic mirroring continues to be an important part of the way in which the individual knows herself and her potential long after the earliest experiences of seeing oneself in the gleam of a loving parent's eye. Pre-pubertal and teen years revive a great need for mirroring so the young person can build a healthy narcissism and stable identity. During her early years, it seems Peg received a very poor level of erotic playback (Samuels, 1989, p. 82) from her father. She described him being embarrassed by sexual material if it appeared on television and yet displayed a leering attitude to women when he was drunk. Peg remembers the look on his face as he gazed drunkenly at her young breasts when she was eleven and how he tolerated his drinking pals' comments on her figure.

In her sessions, Peg expressed her anger and disgust at her father directly and also indirectly by attacking all men in general because, in her view, they are allowed to stay desirable as they grow older while women suffer from the loss of their youthful looks. In the early sessions she also recounted memories of her father physically threatening her mother during his rages while Peg begged him to stop until escaping from the house with her.

This material gave me a sense of the abusive home atmosphere and poor support Peg suffered when growing up and reinforced the image of a wounded child which had at first so struck me in contrast to her appearance as an attractive woman in her early thirties. When it came to reflecting this understanding back, however, Peg was resistant to hearing this from me as she wished to hold on to an omnipotent triumphant feeling of "winning through" despite these conditions. This was emphasised by her holding on to the fantasy of smashing a pot over her father's head to stop his raging. By focusing on this omnipotent aspect and on others (like the protection of her mother and sister), she could split off and banish feelings of her own vulnerability and fear.

Her low expectations of loving relationships reveal further her narcissistic damage. She has described a recent boyfriend, who only sees her when he chooses, as a good-looking saxophone player who "dresses like a tramp and lives in a sort of warehouse". "He is just like me", Peg said, with no hint of irony, "on the same plane—we're going in the same direction". She meant this to be a positive statement but I saw it to show that it is her need to identify with the damaged, lost and vulnerable parts, that makes the relationship mean something to her. It has been difficult for Peg to view this type of relationship from her own position. She wants to talk about why the man behaves in that way and only gradually has she addressed what his uncaring behaviour is meeting in herself. In the next section, I will discuss the effect on Peg of growing up with a disabled, sick sister which is mentioned here for the way in which her carrying of the damaged sister part, which she is ashamed of, has contributed to producing the masochistic child part of herself. As Nathan Schwartz-Salant points out, in narcissistically damaged patients, the 'joyful child' gets lost as the result of the self being physically attacked and instead a more compliant and masochistic attitude develops (Schwartz-Salant, 1982, pp. 159–164).

In the course of coming to look at and accept these masochistic parts of herself—themselves the result of failure of her family to support any healthy narcissism and sense of self—Peg got into great rages about films that showed man as predator to woman as victim. She raged against De Niro and Scorsese for the film *Cape Fear* but, in spite of this still viewed it and admired the power of the male acting and disparaged the women. Even more central to this theme were her feelings of admiration for Anthony Hopkins as a man and an actor, especially in the role of the cannibalistic serial murderer in *Silence of the Lambs*. Peg said she "wants to be like him" and it is not clear whether she meant the actor or the character. She said: "At one point he looks at Jodie Foster and says he knows her, he understands her. And this is the man who eats human livers with a glass of wine. ... "

I interpreted this directly: "I think what you're telling me is you want that contrast, the tension between the vicious-sadistic and the tender understanding of you. I think it is what you experienced with your father and have repeated with others like your boyfriend, but you feel not able to get it here". The session had focused on how I was giving her nothing, just taking, not understanding her, mixed with her checking whether she was being too brutal in her comments or hurting me. Peg could accept the interpretation. My tolerance of her sadistic attacks together with a growing acceptance of her own masochistic tendencies begin to help her feel that her inner world is less intolerable, that it could be considered and the pain of it shared more, rather than defended against by these relationships and denials and by her denied and disguised self-hatred. Not surprisingly, her other mode of being with men is one in which, when they are not easy to identify with and therefore quite desirable (perhaps for reasons of fame, wealth, or simply by treating her with respect), Peg finds herself behaving foolishly and so making herself easily rejectable.

Identifying, splitting and idealising

Peg's transference towards me has fallen into three areas: identification, splitting and idealisation. I will take them in that order. The demand for identifying from the narcissistically damaged patient is well known. I understand this to be both an attempt to get close and in relationship with another and simultaneously a denial of the other an the possibility of difference as this is so threatening. For several months at the beginning of analysis, Peg wanted aspects of herself confirmed by her being able to identify the exact same in myself. She wanted to know if, like her, I believed in extra-terrestrials, in God, astrology, if I hated celebrity culture, liked hypnosis and if I shared her enthusiasm for certain books. She fantasised that my partner knew her at college or worked with a friend of hers and tried to check this out. (There was no such connection at all). We have struggled a good deal with books (psychology/spirituality-themed) she has brought. They obviously uplifted her while it was clear they did not move me in the same way (I will not name names or titles, here!). Through this, Peg's struggle has been to discover how we might have a relationship not be based on identification and similarity, but one that thrives despite—or, indeed, *because of*—our differences.

From the beginning Peg has controlled any effect the analysis or I might have by splitting it off from the rest of her life. She feels she just does 'talking' with me, while outside sessions she is 'doing'. At times the spacing of her four sessions in the week reflected this. This had partly been to accommodate an acting class which, itself, took on the function of a split-off 'kind of therapy'. Peg brought a deal of personal material to the class and to its charismatic leader until a particular session there left her raw and defenceless, unheld and feeling hopeless. This signalled a sense of her discovering how she had been relying on inflated parts of herself to hold back and hide the mess beneath which had now revealed itself to an audience. Up till then, her acting performance had made the pain worthwhile. If the acting performance would not come, there was nothing to hold it together. There was just herself, in fragments.

It was the most clear impression I had had of Peg unprotected by any leap into an inflated aspect of herself that was going to be 'the answer'. This time she was helpless, feeling 'blurred' and unable to think her thoughts, she said. As well as letting me see this and trusting me with it, she said she was suspending the acting class from now on and devoting herself to analysis.

As might be expected, this led to a return of her other relationship pole when all she saw was an idealised version of me. I was the 'good man', in contrast to the bad men she met, I was the one who is good to his partner and his children. Peg said she knew this to be an idealisation but cried, 'I'm allowed that, aren't I?''

Fragments and links

As I have said, throughout the work with Peg I have been struck by her fragmentation, an experience of her as bits, parts that took on a greater or lesser importance each time she presented herself. My struggle has been to discover how to work with a person, a self, when there has not seemed one present. What needs to be emphasised, it seems to me, is that *the fragments, the parts, are the whole*. To an observer there are fragments of a person, but my patient is not falling apart or collapsing into disintegration. There are no missing pieces that are required to reconstitute a whole. What is missing is the linking, the *relationship* between the parts. I find the concept of linking and of its absence, very useful because it can apply directly to both the inner experience, the relationship between parts of the self and to the outer experience, the relationship with others and the world. And of course these two (the inner and outer) are also in relationship themselves through the mechanisms of projection, introjection and projective identification.

This means that, for example, the tendency of the narcissistically disordered patient towards a regressive fusion is both inwardly directed and outwardly directed. The clamour for identifying with me, for seeking agreement of our views, of intolerance of difference, is the outward relating aspect of an inner tendency to undifferentiation. Undifferentiation is sought from the outer object, in an effort to achieve the inner undifferentiated wholeness. This is different from a Freudian idea of a tendency towards homeostasis (primary narcissism) because a form of outward relationship, (primary love) has to be included. What is 'pathological' about this process of regressive fusion is that it is trying to bypass the necessary stage of differentiation. It is side-stepping the painful process of deintegration into parts which then get linked into a structure that is the (whole) integrated personality. De-integration followed by linking is a life-long process of relationship that occurs both within the individual and between the individual and the outside world. It is central to the process of individuation.

Similarly the inflation and grandiosity in the phenomenology of this patient need not simply be seen as a return to some primary or early state, but as an attempt by the psyche to create a 'whole' out of a 'part', to try to *expand a part to serve as the whole*, again eschewing the problem of the need for differentiating and re-linking the parts.

So, initial to the difficulties in this patient when viewed from a perspective of relationship are difficulties of differentiation, from which follow difficulties with linking. Experience with linking can only be poor if differentiation has not been accomplished. The quality of the early encounters and what we might surmise to have been the effect on the developing self will have important implications for the transference/countertransference aspects of the therapy, which is where Kohut places his emphasis.

A second postulate which derives from Kohut's formulation—and is implied in Jung's—is the teleological nature of the psyche: the view that the narcissistic, fragmented pathology has meaning for the whole personality. This means that defensive grandiosity in fact carries within it the energy for true creativity, while envy and rage are distortions of what could become a true sense of empathy. It will be obvious by now that I am linking the concept of narcissistic disorder with individuation, as do Jacoby and Schwartz-Salant. It is this link that has led analytical psychologists to value Kohut's contribution from the psycho-analytical frame. As Jacoby puts it, the sense of 'specialness' in the individual, so overblown and distorted in narcissistic disorder, is the same 'specialness' that is essential to healthy psychological growth and integration of the self that is individuation. (Jacoby, 1991, p. 19) Moreover, individuation is a life-long process requiring at various stages more or less of the narcissitic elements within us all. To write this, for example, I have needed to encourage my own narcissistic capacity to energise my thoughts and expound my views. At other times, while listening carefully to a patient for example, this would be an intrusion. The corollary of all this is the belief that the patient's narcissism (with its grandiosity and omnipotence) is something to be valued and included, not judged and rejected. When faced with the demands of a narcissistic patient, this is easier said than done, but can be helped by a positive orientation in the analyst towards the value of narcissistic qualities.

The disabled sister:
self-image, reconstruction and mirroring

Peg had a sister ('Molly') only fourteen months younger, who was diagnosed with serious health problems in her infancy and spent many years in and out of hospital. She now has a five year old son and lives about thirty miles away. Peg feels very responsible but ultimately helpless in relation to Molly and she has shed many tears over this in sessions. She has similar feelings for her mother, who, since leaving Peg's father, qualified as a teacher. Peg, despite her own limited work and finances, still wishes she could help them both financially. However, it is Peg's mother who pays for her analysis—money Peg says she would rather see given to her sister. This again brings me into the dynamic of her guilt and what she can take for herself. Peg says she (and not Molly) put her mother 'through torture"—absorbing in this it seems both Molly's suffering and her mother's as Molly grew up undergoing operation after operation.

The experience of growing up with Molly and her image within Peg, featured prominently in her material and came to symbolize Peg's own feeling of handicap. Very early on in the work, Peg spoke of her 'not good enough' feelings in connection with her missed opportunities. She felt, as she used to as a child, that her background, her home and her father within it, all shame her. Her compensatory expression of narcissistic grandiosity was present when she went to a middle-class grammar school, where she told friends she had velvet curtains in her living room, imagining this is what her peers had, while the room did not even have a carpet but only bare floor-boards. It became clear to me that the 'sister' image also referred to Peg herself. She is the one who felt disabled, handicapped, ashamed and hard-done by in life. An identification with her sister seemed to have taken the place of and distorted, a sense of her own healthy self.

Early in the sessions Peg had a dream: "I was in a sort of church with my father and Molly was there. He was leering at a girl with big boobs—she was young and seemed into it. I told him she wouldn't age well. I was disgusted. I ran away holding Molly to my chest—so close I could hear her heart beat". Peg immediately commented–"I suppose I'm carrying Molly still". The image remains of Peg carrying the damaged child/vulnerable Molly part of herself which is being ignored and devalued by her father's behaviour. It seems that, in the absence of good mirroring by her father and mother, Peg has taken Molly in and carries the self-image of a deformed, ugly, handicapped girl. When I tentatively suggest she may have lost out on a great deal in those early years, I am met only with her sympathy for her mother and Molly in their heroic struggles. True, there is a great rage aimed at father for his poor support, weakness and violence, but this seems to reinforce the splitting that protects her mother and Molly.

At this stage it is important to clarify what I understand by mirroring—not only as a function important for the growing personality and throughout life, but also as part of the analytic attitude vital for a patient like Peg. Daniel Stern sums it up well with, "parents invariably treat their infants as understandable beings, that is, as the people they are about to become", (Stern, 1984, p. 43) and quotes Friedmann regarding the related clinical phenomena that "it is not necessary for the analyst to know the exact nature of the development he is encouraging. It is sufficient he treats the patient as though he were roughly the person he is about to become" (Friedmann, 1982, p. 12).

REVALUING FRAGMENTATION AND NARCISSISM

If we cannot sense ourselves reflected in our environment, if there is not that reinforcing of our sense of being there, how alive can we feel? This may occur in our relationship with close individuals, or indeed with our inanimate surroundings that we more or less control by our choices. It may occur with our choice of institution or theoretical frame and inwardly with our relationship to our internal images and symbols. For it not to occur, or to occur thinly in a fragmented, incoherent and distorted fashion, results in a loss of that sense of aliveness. I believe this is the experience, in degrees of severity, of the narcissistically damaged patient. The grandiosity, the need to control, the envy and the fragmented presentation of personality that Peg displayed seems to be her efforts to defend against the deadness and emptiness she feels and to replace these with an aliveness. That the replacement is perfunctory, short-lived and 'fizzling out' each time does not alter its reccurrence. It is only when a sense of desperation breaks through that the psyche can begin to sacrifice these emergency measures to allow for development. As she said when she hit this moment: *"I'm not in my own skin. I want to be in my own skin"*. I understood this as a cry from the self crucially aware of its distance from itself, its authentic sense of aliveness as itself, (cf. Jacoby, 1991: "I really don't know where I am—neither with myself, nor with others, I am totally confused" (p. 164)).

I have come across a comparable view expressed by Zinkin in his paper, 'The Human Dimension in Psychotherapy'. In this discussion of the circular interchange between mother and infant he mentions that this " ... is basic. It is one of a number of reciprocal interchanges that must take place *from the beginning* to establish the humanity of the individual". (Zinkin, 1978, p. 28) Zinkin uses 'humanity' where I have used 'aliveness' and he goes on to cite Winnicott's ideas on mirroring which he points out are illustrated by cases of "patients who had difficulty in feeling themselves to be real". (Zinkin, 1978, p. 30) One of Zinkin's central points refers to the analytical situation: "Sometimes this conversation [interchange between patient and analyst] can have the same miraculous significance as in the baby's conversation with the mother, when the patient and the analyst are understanding each other and enhancing each other's existence". (Zinkin, 1978, p. 32) Winnicott, in his seminal paper puts it even more succinctly:

This glimpse of the baby's and child's seeing the self in the mother's face ... gives a way of looking at analysis and the psychotherapeutic task. Psychotherapy is not making clever and apt interpretations; by and large it is a long term giving the patient back what the patient brings. It is a complex derivative of the face that reflects what is there to be seen (Winnicott, 1971, p. 117).

Of course the 'understanding each other' and the 'giving back' and reflecting go on at a more or less unconscious transference/countertransference level. Narcissistically damaged patients are very sensitive to interpretations and interjections from the analyst as many commentators note (e.g., Ledermann, 1982) and a great deal of work has to be done before, as Ledermann says, more typical analytical work can proceed.

This has certainly been true of the present patient. Moreover, some of what she brings seems to concretise the mirroring metaphor. On many occasions she has told me how dissatisfied she is with her face. She has seen it on film and has told me in great detail what she would have altered by plastic surgery. She is anxious about looking older and has fallen into rages about the disadvantages women suffer compared with men when they age. It is as if so much of her sense of self has been cathected to her face, including the fear of the loss of control of it through ageing and fantasises of gaining control through surgery. Importantly, she has always sat opposite me and carefully monitored my reactions to her and what she has read in my face with varying degrees of accuracy. Like the patient Winnicott mentions (1971, p. 117), Peg also relates deeply to the paintings of Francis Bacon—noting their images of dismemberment and disfigurement so that the footnote Winnicott includes comes particularly alive: " ... to look at a painting by Bacon is to look into a mirror and to see there our own afflictions and our fear of solitude, failure, humiliation, old age, death. ... " (Rothenstein, 1964 in Winnicott, p. 117).

As I write it becomes clear that for all its usefulness as a discrete diagnostic category, narcissistic character disorder leads us towards an area of psychological development—parallel to ego-development as Kohut asserts—that is universally present in everyone we see, not just our patients. It is part of what it means to be human. No doubt this explains its attraction as a heuristic, not only a way to organise our thinking about difficult cases, but also because it brings us so close to all the anxieties and fears we humans are heir to.

Sometimes Peg tried to use literal, concrete situations to express how she was mirrored both internally and by me. She complained that the surgeon who removed a small benign lump from her breast promised her it would only leave a small scar. She felt fobbed off and angrily disappointed with the result: the scar was redder, longer and with more tissue removed than she expected. I felt she was saying I was the surgeon too. I was being told I could not hear her concerns. I was leaving her with a scar while attempting to heal her.

This theme of mutilation and harming of her vulnerable self has occurred in several dreams. In one Peg recounted: "I was on a ship on the ocean with B. (a black African woman friend she felt identified with at the time). And we were looking after Molly as a baby and we had a baby each to look after. There were also my two ginger cats and I didn't realise and when we got them back they had had three legs ripped off each of them and I heard that it had taken the men four hours to do this. I knew they couldn't survive so I let them be destroyed and I didn't see it happen. And then we arrived in Africa and the President welcomed us and said, in African, he was glad we had made it. I spoke back in African but then I said I was only pretending to know the language".

In this important dream, Peg could see aspects of her caring for her vulnerable baby self and the threats seem abounding—not least from the analysis and the pain she feels each session will bring. It is not she who is hacking the cats now (as she was in a previous dream): she leaves that to the attacking men. The sea journey to the dark continent suggested the analysis itself, with a sense of being made welcome by the President-analyst indicating the beginnings of trust. However, her admission of only pretending to know the language indicates her great difficulty in getting into dialogue with me and hence within her self. There is only the pretence of doing so.

Gradually Peg was able to use my mirroring interpretations about the damaged sister image she carried and its associated images of the mutilated cats, the scars and the plastic surgery. Peg came to accept and use the idea and feeling of her carrying this damaged child within her and began to observe and comprehend her low self-esteem and its operation in her relationships.

Countertransference:
narcissistic damage and the child motif

Both Nathan Schwartz-Salant and Rushi Ledermann state that patients with narcissistic disorders require a long period at the beginning of analysis of empathic holding before more typical analytical work can be done. This did indeed preceed any success I had with mirroring—whether it functioned as holding and or later was combined with interpretations—which had little effect early in the work. What helped me during this period of poor communication was observation of my own counter-transference processes. Then, as well as later, these have been an extension of the empathic bond so necessary to work with narcissistically damaged people like Peg.

Central to my struggle to offer something back to her was the tension produced by Peg's view of me as being very different from her—with different tastes, experiences, background and values. All the time she made her assumptions known I have been well aware of how much I share with her, but have remained silent on the subject. I think it was right not to join in some sort of reassuring direct understanding, but what I was drawn into—by Peg's own fantasizing—was a rubbishing of all these parts of her for the ostensible aims of grounding, stability and bringing together. Despite claiming these as her aims—she expressed as much in her initial referral letter—they were also what she fought against most. Stability felt so dull and unexciting to her and I become the embodiment of dull unexcitingness: real life happened elsewhere, certainly not in the consulting room!

So my struggle was to allow this image of me as grounded and stable to persist, although it was attacked for being so. I had to remember that in this is the good holding—the reliability that was absent from the abusive atmosphere at home.

Perhaps this area of the work can be illustrated by Peg's material concerning babies. As Peg had two abortions, the images of her aborted foetuses linked with her sister's operations in Peg's own images of internal damage. But Peg has also brought material referring to live, healthy babies and I have had some significant countertransference images along these lines, too. The healthy babies in dreams tended to be alongside Molly, the poorly, wounded child Peg holds inside. In the ship voyage dream, Peg and her friend have a baby each on their journey as well as Molly. This suggests there is a healthy child being carried but not quite born. The kittens stand in for the damaged babies, thus enabling the healthy ones to remain unharmed on the journey.

An event in reality paralleled this. Almost exactly a year after analysis began, Peg arrived for her session with a bright red duffel coat she wanted to give me for one of my children. She said: "It was Molly's little boy's. I was keeping it for a child I might have but you've got a child so I thought I'd give it to you. You can't keep waiting forever". Peg did not want to discuss this gesture further but I interpreted it as confirming we were producing a child between us in the analysis. This could be a re-born Peg, or, equally likely, a newly nurtured and valued child-part of her, existing in relation to a mother-analyst. In Jungian terms and in my own experience, the child image often precedes the birth of new aspects of the personality and the coming together of previously unlinked parts. It very much confirmed a countertransference image that had struck me in a session a few months before, when I imagined a new, wet baby slipping out between Peg's legs onto the floor.

The connection between this new baby and Peg's damaged child and sado-masochism, came later. I could not take the coat home. I left it in my consulting room for some weeks. It reminded me of the significant red child's coat in the film, *Don't Look Now,* where a father loses his child by drowning and in Venice thinks he sees her in her red coat and chases her. But it is a dwarf murderess in the coat and he is stabbed to death. I have not told Peg of this association but I feel it is also contained in her gesture.

The myth

I could not finish this chapter without referring to the myth whose central character has given his name to this part of our human psychology. The universality of our narcissistic path and its detours is confirmed by the Narcissus myth and its presence through the ages. I will begin with a short summary which may help with the points that follow. Ovid's tale speaks of the child Narcissus who is born of a rape of Leiriope by the river god Cesiphus. When Leiriope asks whether her son will have a long life, Tiresias the seer pronounces: "Yes, if he does not come to know himself". Narcissus becomes a hunter, encounters Echo, spurns her advances and is damned to experience unrequited love himself. This he does by falling in love with a reflection in a pool—and when he becomes tragically aware that it is his own reflection cries: " ... What shall I seek by my wooing? What I desire I have. My very plenty makes me poor". What seems to be emphasised is a sense that love and relating has to be object (other)—related. This is affirmed by another version of the tale which explains Narcissus' fate as a punishment by Eros, who Narcissus had previously insulted.

In her book 'Narcissus and Oedipus—The Children of Psychoanalysis' Victoria Hamilton draws our attention to Leiriope's motherly devotion to Narcissus, a "child with whom one could have fallen in love even in his cradle". (Ovid, 1955, p. 83) In her interpretation Narcissus fails at the task of freeing himself from the admiring image of his mother (Hamilton, 1982, p. 123). Citing the struggles of adolescence, with the struggle for independence echoing earlier toddler stages, she points out how the mother-infant relationship had to succumb to the thrusts towards separateness and individuation. This struggle "often takes the form of a preoccupation with ... 'identity' or ... 'image'". (Hamilton, 1982, p. 118) Bringing together the problems of the mother-infant relationship and the struggle for individuation with the importance and pathology of mirroring she notes: "A preoccupation with one's image in the context of acute interpersonal insecurity is the hallmark of narcissism. The image in the mirror is used as an antidote to feelings of fragmentation and insignificance". (Hamilton, 1982, p. 123) In Peg's case this may point us towards an over-closeness with her mother and her mother's admiration of her—both positions born less out of sincere knowledge of each other than out of the emergency situation in the family where these two were more functioning (but of course unequal as adult and child) than the violent, drunk father or the sickly sister. The evidence of Peg's present degree of contact with and support from the mother (who in fact paid for her analysis), may indicate this fusion still persisted.

Hamilton reads the element of the myth concerning Tiresias' prophecies as indicating the failure of Narcissus to survive the first taste of knowledge. "For Narcissus, to be is not to know". (Hamilton, 1982, p. 116) She finds that with narcissistic children, "their exis-tence depends on the closeness of a two-person relationship which shuts out otherness, the third term, the intrusion of anything (or anyone) new and different" (Hamilton, 1982, p. 116). By staring into the pool Narcissus tries to possess an other—he tries to break through the wall between him and the 'external object' (Hamilton, 1982, p. 116). But the image is impossible to relate to–"Narcissus realises that it is his self-sufficiency which renders him utterly deficient" (Hamilton, 1982, p. 133). Hamilton also offers another idea, that Narcissus becomes aware that the self in the mirror is, in Winnicott's terms, a 'false self'. This would mean that, for some individuals, true self-knowledge would involve "the destruction of the perfect image and that liberation lay in the separation, the prising apart, of two images—one self, one other—which had been condensed into one". (Hamilton, 1982, p. 135)

Put another way, Narcissus stares into the pool but sees only its surface reflection: he cannot see deeper into himself; he is stuck with his conscious reflection and almost the horror of his aloneness. Both Echo, with her repetition of part of what Narcissus utters and the surface reflection in the pool prove to be inadequate 'mirroring' for Narcissus. He starves and dies. Similarly an individual like the present patient, in whom the Narcissus principle has not yet sufficient conditions for its development, shrivels in his or her creativity and connection with life. There is a sense of ungroundedness and failure to engage, despite abundant evidence of creative potential. There is a sense of impotence and loss of direction and control over life, replaced by a grandiosity and omnipotence. In therapeutic work, the mirroring that has been missed is constantly demanded of the analyst. Peg demanded, "Agree with me", in her relating to me: "Reflect me without any interruption from yourself", thus controlling and rendering impotent my presence in her life.

Such a demand is problematic for the analyst. If we accede to the demand, the patient will succeed in maintaining an unsatisfactory fragmented and undeveloped state. If we refuse, the patient feels abandoned and justified in rejecting the analyst and the work. *What needs to be discriminated is a reflection of the self in contrast to a reflection of the inflated ego 'parts'*. This is achieved, in the main, through a recognition of the striving for wholeness, the *telos* of the self, within the various ego parts themselves, even when their initial presentation is inflated and 'narcissistic'. Thus, it is the analyst's interpretation/recognition of the inflated ego parts as representing the patient's striving for wholeness that helps the narcissistic patient. Central to the narcissistically damaged patient is the inadequate separation of the ego structure from the self. Thus the dialogue between these aspects (self and ego) is not at first possible. This work becomes enacted in the relationship with the analyst. It is within the analyst him- or herself that the validating dialogue and the implicate linking of ego demands to the wider purposes of the self needs to begin. The analyst has to carry this 'preverbally' for some time through the transference/countertransference processes. To quote Lacan: "Not so long ago, a little girl said to me sweetly that it was about time somebody began to look after her so that she might seem loveable to herself. In saying this, she provided the innocent admission of the mainspring that comes into play in the first stage of the transference" (Lacan, 1979, p. 257). In other words, true self-love, as opposed to the Narcissus short circuit, arises out of relationship with the other.

Acknowledgements

I wish to express my thanks to Andrew Samuels, 'Peg', Anastasios Gaitanidis and Polona Curk for their comments on early drafts of this chapter.

This chapter is a completely revised version of the paper originally published as 'Fragmentation and Narcissism: A Revaluation' in *The Journal of Analytic Psychology*, Vol. 40, No. 4, October 1995, pp. 497–522.

REFERENCES

Abram, J. (1996). *The Language of Winnicott*. London: Karnac.

Adorno, T.W. & Horkheimer, M. (1944). *Dialectic of Enlightenment*. J. Cumming (Trans.), London: Verso, 1979.

Adorno, T.W. (1951). Freudian theory and the pattern of fascist propaganda. In: A. Arato & E. Gebhardt (Eds.), *The Essential Frankfurt School Reader*. Oxford: Blackwell, 1978.

Adorno, T.W. (1968). Sociology and psychology. *New Left Review*, 46 & 47.

Adorno, T.W. (2001). *The Culture Industry: Selected Essays on Mass Culture*. J.M. Bernstein (Ed.), London: Routledge.

Amis, M. (1987). *Einstein's Monsters*. London: Penguin Fiction.

Badiou, A. (2002). *Badiou: Infinite Thought*. London: Continuum.

Bakewell, J. (2004). Article in *The Guardian G2*—31.01.04.

Balint, M. (1991). Contribution to discussion of Isaacs' Paper, In: P. King & R. Steiner (Eds.), *The Freud-Klein Controversies*. London: Bruner-Routledge.

211

Baron-Cohen, S. (2000). Theory of mind and autism: a fifteen year review, In: Baron-Cohen, S., Tager-Flusberg, H., & Cohen, D.J. (Eds.), *Understanding Other Minds, Perspectives from Developmental Neuroscience.* Oxford: Oxford University Press.

Bassin, D., Honey, M., & Kaplan, M.M. (Eds.) (1994). *Representations of Motherhood.* New Haven and London: Yale University Press.

Bataille, G. (1986). Attraction and repulsion II: Social structure, In: D. Hollier (Ed.), *The College of Sociology 1937–39.* Minneapolis: University of Minnesota Press.

Bateman, A., & Holmes, J. (1995). *Introduction to Psychoanalysis.* London: Routledge.

Baudelaire, C. (2002). *On Wine and Hashish.* London: Hesperus Press.

Baudrillard, J. (1983). *Simulations.* New York: SemioText(e).

Beck, U. (1992). *The Risk Society.* London: Sage.

Benjamin, J. (1988). *Bonds of Love: Psychoanalysis, Feminism and the Problem of Domination.* New York: Pantheon Books.

Benjamin, J. (1994). The omnipotent mother: a psychoanalytic study of fantasy and reality, In: Bassin, D., Honey, M., & Kaplan, M.M. (Eds.), *Representations of Motherhood.* New Haven and London: Yale University Press.

Benjamin, J. (1998). *Shadow of the Other—Intersubjectivity and Gender in Psychoanalysis.* New York and London: Routledge.

Benjamin, J. (2004). Beyond doer and done to: an intersubjective view of thirdness. *Psychoanalytic Quarterly,* LXXIII.

Berkely-Hill, O. (1921). The anal erotic factor in the religion, philosophy and character of the hindus. *International Journal of Psychoanalysis,* pp. 310–322.

Bion, W. (1957). Differentiation of the psychotic from the non-psychotic personalities, *International Journal of Psychoanalysis,* 38. Also in *Second Thoughts,* London: Heinemann, 1967.

Blakemore, S.J., & Frith, U. (2005). *The Learning Brain: Lessons for Education.* Oxford: Blackwell Publishing.

Bourdin, D. (2000). *La Psychanalyse de Freud à Aujourd'hui.* Paris: Editions Breal.

Bradley, R., & Westen, D. (2005). The psychodynamics of borderline personality disorder: a view from developmental psychopathology. *Development and Psychopathology, 17,* pp. 927–57.

Britton, R. (2003). *Sex, Death and the Superego: Experiences in Psychoanalysis*. London: Karnac.

Broucek, F.J. (1982). Shame and its relationship to early narcissistic developments. *International Journal of Psychoanalysis, 63*: 369–378.

Butler, J. (2000). Longing for recognition: commentary on the work of Jessica Benjamin. *Studies in Gender and Sexuality*, Vol. 1, no. 3.

Capra, F. (2001). *Where Have All The Flowers Gone*. Fritjof Capra home page: http://www.fritjofcapra.net/articles1201.html

Chasseguet-Smirgel, J. (1975). *The Ego Ideal*. London: Free association books, 1985.

Chasseguet-Smirgel, J. (1984). *Creativity and Perversion*. London: Free Association Books, 1985.

Cherki, A. (2001). *Frantz Fanon—Portrait*. Paris: Seuil.

Chessick, R.D. (1983). Mental health in search of the soul in mid-life. Quoted in Jacobs, M. (1998). *The Presenting Past*. Milton Keynes: Open University Press.

Colarusso, C. & Nemiroff, R. (1981). *Adult Development: A New Dimension in Psychodynamic Theory and Practice*. New York: Plenum Press.

Cooper, A.M. (1999). Narcissism, in Morrison, A. P. (Ed.), *Essential Papers on Narcissism*. New York: New York University Press.

Debord, G. (1994). *The Society of Spectacle*. New York: Zone Books.

Decety, J. & Sommerville, J.A. (2003). Shared representations between self and others: a social cognitive neuroscience view. *Trends in Cognitive Science, 7*: 527–533.

Derrida, Jacques (1998). Geopsychoanalysis. ... and the Rest of the World in Lane, C. (Ed.), *The Psychoanalysis of Race*. New York: Columbia University Press.

Elise, D. (2000). Women and desire: why women may not want to want. *Studies in Gender and Sexuality*, 1(2).

Elliott, A. (2002). *Psychoanalytic Theory—An Introduction*. London: Palgrave.

Elman, J.L., Bates, E.A., Johnson, M.H., Karmiloff-Smith, A., Parisi, D., & Plunkett, K. (1999). *Rethinking Innateness: A Connectionist Perspective on Development*. Cambridge, Mass: The MIT Press.

Erikson, E.H. (1973). *Identity, Youth and Crisis*. London: Faber.

Erikson, E.H. (1977). *Childhood and Society*. London: Paladin.

Fanon, F. (1986). *Black Skin, White Masks*. Charles Lam Markmann (Trans.). London: Pluto Press.

Fanon, F. (1988). *Toward the African Revolution*. Haakon Chevalier (Trans.). New York: Grove Press.

Fanon, F. (1990). *The Wretched of the Earth*. Constance Farrington (Trans.). Harmondsworth: Penguin.

Featherstone, M. (1995). The body in consumer culture, In: M. Featherstone (Ed.), *The Body: Social Processes and Cultural Theory*. London: Sage.

Ferenczi, S. (1926). The problem of the acceptance of unpleasure, In: *Final Contributions to the Theory and Technique of Psychoanalysis*. (Ed.), Michael Balint. London: Tavistock, 1955.

Flax, J. (1990). *Thinking Fragments; Psychoanalysis, Feminism and Postmodernism in the Contemporary West*. California and Oxford: University of California Press.

Fletcher, J. (1999). Psychoanalysis and the question of the other–editor's Introduction, In: J. Laplanche (1999a) *Essays on Otherness*, London and New York: Routledge.

Fonagy, P. (2003). Genetics, developmental psychopathology and psychoanalytic theory: the case for ending our (not so) splendid isolation. *Psychoanalytic Inquiry, 23(2)*, pp. 218–47.

Fonagy, P., & Target, M. (2003). *Psychoanalytic Theories: Perspectives from Developmental Psychopathology*. London: Whurr Publishers.

Fordham, M. (1957). *New Developments in Analytical Psychology*. London: Routledge & Keegan Paul.

Fordham, M. (1973). Maturation of ego and self in infancy, in *Analytical Psychology: A Modern Science*. London: Academic Press.

Foucault, M. (1967). *Madness and Civilisation*. London: Routledge, 2001.

Foucault, M. (1970). *The Order of Things*. London: Tavistock.

Freud, A. (1991). Contribution to discussion of Isaacs' Paper at a Scientific Meeting of April 4th 1943, In: P. King and R. Steiner (Eds.), *The Freud-Klein Controversies*. London: Bruner-Routledge.

Freud, S. (1895). The project for a scientific psychology. *The Standard Edition of The Complete Psychological Works of Sigmund Freud (S.E.)*, Vol. I. James Strachey (Trans. and Ed.), London: Hogarth Press.

Freud, S. (1905d). *Three Essays on the Theory of Sexuality, S.E.*, Vol. VII.

Freud, S. (1910). *Five Lectures on Psycho-Analysis S.E.*,Vol. XI.

Freud, S. (1910c). *Leonardo Da Vinci and a Memory of his Childhood, S.E.*, Vol. XI.

Freud, S. (1911b). *Formulations on the Two Principles of Mental Functioning*, *S.E.*, Vol. XII.

Freud, S. (1911c). Psychoanalytic notes on an autobiographical account of a case of paranoia (dementia paranoides), *S.E.*, Vol. XII.

Freud, S. (1912–13). *Totem and Taboo*. *S.E.*, Vol. XIII.

Freud, S. (1914c). *On Narcissism: An Introduction*. *S.E.*, Vol. XIV.

Freud, S. (1917d). *A Metapsychological Supplement to the Theory of Dreams*, *S.E.*, Vol. XIV.

Freud, S. (1917e). *Mourning and Melancholia*. *S.E.*, Vol. XIV

Freud, S. (1920g). *Beyond the Pleasure Principle*, *S.E.*, Vol. XVIII.

Freud, S. (1921c). *Group Psychology and the Analysis of the Ego*, *S.E.*, Vol. XVIII.

Freud, S. (1923b). *The Ego and the Id*, *S.E.*, Vol. XIX.

Freud, S. (1926d). *Inhibitions, Symptoms and Anxiety*, *S.E.*, Vol. XX.

Freud, S. (1928). Dostoesvsky and parracide, *S.E.*, Vol. XXI.

Freud, S., & Breuer, J. (1895d). *Studies on Hysteria*, *S.E.*, Vol. II.

Friedlander, K. (1991). Contribution to discussion of Paula Heimann's paper, some aspects of the role of projection and introjection in early development at a scientific meeting of October 20th 1943. In: P. King and R. Steiner (Eds.), *The Freud-Klein Controversies*. London: Bruner-Routledge.

Friedmann, V. (1982). The interplay of evocation. Paper presented at the Postgraduate Centre for Mental Health. New York.

Fromm, E. (1991). *The Sane Society*. London: Routledge.

Gabbard, G. (2000). *Psychodynamic Psychiatry in Clinical Practice*. Washington, DC: American Psychiatric Press Inc.

Garner, J. (2002). Psychodynamic work with older adults. *Advances in Psychiatric Treatment*, 8, pp. 128–135.

Gerard, R. (1979). *Violence and the Sacred*. Baltimore: John Hopkins University Press.

Gibson, N. (2003). *Fanon: The Postcolonial Imagination*. Cambridge: Polity.

Gotlieb, G. (1996). *Synthesizing Nature-Nurture: Prenatal Roots of Instinctive Behavior*. New York: Erlbaum.

Green, A. (1974). L'analyste, la symbolization et l'absence dans le cadre analytique. *Nouvelle Revue Psychanalytique*, 10, pp. 237–8.

Green, A. (2001). Primary narcissism: structure or state? In: *Life Narcissism, Death Narcissism*. A. Weller (Trans.). London: Free Association Books.

Green, A. (2001). The dead mother. In: *Life Narcissism, Death Narcissism*. A. Weller (Trans.). London: Free Association Books.

Green, A. (2001). *Life Narcissism, Death Narcissism*. A. Weller (Trans.). London: Free Association Books.

Green, A. (2004). *Key Ideas for a Contemporary Psychoanalysis: Misrecognition and Recognition of the Unconscious*. London: Routledge & The Institute of Psychoanalysis.

Green, J. (1994). *All Dressed Up: The Sixties and Counter Culture*. London: Pimlico Press.

Greenberg, J.R., & Mitchell, S.A. (1983). *Object Relations in Psychoanalytic Theory*. Cambridge, Mass.: Harvard University Press.

Grob, C.S. (Ed.), (2002). *Hallucinogens: A Reader*. New York: Penguin Putnams Inc.

Hamilton, V. (1982). *Narcissus and Oedipus: The Children of Psychoanalysis*. London: Routledge & Keegan Paul.

Hardy, T. (1990). Shut out that moon. In: *Selected Poems*. London. Penguin.

Hartmann, H. (1958). *Ego Psychology and the Problem of Adaptation*. New York: International Universities Press.

Hartmann, H. (1964). Comments on the psychoanalytic theory of the ego in *Essays in Ego Psychology: Selected Problems in Psychoanalytic Theory*. New York: International Universities Press.

Hesse, H. (1988). *Siddhartha*. London: Picador.

Hinshelwood, R. (1989). *A Dictionary of Kleinian Though*. London and New York: Free Association Books.

Horney, K. (1945). *Our Inner Conflicts. A Constructive Theory of Neurosis*. London: W. W. Norton & Company.

Horney, K. (c1951/1991). *Neurosis and Human Growth: The Struggle Toward Self-realization*. New York: Norton.

Ibsen, H. (1875). *A Verse Letter*. www.ibsen.net (19.08.2002).

Isaacs, S. (1991). The nature and function of phantasy, paper delivered at the first of the discussions on January 27th 1943, in P. King and R. Steiner (Eds.), *The Freud-Klein Controversies*. London: Bruner-Routledge.

Isaacs, S. (1991). Response to discussion of her paper at a scientific meeting of May 19th 1943. In: P. King and R. Steiner (Eds.), *The Freud-Klein Controversies*. London: Bruner-Routledge.

Jacobs, M. (1998). *The Presenting Past*. Milton Keynes: Open University Press.

Jacoby, M. (1989). Heinz Kohut's concept of narcissism. In: Samuels, A. (Ed.), *Psychopathology: Contemporary Jungian Perspectives*. London: Karnac, pp. 140–156.

Jacoby, M. (1990). *Individuation and Narcissism—The Psychology of Self in Jung and Kohut*. London and New York: Routledge.

Jacques, E. (1965). Death and the mid-life crisis. *International Journal of Psychoanalysis*, 46, pp. 502–14. Quoted in Bateman, A. & Homes, J. (1995). *Introduction to Psychoanalysis*. London: Routledge.

Jones, E. (1954–7). *Sigmund Freud–Life and Work*, London: The Hogarth Press, 1980.

Jung, C.G. (1963). *Memories, Dreams and Reflections*. London: Routledge.

Jung, C.G. (1966). The relations between the ego and the unconscious, *The Collected Works of C.G. Jung(1953–78)*, H. Read, M. Fordham and G. Adler (Ed.), London: Routledge.

Keller, H., Yovsi, R., Borke, J., Kartner, J., Jensen, H., & Papaligoura, Z. (2004). Developmental differences of early parenting experiences: Self-Recognition and Self-Regulation in Three Cultural Communities. *Child Development*, 75(6), pp. 1745–60.

Kernberg, O. (1975). *Borderline Conditions and Pathological Narcissism*. New York: Jason Aronson.

Kernberg, O. (1977). Pathological narcissism in old age. Quoted in Colarusso, C. & Nemiroff, R. (1981). *Adult Development—A New Dimension in Psychodynamic Theory and Practice*. New York: Plenum Press.

Kernberg, O.F. (1984). *Severe Personality Disorder: Psychotherapeutic Strategies*. New Haven: Yale University Press.

Kernberg, O.F. (1989). Projection and projective identification: developmental and clinical aspects. In: Sandler, J. (Ed.), *Projection, Identification, Projective Identification*. London: Karnac.

Kernberg, O.F. (1995). *Love Relations, Normality and Pathology*. New Haven: Yale University Press.

Kernberg, O.F. (2001). Object relations, affects and drives: toward a new synthesis. *Psychoanalytic Inquiry, 21:* 604–19.

King, P. and Steiner, R. (1991). *The Freud-Klein Controversies 1941–5.* London: Brunner-Routledge.

Klee, P. (1923). *Pedagogical Sketchbook.* London: Faber and Faber, 1953.

Klein, M. (1945–1946) *Love, Guilt and Reparation and Other works.* London: Virago Press, 1988.

Kohon, G. (Ed.), (1999). *The Dead Mother: The Work of André Green.* London: Brunner-Routledge.

Kohut, H. (1966). Forms and transformations of narcissism. *Journal of the American Psychoanalytic Association, 14,* pp. 243–72.

Kohut, H. (1971). *The Analysis of the Self.* Connecticut: International Universities Press.

Kohut, H. (1977). *The Restoration of the Self.* New York: International Universities Press.

Kohut, H. (1984). *How Does Analysis Cure?* Chicago: University of Chicago Press.

Kohut, H. (1996). *The Chicago Institute Lectures.* P. & M. Tolpin (Ed.), Chicago: The Analytic Press.

Kohut, H., & Wolf, E.S. (1978). The disorders of the self and their treatment: an outline. *International Journal of Psycho-Analysis, 59:* 413–26.

Kristeva, J. (1980). *Desire in Language: A Semiotic Approach to Literature and Art.* T. Gora, A. Jardine & L. Roudiez (Trans.), England: Basil Blackwell, 1981.

Lacan, J. (1932). *De la Psychose Paranoïaque dans ses rapports avec la Personnalité.* Paris: Points, 1975.

Lacan, J. (1949). The mirror stage as formative of the function of the 'I' as revealed in psychoanalytic experience in *Écrits: A Selection.* A. Sheridan (Trans.), London: Tavistock, 1977, pp. 1–7.

Lacan, J. (1953). Some reflections on the ego. *The International Journal of Psycho-Analysis, 34,* (1), pp. 11–17.

Lacan, J. (1966). *Écrits.* Paris: Seuil.

Lacan, J. (1977). *Écrits: A Selection.* A. Sheridan (Trans.), London: Tavistock.

Lacan, J. (1977). *The Four Fundamental Concepts of Psychoanalysis.* [*Seminar XI—1964*]. A. Sheridan (Trans.), London: Hogarth Press and Institute of Psycho-analysis.

Lacan, J. (1988). *Seminar II: The Ego in Freud's Theory and in the Technique of Psychoanalysis—1954–55*. S. Tomaselli (Trans.), Cambridge: Cambridge University Press.

Lacan, J. (1992). *Seminar VII: The Ethics of Psychoanalysis—1959–1960*. D. Potter (Trans.), London: Routledge, 1992.

Lacan, J. (2006). Aggressiveness in psychoanalysis in *Écrits*. B. Fink (Trans.), New York: W. W. Norton.

Laing, R.D. (1960). *The Divided Self*. London: Penguin, 1990.

Lane, C. (Ed.), (1998). *The Psychoanalysis of Race*. New York: Columbia University Press.

Laplanche, J. (1976). *Life and Death in Psychoanalysis*. J. Mehlman (Trans.). Baltimore: Johns Hopkins University Press.

Laplanche, J. (1987). *New Foundations for Psychoanalysis*. David Macey (Trans.), Oxford: Basil Blackwell, 1989.

Laplanche, J. (1999). Implantation, intromission. In: *Essays on Otherness*. J. Fletcher (Trans. and Ed.). London: Routledge.

Laplanche, J. (1999a). *Essays on Otherness*. John Fletcher (Ed.), London and New York: Routledge.

Laplanche, J. (1999b). A short treatise on the unconscious. In: Laplanche, J. (1999a), pp. 52–83.

Laplanche, J. (1999d). Seduction, persecution, revelation. In: Laplanche, J. (1999a), pp.166–96.

Laplanche, J., & Pontalis, J.-B. (1983). *The Language of Psychoanalysis*, London: Karnac.

Lasch, C. (1979). *The Culture of Narcissism: American Life in the Age of Diminishing Expectations*. New York: Norton Paperbacks, 1999.

Le Figaro in *The Guardian*, 17.05.05.

Lebeau, V. (2005). Children of violence, In: Max Silverman (Ed.), *Frantz Fanon's Black Skin, White Masks: New Interdisciplinary Essays*, Manchester: Manchester University Press, pp. 112–127.

Lebovici, S. (1999). Importance of narcissistic cathexes in the earliest aspects of the object relationship, In: Fonagy, P., Cooper, A., & Wallerstein, R.S. (Eds.), *Psychoanalysis on the Move: The Work of Joseph Sandler*. London: Routledge & The Institute of Psychoanalysis.

Leclaire, S. (1998). *A Child Is Being Killed: On Primary Narcissism and the Death Drive*, M.-C. Hays (Trans.), Stanford, CA: Stanford University Press.

Ledermann, R. (1979). The infantile roots of narcissistic personality disorder, in *Journal of Analytical Psychology, 24,* 2.

Ledermann, R. (1989). Narcissistic disorder and treatment. In: Samuels, A. (Ed.), *Psychopathology: Contemporary Jungian Perspectives.* London: Karnac, pp. 111–126.

Ledermann. R. (1982). Narcissistic disorder and its treatment. *Journal of Analytical Psychology, 27,* 4.

Levy, K.N., Clarkin, J.F., Yeomans, F.E., Scott, L.N., Wasserman, R.H., & Kernberg, O.F. (2006). The mechanisms of change in the treatment of borderline personality disorder with transference focused psychotherapy. *Journal of Clinical Psychology, 62(4),* pp. 481–501.

Lewes, K. (1989). *The Psychoanalytic Theory of Male Homosexuality.* New York: Basic Books.

Lewis, M. (1991). Ways of knowing: objective self-awareness or consciousness. *Developmental Review, 11,* pp. 231–43.

Lorentzen, J. (1995). Reich Dreams, In: C. Jenks (Ed.), *Visual Culture.* London: Routledge.

McCabe, C. (1998). *Performance.* London: BFI Publishing.

MacDonald, I. (1997). *Revolution in the Head: The Beatles' Records and the Sixties.* London: Pimlico Press.

Macey, D. (2000). *Frantz Fanon: A Life.* London: Granta Books.

MacIntyre, A. (1970). *After Virtue–A Study in Moral Theory,* London: Duckworth.

Mahler, M. (1975). *The Psychological Birth of the Human Infant: Symbiosis and Individuation.* London: Maresfield.

Mannoni, O. (1984). *Prospéro et Caliban: Psychologie de la Colonisation.* Paris: Editions Universitaires.

Marcuse, H. (1956). *Eros and Civilization.* London: Ark.

Masson, G. (1984). *The Assault on Truth: Freud's Suppression of the Seduction Theory,* Harmandsworth: Penguin Books, 1985.

Mayes, L.C., & Spence, D.P. (1994). Understanding therapeutic action in the analytic situation: a second look at the developmental metaphor. *Journal of the American Psychoanalytic Association, 42,* pp. 789–816.

McCulloch, J. (1995). *Colonial Psychiatry and the African Mind.* Cambridge: Cambridge University Press.

McLuhan, M. (1964). *Understanding Media*. London: Routledge, 2004.

Miller, P.H. (2002). *Theories of Developmental Psychology, 4th (Ed.)*, New York: Worth Publishers.

Miller-Kuchanek, H. (2004) *Autism: A Comprehensive Occupational Therapy Approach*. Bethesda, MD: American Occupational Therapy Association.

MIND (2005). *Access All Ages*. Press Release via Internet Website.

Mitchell, S. (1998). Attachment theory and the psychoanalytic tradition: reflections on human relationality. *British Journal of Psychotherapy, 15*, pp. 177–93.

Modell, A.H. (1985). A narcissistic defense against affects and the illusion of self-sufficiency, in morrison, A.P. (Ed.), *Essential Papers on Narcissism*. New York: New York University Press.

Modell, A. H. (1999) A narcissistic defense against affects and the illusion of self-sufficiency, in morrison, A.P. (Ed.), *Essential Papers on Narcissism*. New York: New York University Press.

Mollon, P. (2001). *Releasing the Self: The Healing Legacy of Heinz Kohut*. London: Whurr Publishers.

Neumann, E. (1973). *The Child: Structure and Dynamics of the Nascent Personality*. R. Manheim (Trans.), London: Maresfield.

Office of National Statistics (2005). *Social Trends*, in *The Guardian*— 22.03.05.

Ogden, T.H. (2002). A new reading of the origins of object-relations theory. *International Journal of Psychoanalysis, 83*.

Oury, J. (2005). Psychiatry in post-war France. Lecture given at the French Institute, London, on the 13th of October.

Ovid (1955). *The Metamorphoses*, Book III, Echo and Narcissus. M. Innes (Trans.), Harmondsworth: Penguin.

Oyama, S. (1985). *The Ontogeny of Information: Developmental Systems and Evolution*. Cambridge, Mass: Cambridge University Press.

Panksepp, J. (1998). *Affective Neuroscience: The Foundations of Human and Animal Emotions*. New York: Oxford University Press.

Perlow, M. (1995). *Understanding Mental Objects*. London: The New Library of Psychoanalysis, Routledge.

Phillips. A. (2000). *Promises Promises*. London: Faber and Faber.

Pontalis, J.B. (1981). The birth and recognition of the "Self" in *Frontiers in Psychoanalysis: Between Dream and Psychic Pain*. C. and P. Cullen (Trans.), London: Hogarth.

Pulver, S.E. (1970). Narcissism: the term and the concept. *Journal of the American Psychoanalytic Association, 18*, pp. 319–41.

Ricoeur, P. (1974). The question of the subject: the challenge of semiology, in D. Ihde (Ed.), *The Conflict of Interpretations: Essays on Hermeneutics*. Evanston, IL: Northwestern University Press.

Ricouer, P. (1970). *Freud and Philosophy: An Essay on Interpretation*. D. Savage (Trans.), New Haven: Yale University.

Rieffe, C.N.J., Meerum-Terwogt, M., & Stockmann, L. (2000). Understanding atypical emotions among children with autism. *Journal of Autism and Developmental Disorders, 30*, pp. 195–203.

Rutgers, A.H., Bakermans-Krannenburg, M.J., van Ijzendoorn, M.H., & van Berckelaer-Onnes, M.A. (2004). Autism and attachment: a meta-analytic review. *Journal of Child Psychology and Psychiatry, 45(6)*, pp. 1123–34.

Rycroft, C. (1968). *A Critical Dictionary of Psychoanalysis*. London: Penguin, 1995.

Said, E. (2002). *Freud and the Non-European*. London: Verso.

Samuels, A. (1985). *Jung and the Post-Jungians*. London: Routledge & Kegan Paul.

Samuels, A. (1989). *The Plural Psyche*. London: Routledge & Keegan Paul.

Samuels, A. Shorter, B. & Plaut, F. (Eds.) (1986). *A Critical Dictionary of Jungian Analysis*. London: Karnac.

Sandler, J., Holder, A., Dare, C., & Dreher, A.U. (1997). *Freud's Models of the Mind: An Introduction*. London: Karnac.

Sartre, J.P. (1943). *Being and Nothingness*. London: Methuen and Co., 1977.

Schore, A.N. (2003). *Affect Regulation and the Repair of the Self*. New York: W.W. Norton & Co.

Schur, M. (1957). *The Id and the Regulatory Principles of Mental Functioning*. London.

Schwartz-Salant, N. (1982). *Narcissism and Character Transformation: The Psychology of Narcissistic Character Disorders*. Toronto: Inner City Books.

Segal, H. (1975). Art and the inner world, in *The Times Literary Supplement*, No. 3827, 1975 (17 July).

Segal, H. (1991). *Dream, Phantasy and Art*. London: Routledge.

Segal, L. (1990). *Slow Motion: Changing Masculinity, Changing Men*. London: Virago.

Segal, L. (1999). *Why Feminism? Gender, Psychology, Politics*. Cambridge: Polity Press.

Silverman, M. (2005). Reflections on the human question. In: Max Silverman (Ed.), *Frantz Fanon's Black Skin, White Masks: New Interdisciplinary essays*, Manchester: Manchester University Press, pp. 112–127.

Smith, L.B., & Thelen, E. (2003). Development as a dynamic system. *Trends in Cognitive Science, 7(8)*, pp. 343–8.

Solms, M., & Turnbull, O. (2002). *The Brain and the Inner World: An Introduction to the Neuroscience of Subjective Experience*. New York: Other Press.

Spitzer, S.L. (2003). With and without words: exploring occupation in relative to young children with autism. *Journal of Occupational Science 10(2):67–79*.

Sroufe, A.L. (1995). *Emotional Development: The Organization of Emotional Life in the Early Years*. Cambridge, Mass.: Cambridge University Press.

Steiner, J. (1993). *Psychic Retreats–Pathological Organizations in Psychotic, Neurotic and Borderline Patients*. London and New York: Routledge.

Stern, D.N. (1984). *The Interpersonal World of the Infant—A View from Psychoanalysis and Developmental Psychology*. London: Karnac, 2003.

Sternberg, R.J. (1984). *Mechanisms of Cognitive Development*. New York: Freeman.

Stevens, A. (1990). *On Jung*. London. Routledge.

Stevens, A. (2001). *Jung: A Very Short Introduction*. Oxford: Oxford University Press.

Stoller, R. (1975). *Perversion–The Erotic Form of Hatred*, London: Karnac Books.

Storr, A. (1987). Creative solitude, *The Midland Journal of Psychotherapy*, West Midlands Institute of Psychotherapy, 2.

Stubrin, J. (1994). *Sexualities and Homosexualities*, London: Karnac Books.

Symington, N. (1993). *Narcissism—A New Theory*. London: Karnac.

Szasz, T. (1960). *The Myth of Mental Illness*. London: Harper Collins, 1984.

Thelen, E., & Smith, L.B. (2000). *A Dynamic Systems Approach to the Development of Cognition and Action*. Cambridge, Mass: The MIT Press.

Todorov, T. (2002). *The Imperfect Garden: The Legacy of Humanism*. Carol Cosman (Trans.), Princeton: Princeton University Press.

Tomasello, M. (1999). *The Cultural Origins of Human Cognition*. Harvard: Harvard University Press.

Tronick, E.Z., & Members of the change process study group (1998). Dyadically expanded states of consciousness and the process of therapeutic change. *Infant Mental health Journal, 19(3)*, pp. 290–9.

Turner , G. (2004). *Understanding Celebrity*. London: Sage.

Vaughn, M. (1991). *Curing Their Ills: Colonial Power and African Illness*. Cambridge: Polity.

Verges, F. (1996). To cure and to free in gordon, L., Denean Sharpley-Whiting and White, R. (Eds.), *Fanon: A Critical Reader*, London: Blackwell.

Volkmar, F.R. (2000). Understanding autism: implications for psycho-analysis. *Psychoanalytic Inquiry, 20*, pp. 660–74.

Westen, D. (1997). Towards a clinically and empirically sound theory of motivation. *International Journal of Psycho-Analysis, 78*, pp. 521–48.

Whitbourne, S.K. (2001). *Adult Development and Ageing*. London: J. Wiley.

Whitebook, J. (1995). *Perversion and Utopia: A Study in Psychoanalysis and Critical Theory*. Cambridge, Mass: The MIT Press.

Winnicott, D.W. (1963). The fear of breakdown. In: Winnicott, D.W., Shepherd, R. & Davis, M. (Eds.), (1989). *Psycho-analytic Explorations*. London: Karnac.

Winnicott, D.W. (1965). The theory of the parent-infant relationship. In: *The Maturational Processes and the Facilitating Environment—Studies in the Theory of Emotional Development*. London: Hogarth. Also Published by Karnac & The Institute of Psycho-Analysis, 1990.

Winnicott, D.W. (1971). Mirror-role of mother and family in child development. In: *Playing and Reality*. London: Pelican Books.

Winnicott, D.W. (1971). The use of an object and relating through identifications. In: *Playing and Reality*. London: Pelican Books.

Winnicott, D.W. (1971). *Playing and Reality*. London: Pelican Books.

Yalom, I. (1989). *Love's Executioner and Other Tales of Psychotherapy*.
London: Penguin.

Zinkin, L. (1978). Person to person: the search for the human dimension
in psychotherapy. *British Journal of Medical Psychology, 51*, pp. 25–34.

Žižek, S. (2003). *Live Theory*. Rex Butler (Trans.), London: Continuum.

INDEX

227